Joseph Gerald Pease, Herbert Chitty

A Treatise on the Law of Markets and Fairs

With the principal Statutes relating thereto

Joseph Gerald Pease, Herbert Chitty

A Treatise on the Law of Markets and Fairs
With the principal Statutes relating thereto

ISBN/EAN: 9783337107208

Printed in Europe, USA, Canada, Australia, Japan

Cover: Foto ©ninafisch / pixelio.de

More available books at **www.hansebooks.com**

A TREATISE

ON THE LAW OF

MARKETS AND FAIRS

WITH THE

PRINCIPAL STATUTES RELATING THERETO

BY

J. G. PEASE
OF THE INNER TEMPLE AND WESTERN CIRCUIT, BARRISTER-AT-LAW
B.A. (LOND.)

AND

HERBERT CHITTY
OF THE INNER TEMPLE AND WESTERN CIRCUIT, BARRISTER-AT-LAW
M.A. (OXON.)

LONDON
KNIGHT AND CO.
4 & 4A LA BELLE SAUVAGE YARD, LUDGATE HILL
(LATE OF 90 FLEET STREET)
1899

DEDICATED

BY PERMISSION

TO THE

RIGHT HON. SIR NATHANIEL LINDLEY

MASTER OF THE ROLLS

PREFACE.

OUR aim has been to state in a book of moderate size the whole of the English law of markets and fairs.

Most of the materials were collected by one of us more than ten years ago, but their arrangement for the press was postponed upon the appointment of the Royal Commission on Market Rights and Tolls.

The first Report of the Commissioners was published in 1889. It contains materials for a history of markets and fairs, prepared by Mr. Elton, Q.C., and Mr. B. F. C. Costelloe, from which we have derived assistance. In the final Report, published in 1891, considerable alterations in the law were recommended ; but Parliament has shown no inclination to carry them out.

This book consists of an Introduction and two Parts, with an Appendix. Part I. contains the common law of markets and fairs, and shows how it has been modified by statute.

In Part II. we have set out and commented on the enactments under which in recent times markets have usually been established. The common law seems to be applicable to markets established under statutory powers, except in so far as it is inconsistent with those powers. Part II., therefore, does not contain the whole law of statutory markets, but only such additions and modifications as are contained in the Markets and Fairs Clauses Act, 1847, and the general enactments conferring on local authorities power to establish or regulate markets. It is hoped that the cross-references and explanations will be sufficient to enable the reader to discover to what classes of markets the various provisions of the law apply.

The Appendix consists of the principal Acts whereby the common law has been modified other than those set out in Part II.

We have endeavoured to refer to every reported case on the law of markets decided in the English Courts since the seventeenth century. Earlier cases, including those in the Year Books, have been utilised somewhat more sparingly, but all have been noticed which seem to be still useful to lawyers. The printed volumes of early records, such as the *Placita de Quo Warranto* and the *Abbrevatio Placitorum*, contain many cases upon markets and fairs, but most of these are only summaries of the pleadings and the findings of juries, and are of little importance as legal authorities, however valuable they may be to the antiquary or to the historian of particular franchises. From these records we have only cited typical cases to illustrate the law as understood in the thirteenth and fourteenth centuries.

After the Introduction had been printed our attention was drawn to the passages in Professor Maitland's ' Domesday Book and Beyond ' in which the origin of market-rights is explained. We are glad to find that the views we have adopted do not differ widely from those of Professor Maitland, and we refer our readers to his learned discussion of the subject.

Preface.

We hope that this work will prove to be both a concise treatise on a branch of the law about which but little has been written in recent years, and a practical handbook for clerks of urban authorities and other persons concerned in the management of markets.

We desire to acknowledge our indebtedness to Mr. Stuart Moore, of the Inner Temple, for advice and information readily given to us.

J. G. P.
H. C.

December, 1898.

CONTENTS.

	PAGE
TABLE OF CASES	XV
TABLE OF STATUTES	xxvii

INTRODUCTION.

§ 1. NATURE OF MARKETS AND FAIRS	1
§ 2. COURTS OF PIE POWDER	6
§ 3. CORRECTION OF THE MARKET	8
§ 4. EXTRAORDINARY JURISDICTION	9
§ 5. THE CLERK OF THE MARKET	10

PART I.

THE LAW OF MARKETS AND FAIRS GENERALLY.

CHAPTER I.

TITLE TO THE FRANCHISE.

§ 1. ACQUISITION BY GRANT	19
§ 2. ACQUISITION BY PRESCRIPTION OR USAGE	22
§ 3. ACQUISITION BY STATUTE	25
§ 4. DEVOLUTION OF MARKET-RIGHTS	27

CHAPTER II.

THE MARKET-PLACE AND PLACE FOR HOLDING FAIRS.

§ 1. THE RIGHTS OF THE PUBLIC	31
§ 2. THE RIGHTS AND DUTIES OF THE OWNER	33

		PAGE
§ 3.	THE RIGHT OF REMOVAL	37
§ 4.	UPON WHAT LANDS A MARKET OR FAIR MAY BE HELD	39
§ 5.	MARKETS AND FAIRS IN CHURCHYARDS AND HIGHWAYS	42

CHAPTER III.
THE DAYS AND HOURS FOR HOLDING MARKETS AND FAIRS.

§ 1.	THE DAYS	48
§ 2.	CHANGE OF THE DAYS	50
§ 3.	THE HOURS	53

CHAPTER IV.
TOLL AND STALLAGE.

§ 1.	THE NATURE OF TOLL, STALLAGE AND OTHER CHARGES	55
§ 2.	THE RIGHT TO TOLL	56
§ 3.	THE RIGHT TO STALLAGE	63
§ 4.	TOLLS AND STALLAGE IN KIND	65
§ 5.	VARIABLE AND DIFFERENTIAL TOLLS	66
§ 6.	THE RECOVERY OF TOLL AND STALLAGE	66
§ 7.	THE REMEDIES FOR TOLL WRONGFULLY TAKEN	68
§ 8.	EXEMPTIONS FROM TOLL	69

CHAPTER V.
DISTURBANCE OF THE FRANCHISE.

§ 1.	DISTURBANCE BY LEVYING A RIVAL MARKET OR FAIR	74
§ 2.	DISTURBANCE BY ACTS OTHER THAN LEVYING A RIVAL MARKET OR FAIR	82
§ 3.	DISTURBANCE OF MARKET-RIGHTS VESTED IN PERSONS OTHER THAN THE LORD	86
§ 4.	NATURE OF ACTION FOR DISTURBANCE	86
§ 5.	REMEDIES FOR DISTURBANCE OF STATUTORY MARKETS AND FAIRS	87

CHAPTER VI.
HOW THE FRANCHISE MAY BE LOST.

		PAGE
§ 1.	FORFEITURE	90
§ 2.	SURRENDER	93
§ 3.	EXTINCTION BY ACT OF PARLIAMENT	93
§ 4.	THE FAIRS ACT, 1871	94

CHAPTER VII.
THE ADMINISTRATION OF MARKETS AND FAIRS.

§ 1.	REGULATION AND BY-LAWS	96
§ 2.	WEIGHTS AND MEASURES	98
§ 3.	SALE OF UNWHOLESOME MEAT AND PROVISIONS	104
§ 4.	DISEASES OF ANIMALS	106
§ 5.	LICENCES FOR SALE OF INTOXICATING DRINKS	107
§ 6.	LICENCES FOR THEATRICAL PERFORMANCES AT FAIRS	109
§ 7.	ACCOUNTS	111

CHAPTER VIII.
RATES AND TAXES.

§ 1.	LAND TAX	114
§ 2.	INCOME TAX	115
§ 3.	RATES	117

CHAPTER IX.
SALES IN MARKETS AND FAIRS.

§ 1.	THE LAW AS TO SALE OF GOODS IN MARKET OVERT	120
§ 2.	SALE OF HORSES	126
§ 3.	SALE OF HAY AND STRAW IN MARKETS IN AND NEAR THE METROPOLIS	128

CHAPTER X.
PROCEDURE AND EVIDENCE.

§ 1.	SCIRE FACIAS	130
§ 2.	QUO WARRANTO	131

xiv *Contents.*

	PAGE
§ 3. SUMMARY PROCEEDINGS UNDER THE METROPOLITAN FAIRS ACT, 1868	134
§ 4. EVIDENCE	134

PART II.

PUBLIC STATUTES RELATING TO THE ESTABLISHMENT OF MARKETS AND FAIRS.

THE MARKETS AND FAIRS CLAUSES ACT, 1847, AND THE INCORPORATED SECTIONS OF THE RAILWAYS CLAUSES CONSOLIDATION ACT, 1845	141
THE PUBLIC HEALTH ACT, 1875, SS. 166–168 AND 316	181
THE DISEASES OF ANIMALS ACT, 1894, S. 32	189

APPENDIX.

PRINCIPAL STATUTES RELATING TO MARKETS AND FAIRS.

1. The Fairs Act, 1871 193
2. The Fairs Act, 1873 194
3. The Weights and Measures Act, 1878, Sixth Schedule, Second Part (re-enacting 22 & 23 Vict. c. 56, ss. 6, 7, 8, and 12) 195
4. The Markets and Fairs (Weighing of Cattle) Act, 1887 . 196
5. The Markets and Fairs (Weighing of Cattle) Act, 1891 . 198
6. The Public Health (Confirmation of By-laws) Act, 1884 . 200
7. The Local Taxation Returns Act, 1860 202
8. The Local Taxation Returns Act, 1877 203
9. The Metropolitan Police Act, 1839, ss. 38–40 . . . 204
10. The Metropolitan Fairs Act, 1868 206

MODEL BY-LAWS ISSUED BY THE LOCAL GOVERNMENT BOARD 208

INDEX 215

TABLE OF CASES CITED.

[THIS table does not contain the cases cited from the *Placita de Quo Warranto, Abbrevatio Placitorum*, or *Rotuli Hundredorum*. In citing cases from these records, it has been thought sufficient to refer to the pages of the printed volumes. These volumes are referred to respectively by the abbreviations, Plac. Quo. Warr. (or P.Q.W.), Abb. Plac., and Rot. Hund.]

	PAGE
Abergavenny Improvement Commissioners *v.* Straker, 42 Ch.D. 83; 58 L.J. Ch. 717; 60 L.T. 756; 38 W.R. 158	89
Addington *v.* Clode, 2 W. Bl. 989	xxxi
Agar *v.* Lisle, Hob. 187; Hutt. 10	67, 68
Aiton *v.* Stephen, 1 App. Cas. 456	38
Andrew *v.* Hancock, 1 Bro. & Bing. 37; 3 Moore, 278.	115
Anon., 12 Mod. 225	132
——, 12 Mod. 521	122
Ashby *v.* White, 6 Mod. 49; 2 Ld. Raym. 938; 1 Salk. 19; Holt. 524	85
Ashworth *v.* Heyworth, L.R. 4 Q.B. 316; 38 L.J.M.C. 91; 20 L.T. 439; 17 W.R. 668; 10 B. & S. 309	152, 153
Attorney-General *v.* Brecon (Mayor of), 9 Ch.D. 204; 48 L.J.Ch. 153; 40 L.T. 52; 27 W.R. 332	25
—— *v.* Cambridge (Mayor of), L.R. 6 H.L. 303; 22 W.R. 37	145
—— *v.* Great Eastern Railway Co., 5 App. Cas. 473; 49 L.J.Ch. 545; 42 L.T. 810; 28 W.R. 769; 44 J.P. 648	29
—— *v.* Horner, 11 App. Cas. 66; 14 Q.B.D. 245; 55 L.J.Q.B. 193, 54 Id. 227; 54 L.T. 281; 34 W.R. 641, 33 Id. 93; 50 J.P. 564, 49 Id. 326	24, 31, 34, 41, 43, 44, 49
—— *v.* Metropolitan Railway Co., [1894] 1 Q.B. 384; 69 L.T. 811; 42 W.R. 381; 58 J.P. 342; 9 R. 598	146
—— *v.* Scott, 28 L.T. 302; 21 W.R. 265	112, 116
Austin *v.* Whittred, Willes, 623	31, 40, 57
Ayr Harbour Trustees *v.* Oswald, 8 App. Cas. 623	182
Bailey *v.* Appleyard, 8 A. & E. 161; 2 N. & P. 257; 1 W., W. & H. 208; 2 Jur. 872	24
Ball *v.* Ward, 33 L.T. 170	45
Barker *v.* Reading, W. Jones, 163; Palm. 485	127
Barraclough *v.* Johnson, 8 A. & E. 99; 3 N. & P. 233; 2 Jur. 839	136
Barry *v.* Midland Railway Co., I.R. 1 C.L. 130	179
Basset's Case, Dyer, 276 b	131
Beaufort (Duke of) *v.* Smith, 4 Exch. 450; 19 L.J.Ex. 97	60, 136, 137
Beckett *v.* Midland Railway Co., L.R. 3 C.P. 82; 37 L.J.C.P. 11; 17 L.T. 499; 16 W.R. 221	146

Table of Cases.

	PAGE
Bedford (Duke of) v. Emmett, 3 B. & Ald. 366	55, 64, 66
———— v. Overseers of St. Paul, Covent Garden, 51 L.J.M.C. 41; 45 L.T. 616; 30 W.R. 411; 46 J.P. 581	55, 64, 118
Benjamin v. Andrews, 5 C.B.N.S. 299; 27 L.J.M.C. 310; 4 Jur. N.S. 41	24
———— v. Storr, L.R. 9 C.P. 400; 43 L.J.C.P. 162; 30 L.T. 362; 22 W.R. 631	155
Bennington v. Taylor, 2 Lutw. 1517	55, 62, 64, 65, 68
Bentley v. Vilmont, 12 App. Cas. 471; 18 Q.B.D. 322; 57 L.J.Q.B. 18; 57 L.T. 854; 36 W.R. 481; 52 J.P. 68	121, 124, 125
Birmingham, In re Corporation of, 1 Tax Cas. 26	116
———— (Mayor of) v. Foster, 70 L.T. 371	87, 88, 89
Biscoe v. Great Eastern Railway Co., L.R. 16 Eq. 636; 21 W.R. 902	146
Black v. Sackett, 10 B. & S. 639	152
Blackburn (Mayor of) v. Parkinson, 1 E. & E. 71; 28 L.J.M.C. 7; 5 Jur. N.S. 572	175
Blaker v. Herts & Essex Waterworks Co., 41 Ch.D. 399; 58 L.J. Ch. 497; 60 L.T. 776; 37 W.R. 601; 1 Meg. 217	30
Blakey v. Dimsdale, 2 Cowp. 661	68, 82, 83
Bourne v. Lowndes, 22 J.P. 354	152
Brecon Markets Co. v. Neath & Brecon Railway Co., L.R. 8 C.P. 157; 42 L.J.C.P. 63	56
———— v. St. Mary's (Brecon), 36 L.T. 109	117
———— (Mayor of) v. Edwards, 1 H. & C. 51; 31 L.J. Ex. 368; 8 Jur. N.S. 461; 6 L.T. 293	83, 84
Brett v. Beales, M. & M. 416	136
Bridgland v. Shapter, 5 M. & W. 375	28, 82
Briscoe v. Lomax, 8 A. & E. 198; 3 N. & P. 308; 2 Jur. 682	137
Bristow v. Cormican, 3 App. Cas. 641	135
Broadbent v. Imperial Gaslight Co., 7 H.L.C. 600; 7 De G. M. & G. 436; 26 L.J. Ch. 276, 29 Id. 377; 3 Jur. N.S. 221, 5 Id. 1319	146
Brune v. Thompson, 4 Q.B. 543; D. & M. 221; 12 L.J.Q.B. 251; 7 Jur. 395	61
Bryant v. Foot, L.R. 3 Q.B. 497; 37 L.J.Q.B. 217; 9 B. & S. 444	61
Burdett's Case, 1 Salk. 327	11
Caledonian Railway Co. v. Walker's Trustees, 7 App. Cas. 259; 46 L.T. 826; 30 W.R. 569; 46 J.P. 676	146
Campbell v. Wilson, 3 East, 294	87
Carlisle (Mayor of) v. Wilson, 5 East, 2; 1 Smith, 297	61
Carnarvon (Earl of) v. Villebois, 13 M. & W. 313; 14 L.J. Ex. 233	xxxi, 136, 137
Carter v. Parkhouse, 22 L.T. 788	153
Caswell v. Cook, 11 C.B.N.S. 637; 31 L.J.M.C. 185	151, 153
Charing Cross Bridge Co. v. Mitchell, 4 E. & B. 549; 24 L.J.Q.B. 249; 1 Jur. N.S. 608	114
Chasin v. Betsworth, 3 Lev. 190	65
Chelsea (Vestry of) v. Stoddard, 43 J.P. 782	46
Clifton v. Chancellor, Moore, 122	122
Clowes v. Staffordshire Potteries Waterworks Co., L.R. 8 Ch. 125; 42 L.J.Ch. 107; 27 L.T. 521; 21 W.R. 32	146
Collier v. North, 35 L.T. 345	151

Table of Cases.

xvii

	PAGE
Collins v. Cooper, 68 L.T. 450; 57 J.P. 248; 5 R. 256	1, 2
—— v. Wells (Corporation of), 1 T.L.R. 328	98, 165
Colonial Bank of Australia v. Willan, L.R. 5 P.C. 417; 43 L.J.P.C. 39; 30 L.T. 237; 22 W.R. 516	179
Coltness Iron Co. v. Black, 6 App. Cas. 315; 51 L.J.Q.B. 626; 45 L.T. 145; 29 W.R. 717; 46 J.P. 20	116
Comyns v. Boyer, Cro. Eliz. 485	51, 121, 122
Consolidated Co. v. Curtis, [1892] 1 Q.B. 495; 61 L.J.Q.B. 325; 40 W.R. 426; 56 J.P. 565	123
Cooper v. Whittingham, 15 Ch. D. 501; 49 L.J. Ch. 752; 43 L.T. 16; 28 W.R. 720	88
Cork (Corporation of) v. Shinkwin, Smith & B. 395	51, 75, 76, 80, 81
Cowper Essex v. Acton Local Board, 14 App. Cas. 153; 58 L.J.Q.B. 594; 61 L.T. 1; 53 J.P. 756	146
Crane v. London Dock Co., 5 B. & S. 313; 33 L.J.Q.B. 224; 10 Jur. N.S. 984; 10 L.T. 372; 12 W.R. 745	120, 122
Crease v. Barrett, 1 C.M. & R. 919, 2 Id. 738; 5 Tyr. 458; 1 T. & G. 112; 4 L.J. Ex. 297, 5 Id. 8	136
Crump v. Lambert, L.R. 3 Eq. 409; 15 L.T. 600, 17 Id. 133; 15 W.R. 417	155
Cundy v. Lindsay, 3 App. Cas. 459; 47 L.J.Q.B. 481; 38 L.T. 573; 26 W.R. 406	120, 125
Curtis v. Embery, L.R. 7 Ex. 369; 42 L.J.M.C. 39; 21 W.R. 143	44, 45
Curwen v. Salkeld, 3 East, 538	37, 38, 39
Dartford Rural Council v. Bexley Heath Railway Co., [1898] A.C. 210; 67 L.J.Q.B. 231; 77 L.T. 601; 46 W.R. 235; 62 J.P. 227	141
Davies v. Williams, 16 Q.B. 546; 20 L.J.Q.B. 330; 15 Jur. 752	32
Davys v. Douglas, 4 H. & N. 180; 28 L.J.M.C. 193; 7 W.R. 327	110
Delaney v. Wallis, 14 L.R. Ir. 31; 15 Cox C.C. 525	123
Dent v. Oliver, Cro. Jac. 43, 122	85, 86
De Rutzen v. Farr, 4 A. & E. 53; 5 N. & M. 617; 1 H. & W. 735	136
—— v. Lloyd, 5 A. & E. 456; 6 N. & M. 776	37, 39, 86
Devizes (Mayor of) v. Clark, 3 A. & E. 506	80
De Winton v. Brecon (Mayor of), 26 Beav. 533	30
Dixon v. Robinson, 3 Mod. 107	33
Doe v. Catomore, 16 Q.B. 745; 20 L.J.Q.B. 728	92
—— v. Cowley, 1 C. & P. 123	63
—— v. Michael, 17 Q.B. 276	136
—— v. Roberts, 13 M. & W. 520; 14 L.J.Ex. 274	137
—— v. Thynne, 10 East, 206	136
Dorchester (Mayor of) v. Ensor, L.R. 4 Ex. 335; 39 L.J. Ex. 11	38, 75, 78, 79, 80, 86
Downshire (Marquis of) v. O'Brien, 19 L.R. Ir. 380	1, 75, 86, 91
Draper v. Sperring, 10 C.B.N.S. 131; 30 L.J.M.C. 225; 4 L.T. 365; 9 W.R. 656	46, 96
Drewry v. Barnes, 3 Russ. 94; 5 L.J.Ch. 47	30
Drinkwater v. Porter, 7 C. & P. 181	136
Dungey v. London (Mayor of), 38 L.J.C.P. 298; 20 L.T. 921; 17 W.R. 1106	144
Dyson v. London & North-Western Railway Co., 7 Q.B.D. 32; 50 L.J.M.C. 78; 44 L.T. 609; 29 W.R. 565; 45 J.P. 650	98, 168

a

Table of Cases.

	PAGE
Eastern Archipelago Co. v. The Queen, 2 E. & B. 856, 1 Id. 310; 23 L.J.Q.B. 82 ; 18 Jur. 481	130, 131
Egremont (Earl of) v. Keene, 2 Jones, Ir. Exch. 307	28
———————— v. Saul, 6 A. & E. 924	57, 137
Elias v. Nightingale, 8 E. & B. 698; 27 L.J.M.C. 151 ; 4 Jur. N.S. 166	155
Ellis v. Bridgenorth (Mayor of), 15 C.B.N.S. 52; 32 L.J.C.P. 273; 9 Jur. N.S. 1078; 8 L.T. 668 ; 12 W.R. 56	38, 39, 86, 183
———————— 2 Johns. & H. 67 ; 4 L.T. 112; 9 W.R. 331	97, 184, 186
Elwes v. Payne, 12 Ch. D. 468; 48 L.J.Ch. 831 ; 41 L.T. 118 ; 28 W.R. 234	74, 75, 76, 78
Elwood v. Bullock, 6 Q.B. 383; 13 L.J.Q.B. 330; 8 Jur. 1044	42, 43, 44, 46, 65, 98, 168
Escot v. Lanreny, Owen, 109	57
Exeter (Mayor of) v. Heaman, 37 L.T. 534	152
———————— v. Warren, 5 Q.B. 773; D. & M. 524; 8 Jur. 441	136
Fazerkerly v. Wiltshire, 1 Stra. 462	98
Fearon v. Mitchell, L.R. 7 Q.B. 690; 41 L.J.M.C. 170; 27 L.T. 33	80, 89, 152, 153, 183
Fenwick v. East London Railway Co., L.R. 20 Eq. 544; 44 L.J.Ch. 602; 33 W.R. 901	146
Ferrar v. Commissioners of Sewers, L.R. 4 Ex. 227 ; 38 L.J.Ex. 102; 21 L.T. 295; 17 W.R. 709	144
Fitzgerald v. Connors, 5 Ir. R. C.L. 191	86
Fowkes v. Joyce, 3 Lev. 260 ; 2 Lutw. 1161	33
Fredericks v. Payne, 1 H. & C. 584; 32 L.J.M.C. 14; 8 Jur. N.S. 1109; 7 L.T. 329; 11 W.R. 36	110
Freeman v. Phillips, 4 M. & S. 486	136
Fripp v. Chard Railway Co., 11 Hare, 241 : 22 L.J.Ch. 1084; 17 Jur. 887	30
Ganly v. Ledwidge, 10 Ir. R. C.L. 33	121, 123
Gard v. Callard, 6 M. & S. 69	60
Gardiner v. Williamson, 2 B. & Ad. 336	28
Gardner v. London, Chatham & Dover Railway Co., L.R. 2 Ch. 201 ; 36 L.J.Ch. 323; 15 W.R. 324 ; 15 L.T. 552	29, 30
Gerring v. Barfield, 16 C.B.N.S. 597; 11 L.T. 270	44
Gibb's Case, Owen, 27 ; 1 Leon. 158	127
Gibson v. Doeg, 2 H. & N. 615; 27 L.J.Ex. 37	23
Golightly v. Reynolds, Lofft, 88	124
Goodson v. Duffield, Cro. Jac. 313, 2 Bulstr. 21 ; Moore, 830	6, 7, 93
Great Eastern Railway Co. v. Goldsmid, 9 App. Cas. 927. 25 Ch. D. 511 ; 54 L.J.Ch. 162, 53 Id. 371 ; 52 L.T. 270, 47 Id. 727 ; 33 W.R. 81, 32 Id. 341 ; 49 J.P. 260	25, 36, 43, 44, 77, 78, 80, 81, 83, 87, 130
Great Western Railway Co. v. Swindon & Cheltenham Railway Co., 9 App. Cas. 787 ; 53 L.J.Ch. 1075 ; 51 L.T. 798 ; 32 W.R. 957 ; 48 J.P. 821	29, 144, 147, 182
Gregson v. Potter, 4 Ex.D. 142 ; 27 W.R. 840	164
Hall v. Jones, Cro. Eliz. 773, Moore, 623; 10 Co. Rep. 73a; 2 Bulstr. 21	6, 7
———— v. Metcalfe, [1892] 1 Q.B. 208 ; 61 L.J.Q.B. 53 ; 66 L.T. 498	119

Table of Cases.   xix

Hammersmith Railway Co. v. Brand, L.R. 4 H.L. 171; 38 L.J.Q.B.
   265; 21 L.T. 238; 18 W.R. 12 . . . 80, 142, 146
Hargreave v. Spink [1892] 1 Q.B. 25; 61 L.J.Q.B. 318; 65 L.T.
   650; 40 W.R. 254 122
Harris v. Hawkins, 1 Keb. 342 68
Harvey v. Facy, 2 And. 115; Godb. 131; Poph. 61 . . . 122
Heddy v. Weelhouse, Cro. Eliz. 558, 591; Moore, 474
   . . 28, 41, 57, 58, 61, 67, 68
Hickman's Case, Noy, 37; 2 Roll. Abr. 123 . . . . 64, 65, 68
Hill v. Hawker, Haukes, or Hank, Moore, 835; 2 Bulstr. 201; 1
   Roll. Rep. 1, 44 . . . . 56, 63, 65
Hill v. Midland Railway Co., 21 Ch. D. 143; 51 L.J.Ch. 774; 47
   L.T. 225; 30 W.R. 774 . . . . 147, 182
— — v. Priour, 2 Show. 34 72
— — v. Smith, 4 Taunt. 520; 10 East 476 . . . . 62, 122
Hitchman v. Watt, 58 J.P. 720 45
Hobbs v. Midland Railway Co., 20 Ch. D. 418; 51 L.J.Ch. 320;
   46 L.T. 270; 30 W.R. 516 29
Holcroft v. Heel, 1 B. & P. 400 . . . . . . 86, 87
Holloway v. Smith, 2 Stra. 1171 57
Hooper v. Kenshole, 2 Q.B.D. 127; 46 L.J.M.C. 160; 36 L.T.
   111; 25 W.R. 368 . . . . . . 150, 151, 153
Hopkins v. Great Northern Railway Co., 2 Q.B.D. 224; 46
   L.J.Q.B. 265; 36 L.T. 898 147
——— v. Worcester & Birmingham Canal Co., L.R. 6 Eq. 437;
   37 L.J.Ch. 729 30
Horner v. Whitechapel Board of Works, 55 L.J.Ch. 289; 53 L.T.
   842 46
Horwood v. Smith, 2 T.R. 750 125
Howel v. Johns. See Hall v. Jones.
Hull (Mayor of) v. Horner, 1 Cowp. 102 . . . . 23, 24
Hungerford Market Co. v. City Steamboat Co., 3 E. & E. 365; 30
   L.J.Q.B. 25; 7 Jur. N.S. 67; 3 L.T. 732 66
Hunt v. Burn, 1 Salk. 57; Holt, 60; 1 Comyns Rep. 93 . . 70

Islington Market Bill, 3 Cl. & F. 513; 12 M. & W. 20, n; H. of L.
   Jo. 285, 295, 583. . . 20, 21, 34, 35, 36, 75, 78, 80, 81, 83

Jenkins v. Harvey, 1 C.M. & R. 877, 2 Id. 393 23
Jewel's Case, 5 Co. Rep. 3 28
Jewel v. Stead, 6 E. & B. 350; 25 L.J.Q.B. 70; 1 Jur. N.S. 1136 . 78
Jones v. Matthews, 1 T.L.R. 482 45
Josephs v. Adkins, 2 Stark. 76 128

Keep v. St. Mary's Newington (Vestry of), [1894] 2 Q.B. 524; 63
   L.J.Q.B. 369; 70 L.T. 509; 58 J.P. 748; 9 R. 346 . . 6, 45
Kemp v. West End of London Railway Co., 1 K. & J. 681; 1 Jur.
   N.S. 1012 147
Kerby v. Wychelow, 2 Lutw. 1498 . . . . . . 36, 62
Kilminster v. Fitton, 53 L.T. 959. 151
Knight's Case, 5 Co. Rep. 56 a 28
Kruse v. Johnson, [1898] 2 Q.B. 91; 67 L.J.Q.B. 782; 78 L.T.
   647; 46 W.R. 630; 62 J.P. 469 . . . . . . 98, 168

xx   *Table of Cases.*

PAGE

Lambton *v.* Mellish, [1894] 3 Ch. 163 ; 63 L.J.Ch. 929 ; 71 L.T.
   385 ; 43 W.R. 5 ; 58 J.P. 835 ; 8 R. 807 . . . 111
Lancum *v.* Lovell, 6 C. & P. 437 58
Lawes' Case, 2 Co. Rep. 16 b 134
Lawnson's (Mayor of) Case, Cro. Eliz. 75 . . . 31, 64
Lawrence *v.* Great Northern Railway Co., 16 Q.B. 643 ; 20 L.J.Q.B.
   293 ; 15 Jur. 652 ; 6 Railw. Cas. 656 146
   —— *v.* Hitch, L.R. 3 Q.B. 521 ; 37 L.J.Q.B. 209; 9 B. & S.
   467 . . . . 59, 61, 136
Lax *v.* Darlington (Mayor of), 5 Ex. D. 28 ; 49 L.J. Ex. 105, 48
   L.J.Q.B. 143 ; 41 L.T. 489 ; 28 W.R. 221 ; 44 J.P. 312 32, 96
Lee *v.* Bayes *or* Robinson, 18 C.B. 599 ; 25 L.J.C.P. 249 ; 2 Jur.
   N.S. 1093 121
Leicester Forest, Case of, Cro. Jac. 155 ; Jenk. 316 . . 90, 92
Leicester Sanitary Authority *v.* Holland, 57 L.J.M.C. 75 ; 52 J.P.
   788 45
Leicester's (Town of) Case, 2 Leon. 190 71
Leight *v.* Pym, 2 Lutw. 1336 . . . . . 62, 63, 68
Le Neve *v.* Mile End Old Town (Vestry of), 8 E. & B. 1054 ; 27
   L.J.Q.B. 208 ; 4 Jur. N.S. 660 46
Lewis *v.* Hammond, 2 B. and Ald. 206 68
Lightfoot *v.* Lenet, Cro. Jac. 421 ; Bridgm. 88 . . . 58
Llandaff & Canton Market Co. *v.* Lyndon, 8 C.B.N.S. 515 ; 30
   L.J.M.C. 105 ; 6 Jur. N.S. 1344 ; 8 W.R. 693 . 152, 153, 156
Lockwood *v.* Wood, 6 Q.B. 31 ; 15 L.J.Q.B. 37 ; 10 Jur. 158
                                          55, 63, 67, 72
Loftos *v.* Gleave, 55 J.P. 149 151
   —— *v.* Kiggins, 55 J.P. 151 151
London & Brighton Railway Co. *v.* Watson, 4 C.P.D. 118 ; 48
   L.J.C.P. 316 ; 40 L.T. 183 ; 27 W.R. 614 . . . 177
   —— Brighton & South Coast Railway Co. *v.* Truman, 11 App.
   Cas. 45 ; 55 L.J.Ch. 354 ; 54 L.T. 250 ; 34 W.R. 657 ;
   50 J.P. 388 146
   —— (City of) *v.* Vanacre, 12 Mod. 270, 5 Id. 438 ; 1 Salk. 142 ;
   Carth. 480 ; Holt, 431 ; 1 Ld. Raym. 496 . . . 90, 96
   —— (Mayor of) *v.* Greenwich Union (Assessment Committee of),
   48 L.T. 437 ; 47 J.P. 420 118
   —— ——— *v.* Low, 49 L.J.Q.B. 144 ; 42 L.T. 16 ; 28 W.R.
   250 ; 44 J.P. 169 78
   —— ——— *v.* Lynn (Mayor of), 1 H.Bl. 206 ; 1 B. & P. 487 ;
   7 Bro. P.C. 120 71
   —— ——— *v.* St. Sepulchre (Overseers of), L.R. 7 Q.B.
   333 n. 117
London's (Chamberlain of) Case, 5 Co. Rep. 62 b ; 3 Leon. 264 ; 1
   Rol. Rep. 109 ; 8 Mod. 267 96
Londonderry (Mayor of) *v.* McElhinney, 9 Ir. R. C.L. 71 . 152
Lowden *v.* Hierons, 2 B. Mo. 102 . . . . . 57, 58
Lucan (Earl of) *v.* Gildea, 2 Hud. & Br. Ir. K.B. 635 . . 28
Luke *v.* Charles, 25 J.P. 148 152
Lyons *v.* Depass, 11 A. & E. 326 ; 3 P. & D. 177 ; 9 C. & P. 68 ;
   4 Jur. 505 122

Macclesfield (Mayor of) *v.* Chapman, 12 M. & W. 18 ; 13 L.J.Ex.
   32 ; 7 Jur. 1041 . . . . 79, 80
   —— *v.* Pedley, 4 B. & Ad. 397 ; 1 N. & M.
   708 . . . . 79, 80

Table of Cases.   xxi

	PAGE
Malcolmson v. O'Dea, 10 H.L.C. 593; 9 Jur. N.S. 1135; 9 L.T. 93; 12 W.R. 178	135, 136
Manchester (Mayor of) v. Lyons, 22 Ch.D. 287; 47 L.T. 677	27, 53, 79, 87, 94
———— v. Pedley, 22 Ch.D. 294 n. . . .	94
Market Overt, Case of, 5 Rep. 83 b; Cro. Eliz. 454; Moore, 360; Poph. 84	122
McHole v. Davies, 1 Q.B.D. 59; 45 L.J.M.C. 30; 33 L.T. 502; 24 W.R. 343	80, 152
McIntosh v. Romford Local Board, 61 L.T. 185 . .	103
Mercer v. Woodgate, L.R. 5 Q.B. 26; 37 L.J.M.C. 21; 18 W.R. 116	44
Metropolitan Board of Works v. McCarthy, L.R. 7 H.L. 243; 43 L.J.C.P. 385; 31 L.T. 182; 23 W.R. 115 . . .	146
Middleton (Lord) v. Lambert, 1 A. & E. 401; 3 N. & M. 841	69, 71, 72
Midleton (Lord) v. Power, 19 L.R. Ir. 1 .	38, 49, 53, 81, 90, 93
Mills v. Colchester (Mayor of), L.R. 3 C.P. 575; 37 L.J.C.P. 278	60
Mogul Steamship Co. v. McGregor Gow & Co., 23 Q.B.D. 598; [1892] A.C. 25; 58 L.J.Q.B. 465, 61 Id. 295; 61 L.T. 820, 66 Id. 1; 37 W.R. 756, 40 Id. 337; 53 J.P. 709, 56 Id. 101	33
Moran v. Pitt, 42 L.J.Q.B. 47; 28 L.T. 554; 21 W.R. 525	122, 127
Morgan v. Kingdon, 39 J.P. 471	153
Mosley v. Pierson, 4 T.R. 104	62, 83
———— v. Walker, 7 B. & C. 40; 9 D. & R. 863	34–42, 79–81, 136, 137
Motteram v. Eastern Counties Railway Co., 7 C.B.N.S. 58; 29 L.J.M.C. 59; 6 Jur. N.S. 583	169, 170
Mouflet v. Cole, L.R. 7 Ex. 70, 8 Id. 32; 41 L.J. Ex. 28, 42 Id. 62; 25 L.T. 839, 28 Id. 678; 20 W.R. 339, 21 Id. 175	78
Mountjoy's (Lord) Case, 5 Co. Rep. 3 b	28
Moyce v. Newington, 4 Q.B.D. 32; 48 L.J.Q.B. 125; 39 L.T. 535; 27 W.R. 319	121
Mulliner v. Midland Railway Co., 11 Ch.D. 611; 48 L.J. Ch. 258; 40 L.T. 121; 27 W.R. 330	29
Muspratt v. Gregory, 1 M. & W. 633, 3 Id. 677; 1 T. & G. 1086; 7 L.J. Ex. 385	33

m L f , ,

Newington Fair Case, 2 Roll. Abr. 123	79
Newport (Mayor of) v. Saunders, 3 B. & Ad. 411 . .	63, 67
Newtownards Town Commissioners v. Woods, 11 Ir. R. C.L. 506	87, 89, 152
Norman v. Bell, 2 B. & Ad. 190	65, 66, 68
Norris v. Staps, Hob. 211; Moore, 869; Hutt. 5; 1 Brownl. 48 .	96
North v. Jackson, 2 F. & F. 198	127
Northampton (Mayor of) v. Ward, 1 Wils. 107; 2 Str. 1238	32, 55, 63, 64
Norwich (Mayor of) v. Swann, 2 W. Bl. 1116 . .	32, 64
Nugent v. Kirwan, 1 Jebb & Symes, 97 . . .	33
Openshaw v. Oakeley, 60 L.T. 929; 53 J.P. 740 . .	151
Osbuston v. James, 2 Lutw. 1377	57
Parry v. Berry, 1 Comyns, 269	98
Payne v. Wilson, [1895] 1 Q.B. 653; 2 Q.B. 537; 64 L.J.Q.B. 328, 65 Id. 150; 72 L.T. 110, 73 Id. 12; 43 W.R. 657	124, 125

Table of Cases.

	PAGE
Peer v. Humphrey, 2 A. & E. 495; 4 N. & M. 430; 4 L.J.K.B. 100	123
Penny, In re, 7 E. & B. 660; 26 L.J.Q.B. 225; 3 Jur. N.S. 957	146
Penryn (Mayor of) v. Best, 3 Ex.D. 292; 48 L.J. Ex. 103; 38 L.T. 805; 27 W.R. 126 . . . . 23, 53, 79, 80, 135,	136
Percy v. Ashford (Union), 34 L.T. 579 117,	118
Perkins v. Arber, 37 J.P. 406	153
Peter v. Kendal, 6 B. & C. 703 . . . . 90, 130, 132,	133
Pim v. Currell, 6 M. & W. 234 136,	137
Pinchin v. London & Blackwall Railway Co., 5 De G.M. & G. 851; 24 L.J.Ch. 417; 1 Jur. N.S. 241 147,	182
Plaxton v. Dare, 10 B. & C. 17; 5 M. & R. 1	136
Player v. Jenkens, 1 Sid. 284; 2 Keb. 420, 501; 1 Ventr. 21; Raym. 288, 324	98
Pletts v. Beattie, [1896] 1 Q.B. 519; 65 L.J.M.C. 86; 74 L.T. 148; 60 J.P. 185; 18 Cox C.C. 264	153
—— v. Campbell, [1895] 2 Q.B. 229; 64 L.J.M.C. 225; 73 L.T. 344; 43 W.R. 634; 59 J.P. 502; 15 R. 493	153
Pope v. Whalley, 6 B. & S. 303; 34 L.J.M.C. 76; 11 Jur. N.S. 444; 11 L.T. 769; 13 W.R. 402 . . . . 89, 152,	153
Prince v. Lewis, 5 B. & C. 363; 3 D. & R. 121; 2 C. & P. 66 34, 35, 38, 81,	83
Prince's Case, 8 Co. Rep. 14 a	25
Quilligan v. Limerick Marke Trustees, 14 L.R. Ir. 265 . .	153
Reading (Mayor of) v. Clarke, 4 B. & Ald. 268	66
Reed v. Jackson, 1 East, 355	137
Reg. v. Aires or Eyre, 10 Mod. 258, 354; 1 Stra. 43 . 21, 75, 76,	131
—— v. Barnard Castle, 27 J.P. 534	117
—— v. Casswell or Caswell, L.R. 7 Q.B. 328; 41 L.J.M.C. 108; 26 L.T. 574; 20 W.R. 624	117
—— v. Crawley, 3 F. & F. 109	104
—— v. Derby J.J., 28 L.T.O.S. 89	117
—— v. East & West India Docks Co., 2 E. & B. 466; 22 L.J.Q.B. 380; 17 Jur. 1181	146
—— v. Edwards, 13 Q.B.D. 586; 53 L.J.M.C. 149; 51 L.T. 586; 49 J.P. 117	149
—— v. Eyre. See Reg. v. Aires.	
—— v. Jarvis, 3 F. & F. 108	104
—— v. London (Mayor of), L.R. 2 Q.B. 292; 16 L.T. 280 .	144
——————, L.R. 4 Q.B. 371; 38 L.J.M.C. 107; 20 L.T. 604; 17 W.R. 722; 11 Cox C.C. 280; 10 B. & S. 341 123,	124
—— v. Prosser, 11 Beav. 316; 18 L.J.Ch. 35; 13 Jur. 71 .	130
—— v. Stevenson, 3 F. & F. 106	104
—— v. Wood, 5 E. & B. 49; 3 C.L.R. 1134; 34 L.J.M C. 130; 1 Jur. N.S. 802 168,	179
—— v. Young, 52 L.J.M.C. 55	45
Rex. v. ——, 2 Show. 201 . . . . . . 4, 5,	132
—— v. Bell, 5 M. & S. 221 63,	117
—— v. Bliss, 7 A. & E. 550; 9 Jur. 959	136
—— v. Bradley, Tremaine, P.C. 449	132
—— v. Burdett, 1 Ld. Raym. 148	64
—— v. Butler, 3 Lev. 220; 2 Ventr. 344; 2 Freem. 50 . 21,	131
—— v. Cotterill, 1 B. & Ald. 67 37,	38
—— v. Cotton, 3 Camp. 444	136

Table of Cases. xxiii

	PAGE
Rex. v. Cross, 2 C. & P. 483	153
— v. Jolliffe, 2 B. & C. 54	23
— v. London (Mayor of), 1 Show. 240; 4 Mod. 53	132
————————, 2 Show. 263	58
v. Maidenhead (Corporation of), Palmer, 76; 2 Roll. Rep. 155	57, 58, 61
v. Marsden, 3 Burr. 1812; 1 W. Bl. 579	4, 5, 55, 133
— v. Miles, 7 T.R. 367	131
— v. Mosley, 2 B. & C. 226; 3 D. & R. 385	118
v. Pease, 4 B. & Ad. 30; 1 N. & M. 690	146
v. Ponsonby, Sayer, 245	132
v. Smith, 4 Esp. 111	44
— v. Starkey, 7 A. & E. 95; W., W. & D. 502	9, 38, 40, 41, 42
— v. Staverton, Yelv. 190	132
- - v. Sutton, 4 M. & S. 532	135, 137
- v. Trinity House, 1 Sid. 54, 86; 1 Keb. 137, 250, 270. 300	132, 133
- v. Watts, 2 C. & P. 486	153

Richards v. Scarborough Public Market Co., 23 L.J.Ch. 110 . 144
Ricket v. Metropolitan Railway Co., L.R. 2 H.L. 175; 36 L.J.Q.B.
205; 16 L.T. 542; 15 W.R. 937 146
Rivers v. Adams, 3 Ex.D. 361; 48 L.J. Ex. 47; 39 L.T. 39; 27
W.R. 381 19
Roberts v. Aylesbury (Churchwardens and Overseers of), 1 E. & B.
423; 22 L.J.M.C. 34; 17 Jur. 236 . . . . 117, 118
Roe v. Parker, 5 T.R. 26 137
Ross v. Taylerson, 62 J.P. 181 188
Rowe v. Brenton, 8 B. & C. 737; 3 M. & R. 133 . . . 137
Rutherford v. Straker, 42 Ch.D. 85 n.; 58 L.J.Ch. 718 n.; 60
L.T. 756 n. 153

St. Mary Newington (Vestry of) v. Jacobs, L.R. 7 Q.B. 47; 41
L.J.M.C. 72; 25 L.T. 800; 20 W.R. 249 46
Saunders v. South-Eastern Railway Co., 5 Q.B.D. 456; 49 L.J.Q.B.
761; 43 L.T. 281; 29 W.R. 56; 44 J.P. 781 . . . 168
Savage v. Brook, 15 C.B.N.S. 264; 33 L.J.M.C. 42; 10 Jur. N.S.
587; 9 L.T. 334; 12 W.R. 81 . . . . 98, 165, 186
Savery v. Smith, 2 Lutw. 1144; 3 Salk. 36 69
Sawyer v. Wilkinson, Cro. Eliz. 627 . . . . . 31, 64
Scattergood v. Sylvester, 15 Q.B. 506; 19 L.J.Q.B. 447; 14 Jur.
977 124
Seward v. Baker, 1 T.R. 616 66
Shephard v. Payne, 16 C.B.N.S. 132; 33 L.J.C.P. 158; 10 Jur.
N.S. 540; 10 L.T. 193; 12 W.R. 581 23
Shepherd v. Folland, 49 J.P. 165 153
Shillito v. Thompson, 1 Q.B.D. 12; 45 L.J.M.C. 18; 33 L.T. 506;
24 W.R. 57 104
Simpson v. Routh, 2 B. & C. 682 178
——— v. Wells, L.R. 7 Q.B. 214; 41 L.J.M.C. 105; 26 L.T. 163 6, 44
Six Carpenters' Case, 8 Rep. 146 a 31
Slade v. Drake, Hob. 295; W. Jones, 6; 1 Roll. Rep. 250; Noy,
97 22
Smith v. Shepherd, Cro. Eliz. 710; Moore, 574 . . 67, 68
Somerset (Duke of) v. Fogwell, 5 B. & C. 875; 1 D. & R. 747 . 27
Spear v. Bodmin (Union), 49 L.J.M.C. 69; 43 L.T. 127; 44 J.P.
764 119

xxiv   *Table of Cases.*

	PAGE
Specot v. Carpenter, Thos. Jones, 207	65
Spice v. Peacock, 39 J.P. 581	45
Sprosley v. Evans, 1 Roll. Abr. 103	83
Spurling v. Bantoft, [1891] 2 Q.B. 384; 60 L.J.Q.B. 745; 65 L.T. 584; 40 W.R. 157	151, 153, 182, 183
Staffordshire & Worcestershire Canal Navigation v. Birmingham Canal Navigations, L.R. 1 H.L. 254; 35 L.J.Ch. 757	29
Stamford (Corporation of) v. Pawlett, 1 Cr. & J. 57, 400; 1 Tyr. 291	57, 58, 67
Stevens v. Emson, 1 Ex. D. 100; 45 L.J.M.C. 63; 33 L.T. 821	107
Stockport, Timperley & Altrincham Railway Co., In re, 33 L.J.Q.B. 251; 10 L.T. 436; 12 W.R. 762; 10 Jur. N.S. 614	146
Strata Mercella's (Abbot of) Case, 9 Co. Rep. 25 b	28
Stretch v. White, 25 J.P. 485	152
Strike v. Collins, 55 L.T. 182; 34 W.R. 459; 50 J.P. 741	98, 165
Stubbs v. Parsons, 3 B. & Ald. 516	115
Summers v. Holborn District Board of Works, [1893] 1 Q.B. 612; 62 L.J.M.C. 81; 68 L.T. 226; 41 W.R. 445; 57 J.P. 326; 5 R. 284	6, 45
Swindon Central Market Co. v. Panting, 27 L.T. 578	62, 63
Talbot v. Lewis, 1 C.M. & R. 495; 6 C. & P. 603	137
Tarling v. Fredericks, 28 L.T. 814; 21 W.R. 785	110
Taunton Market v. Kimberley, 2 W. Bl. 1120	63
Taylor v. Chambers, Cro. Jac. 68	53, 122
—— v. New Windsor Corporation, [1898] 1 Q.B. 186; 67 L.J.Q.B. 96; 77 L.T. 585; 62 J.P. 5	27, 93, 94
Tewkesbury (Bailiffs of) v. Bricknell, 2 Taunt. 120	62, 72, 83, 84
—————— v. Diston, 6 East, 438; 2 Smith, 508	62, 83, 84, 85
Thomas v. Jenkins, 6 A. & E. 525; 1 N. & P. 587; 1 Jur. 261	136
Thompson v. Gibson, 7 M. & W. 456; 9 D.P.C. 717	85
Toronto (Corporation of) v. Vigo, [1896] A.C. 88; 65 L.J.P.C. 4; 73 L.T. 449	98
Torquay Market Co. v. Burridge, 48 J.P. 71	152
Townend v. Woodruff, 5 Ex. 506; 19 L.J.Ex. 315	32, 63
Truro (Mayor of) v. Reynolds, 8 Bing. 275; 1 M. & Scott, 272	72
Turner v. Sterling, 2 Ventr. 26, 1 Id. 206; 2 Lev. 50; 3 Keb. 26, 32	85
Tyson v. Smith, 9 A. & E. 406; 1 P. & D. 307; W., W. & D. 749	65, 68
Vaughan v. Taff Vale Railway Co., 5 H. & N. 679; 29 L.J.Ex. 247; 6 Jur. N.S. 899; 2 L.T. 394; 8 W.R. 594	146
Vauxhall Bridge Co. v. Sawyer, 6 Exch. 504; 20 L.J. Ex. 304	114
Vines v. Reading (Mayor of), 4 Bing. 8; 12 B. Moore, 201; 1 Y. & J. 4	62
Wallasey Tramway Co. v. Wallasey Local Board, 47 J.P. 821	167
Walker v. Matthews, 8 Q.B.D. 109; 51 L.J.Q.B. 243; 46 L.T. 915; 30 W.R. 338	125
Ward v. Knight, Cro. Eliz. 227; 1 Leon. 231	70, 71
Waterhouse v. Keen, 4 B. & C. 200; 6 D. & R. 257	61, 68
Wells v. Miles, 4 B. & Ald. 559	62
Whistler's Case, 10 Co. Rep. 63 a	28
White v. Yeovil (Mayor of), 61 L.J.M.C. 213	152

Table of Cases.   xxv

	PAGE
Whittaker v. Rhodes, 46 J.P. 182	45
Wigley v. Peachy, 2 Ld. Raym. 1589	31, 63, 68
Wikes v. Morefoots, Cro. Eliz. 86	127
Wilkinson v. King, 2 Camp. 335	122
—— v. Nethersol, Cro. Eliz. 530	6, 7
Willingale v. Maitland, L.R. 3 Eq. 103; 36 L.J.Ch. 64	19
Wiltshire v. Baker, 11 C.B.N.S. 237; 31 L.J.C.P. 10 n.; 5 L.T. 355; 10 W.R. 89	153
—— v. Willett, 11 C.B.N.S. 240; 31 L.J.C.P. 8; 5 L.T. 355; 10 W.R. 44	153
Wolverhampton New Waterworks Co. v. Hawkesford, 6 C.B.N.S. 336; 28 L.J.C.P. 242; 5 Jur. N.S. 1104; 7 W.R. 464	88
Wood v. Hankshead, Yelv. 13	68
Woolwich Local Board v. Gardiner, [1895] 2 Q.B. 497; 64 L.J.M.C. 248; 73 L.T. 218; 44 W.R. 46; 18 Cox C.C. 173; 59 J.P. 597; 15 R. 590	151
Worcester's (L'Evesque de) Case, Moore, 360; Poph. 84	122
Worcester v. St. Clement's, 22 J.P. 319	117
Wortley v. Nottingham Local Board, 21 L.T. 582	37, 98, 165
Wright v. Bruister, 4 B. & Ad. 116; Gunning on Tolls, 62	59, 60, 61
Yard v. Ford, 2 Wms. Saund. 172	75, 77, 78, 86
Yarmouth (Mayor of) v. Groom, 1 H. & C. 102; 32 L.J. Ex. 74; 8 Jur. N.S. 677; 7 L.T. 161	32, 63, 64, 67
York's (Archbishop of) Case, 4 Leon. 168, 214	72

YEAR BOOKS CITED.

		PAGE			PAGE
22 Ass. fol. 93 pl. 34.		49	11 Hen. VI. fol. 25 pl. 2		83
13 Edw. III. pl. 20		75	19 —— — — 66b — 9		70
29 —— —— fol. 18b		85	35 ——— — 29 — 33		120, 122
30 —— — 15b		69			
41 —— —— — 24 pl. 17		85	6 Edw. IV. — 3b — 9		7
43 —— — 30 — 4		72	11 —— — 6 — 10		120
7 Hen. IV. — 44b — 11		70	12 —— — 8b — 22		120, 122
11 —— — 5 — 13		75, 80	—— — 12b — 3		120
—— —— — 47b — 21		85	13 —— — 8b — 2		6
9 Hen. VI. — 25b — 20		69, 70	15 ——— — 7 — 12		133
			20 —— — 5 — 4		90
—— —— — 45 — 28		62, 85, 120	2 Hen. VII. — 11b — 10		11, 91
			8 —— — 4b — 1		6
1 —— —— — 19 — 13		9, 83	12 —— — 16b — 1		6
—— —— — 23 — 20		32, 40	21 —— — 5 — 2		93

TABLE OF STATUTES CITED.

	PAGE
51 Hen. III. st. 1 (Ruff.) [Assiza Pan. et Cerv.]	8
—— —— st. 6 (Ruff.) [Judic. Pillorie]	8, 9, 92, 104
3 Edw. I. (St. Westm. I.) c. 31	59, 60, 64, 68, 69, 100
—— —— —— c. 39	23
4 Edw. I. st. 1 (Ruff.) [Extenta Manerii]	137
13 Edw. I. (St. Westm. II.), c. 24	100
—— —— (St. Wynton) [st. 2, c. 5, Ruff.]	77
—————————— [st. 2, c. 6, Ruff.]	42
18 Edw. I. (st. de Quo War.) [st. 2, Ruff.]	23
—— —— (st. de Quo. War. Nov.) [st. 3, Ruff.]	23
18 Edw. II. (Ruff.) [Visus. Francipleg.]	8
2 Edw. III. c. 15	49
5 Edw. III. c. 5	49
14 Edw. III. st. 1, c. 12	12
23 Edw. III. (st. of Labourers)	5
13 Ric. II. st. 1, c. 4	11
16 Ric. II. c. 3	11
25 Hen. VI.	93
27 Hen. VI. c. 5	50, 51
17 Edw. IV. c. 2	6, 7
1 Ric. III. c. 6	6, 7
21 Hen. VIII. c. 11	124
27 Hen. VIII. c. 24	12
32 Hen. VIII. c. 20	12
5 & 6 Edw. VI. c. 3	50
2 & 3 Ph. & M. c. 7	123, 126, 127
5 Eliz. c. 4	5
31 Eliz. c. 12	123, 126, 128
43 Eliz. c. 2	117
21 Jac. I. c. 16	87
—— c. 28	92
16 Car. I. c. 19	12

	PAGE
22 Car. II. c. 8	12
22 & 23 Car. II. c. 12	12
2 Will. & M. sess. 1, c. 8	24
2 Geo. II. c. 25	175
24 Geo. II. c. 23	50, 51
9 Geo. III. c. 16	87
12 Geo. III. c. xxxviii.	44
28 Geo. III. c. lx.	44
36 Geo. III. c. 88	53, 54, 103, 104, 128, 129
38 Geo. III. c. 5	114, 115
—— —— c. 60	114
56 Geo. III. c. 138	92
57 Geo. III. c. xxix.	44, 45
7 & 8 Geo. IV. c. 27	77, 124
—— —— c. 29	124
10 Geo. IV. c. 50	93
2 & 3 Will. IV. c. 64	38
—— —— c. 71	24, 87
3 & 4 Will. IV. c. 27	87
4 & 5 Will. IV. c. 21	54, 103, 128
—— —— c. 85	107
5 & 6 Will. IV. c. 50	44
—— —— c. 76	38, 46, 96
7 Will. IV. & 1 Vict. c. 83	173, 174
1 & 2 Vict. c. 94	135, 137
2 & 3 Vict. c. 47	44, 45, 54, 134
—— —— (ss. 38–40 set out)	204
—— —— c. 71	172
5 & 6 Vict. c. 35	115–117
6 & 7 Vict. c. 68	109–111
7 & 8 Vict. c. 24	33, 92, 104
8 & 9 Vict. c. 18	145–147, 149, 182
—— —— c. 20	142, 145, 147, 162, 163, 171, 172
—— —— (ss. 140–159 set out)	175–180
—— —— c. 113	135, 148, 161

Table of Statutes.

	PAGE
9 & 10 Vict. c. 95	7
10 & 11 Vict. c. 14	25, 26, 80, 88, 100, 103, 105, 112, 113, 175–180, 184–191, 198, 208
————— (set out)	141–174
————— c. 17	145, 147
————— c. 34	105
————— c. 89	44, 45
11 & 12 Vict. c. 43	178
12 & 13 Vict. c. 92	162
————— c. 109	131
13 & 14 Vict. c. 23	50
14 & 15 Vict. c. 99	135, 161, 169, 170
15 & 16 Vict. c. 62	93
16 & 17 Vict. c. 34	115
17 & 18 Vict. c. 60	162
18 & 19 Vict. c. 120	46
————— c. 121	47
19 & 20 Vict. c. 114	103, 104, 128, 129
21 & 22 Vict. c. 98	27, 160, 181, 183, 185, 186
22 & 23 Vict. c. 56	99, 195
23 & 24 Vict. c. 27	107
————— c. 51	113
————— (set out)	202
————— c. 106	147
————— c. 107	107
24 & 25 Vict. c. 62	87
————— c. 95	124
————— c. 96	123–125
25 & 26 Vict. c. 22	107, 108
————— c. 89	187
26 & 27 Vict. c. 33	107, 108
27 & 28 Vict. c. 18	107, 108
29 & 30 Vict. c. 36	116
30 & 31 Vict. c. 125	189
————— c. 134	6, 45, 46, 134
31 & 32 Vict. c. 5	7, 45, 46
————— c. 37	185
————— c. 106	134
————— c. 122	178
32 & 33 Vict. c. 18	147
————— c. 70	189, 191
34 & 35 Vict. c. 12	94, 95
————— (set out)	193
————— c. 70	170, 185
————— c. 96	150, 151
35 & 36 Vict. c. 79	166, 167
————— c. 94	108, 109
36 & 37 Vict. c. 37	51, 52
————— (set out)	194
————— c. 66	144

	PAGE
37 & 38 Vict. c. 49	107–109
————— c. 57	87
————— c. 81	21, 131
38 & 39 Vict. c. 55	19, 27, 30, 47, 80, 88, 97, 103, 104, 112, 149–167, 181–188, 208
————— (ss. 166, 168, 316 set out)	181–188
————— c. 63	105, 106
40 & 41 Vict. c. 66	113
————— (set out)	203
41 & 42 Vict. c. 49	12, 98, 99, 100
————— (Sch. 6, Pt. II., set out)	195
————— c. 74	189, 191
42 & 43 Vict. c. 6	112, 113
————— c. 22	124
————— c. 30	105, 106
————— c. 49	180
————— c. 78	21, 131
43 & 44 Vict. c. 19	115, 116
44 & 45 Vict. c. 45	150, 151
45 & 46 Vict. c. 9	135
————— c. 50	29, 38, 46, 72, 73, 96, 97, 112, 113, 182, 186
46 & 47 Vict. c. 15	147
47 & 48 Vict. c. 12	167, 169, 170
————— (set out)	200
————— c. 13	191
————— c. 43	172, 177–180, 186, 188
————— c. 47	191
————— c. 61	132
————— c. 71	28
48 & 49 Vict. c. 3	119
————— c. 18	45
————— c. 79	93
49 & 50 Vict. c. 32	189–191
50 & 51 Vict. c. 27	100–102, 160, 185
————— (set out)	196–198
————— c. 29	105
————— c. 55	8, 12
————— c. 72	112
51 & 52 Vict. c. 10	119
————— c. 33	150, 151
————— c. 41	98, 99, 106, 110, 111, 113
————— c. 43	7, 67, 163
————— c. 46	144
52 & 53 Vict. c. 21	98
————— c. 30	189
————— c. 63	29, 135
53 & 54 Vict. c. 14	191
————— c. 59	104, 111

Table of Statutes.

	PAGE		PAGE
54 & 55 Vict. c. 70	100–102, 185	56 & 57 Vict. c. 71	120–126
— (set out)	198–200	— c. 73	27, 52, 94, 112, 182, 186
— c. 76	47, 104, 167		
55 & 56 Vict. c. 18	12, 98	57 & 58 Vict. c. 57	27, 30, 80, 97, 103, 106, 112, 113, 142–173
— c. 47	. 191		
— c. 62	. 54	— (s. 32, set out)	189–191
56 & 57 Vict. c. 19	. 98		
— c. 43	. 191	58 & 59 Vict. c. 5	. 54
— c. 61	171, 184	59 & 60 Vict. c. 15	. 106
— c. 67	. 54	60 & 61 Vict. c. 46	. 98

xxxi

ADDENDA.

Hawkers and Pedlars.

Section 23 of the Pedlars Act, 1871 (34 & 35 Vict. c. 96), provides that 'Nothing in this Act shall render it necessary for a certificate to be obtained by .... persons selling, or exposing to sale, goods, wares, or merchandise in any public mart, market, or fair legally established.'
The Hawkers Act, 1888 (51 & 52 Vict. c. 33), contains, in s. 3 (3) a proviso that 'It shall not be necessary for a licence to be taken out under this Act .... by any person selling or exposing for sale, goods, wares, or merchandise in any public mart, market, or fair legally established.'

Change of Fair Days.

(Add at p. 51, at end of the 4th paragraph.)
After the Calendar (New Style) Act, 1750, many fairs which had been granted to be held on fixed feast days were held, not on the days on which the feast days fell according to the new calendar, but eleven days later, as if the fairs had been granted to be held on nominal days of a month. Thus Bartholomew Fair at Smithfield was no longer held upon the eve, day, and morrow of St. Bartholomew (August 23-25), but upon September 3-5, though St. Bartholomew's Day continued to fall on the same nominal day, viz., on August 24.
By an order of the Home Secretary, made in 1895 under the Fairs Act, 1873, the dates of the fairs then held at Dunstable on May 22, August 12, and November 12, were altered to the second Wednesday in May, August, and November. See the 'London Gazette' for June 7, 1895, p. 3260.

Surrender of Prescriptive Franchise.

(Add at p. 93, note *f*.)
See also Addington *v.* Clode (1775) 2 W. Bl. 989 ; Carnarvon (Earl of) *v.* Villebois (1844) 13 M. & W. 313 ; Grant *on Corporations*, 324.

A TREATISE

ON THE LAW OF

MARKETS AND FAIRS

INTRODUCTION

§ 1. *Nature of Markets and Fairs.*

MARKETS and fairs, though probably of different origins,(*a*) have always been treated in English law as possessing nearly the same incidents. Indeed, the word 'market' is sometimes employed to include 'fair': and Lord Coke says that 'every fair is a market, but every market is not a fair.'(*b*) The main distinction between markets and fairs at common law appears to be that, as a rule, fairs are held only once, or at most on but few occasions, during the year, whereas markets are held once, if not on several days, in each week, or at any rate at short intervals measured by weeks. The normal market is a weekly gathering of buyers and sellers: the normal fair is a great annual gathering. If there be any other distinction, it is that the market is given over entirely to business, while amusements have a recognised place in the fair. A 'mart' seems to be the same as a fair; Lord Coke called it 'a great fair holden every year.'(*c*)

A market is defined by Chatterton, V.C.(*d*) to be 'properly

(*a*) Suggestions concerning their origins will be found in the learned First Report of the Royal Commission on Market-rights and Tolls (1889), by Mr. C. I. Elton, Q.C., and Mr. B. F. Costelloe; see also the judgment of Bruce, J., in Collins *v.* Cooper (1893) 9 T.L.R. 250.
(*b*) 2 Inst. 406.
(*c*) 2 Inst. 221.
(*d*) Downshire *v.* O'Brien (1887) 19 L.R. Ir. 380, 390.

speaking, the franchise right of having a concourse of buyers and sellers to dispose of commodities in respect of which the franchise is given.' This is, perhaps, the happiest definition of a market which has come from the Bench.(a) Any person, so long as he does not interfere with existing market-rights, may now make provision for a concourse of buyers and sellers upon his land, but such a concourse is not necessarily a market. It is not strictly a market, in the eye of the law, if there be no franchise; and no person can have a franchise of market, or 'a free market,' as it is sometimes called,(b) without a grant from the crown, or the authority of parliament.

The incident which at the present time constitutes the chief distinction between a franchise market and a mere concourse of buyers and sellers is that the owner of the former enjoys protection, and has within certain limits something akin to a monopoly, that is to say, the sole and exclusive right of holding markets. He has the right to prevent the establishment, within seven miles of his market, of any rival market which will draw customers away from his own. But a franchise of market was formerly much more than a right to provide for a concourse of buyers and sellers and to prevent other persons from doing the same; and the principle that no one can hold a market without the authority of the crown is more fundamental than the principle that when the crown has granted a market to one subject it cannot afterwards derogate from its grant by authorising the establishment of a rival, for the monopoly is but the consequence of the grant.

Even before the Norman Conquest the kings used to make grants of markets and fairs, and at the time of Domesday there were many markets and fairs in existence. The reason why they could not be set up without a grant probably was to secure that trade should be carried on only in places where it could be conducted under proper regulations, where law and order could be enforced, and the publicity of sales (which was looked upon as necessary to their validity) could be ensured. The Anglo-Saxon laws confined buying and selling to cities and

(a) See also per Bruce, J., in Collins v. Cooper (1893) 9 T.L.R. 250.
(b) A 'free market' appears to mean, not a market free to the public, or free of toll, but a franchise-market, a market belonging entirely to the lord, free from the control of other persons; compare the terms 'free court,' 'free fishery,' 'freehold,' 'free warren,' and the comprehensive expressions 'liberties' and 'franchises.'

towns, and required the presence of witnesses.(a) The laws of William the First were conceived in the same spirit :—'We forbid also that any live cattle be sold or bought except within cities, and then before three faithful witnesses.' 'Likewise let no market or fair be, or be permitted to arise, except in the cities of our kingdom, and in boroughs enclosed and walled, and in castles and in very secure places where the customs of our kingdom and our common law and the dignities of our crown, which have been constituted by our good predecessors, cannot perish, or be defrauded or violated ; and all things ought to be done regularly and openly and by judgment and justice.'(b)

To encourage irregular buying and selling of commodities was in direct violation of such a system, and accordingly it was proper to obtain the king's licence before promoting concourses of buyers and sellers—at all events, in cases where they were to be held outside established towns. The grantees of such licences became market-owners, charged with ensuring the due observance of the law. The witnessing of sales would be one of the matters for which the lord would have to provide ; and disputes arising out of such sales would, not unnaturally, be referred to him or his deputy. To this may be ascribed the origin of courts of pie powder ; and there would thus be most intimately connected with the holding of a market the exercise therein of a civil jurisdiction.

By the thirteenth century the mere gathering together of a concourse of buyers and sellers had ceased to be unlawful ; but by this time the holding of a court had become incident to every market or fair. The assumption of civil jurisdiction without a grant from the crown was unlawful. For no one could hold a court except by virtue of a franchise or the tenure of lands.(c) Hence, at this period also, a grant from the king

---

(a) See Laws of Edward the Elder (901-924); Laws of Aethelstan, (circ. 925); Laws of Edgar (959-975); Laws of Cnut (circ. 1017); Laws of Edward the Confessor (1043-1066) ; printed in *The Ancient Laws and Institutes of England* (1840), pp. 68, 88, 90, 117, 167.
(b) See *The Ancient Laws and Institutes of England* p. 212. Cf. Id. p. 209.
(c) See Prof. Maitland's introduction to *Select Pleas in Manorial and other Seignorial Courts*, Selden Soc., vol. i., where the difference between feudal or manorial jurisdictions and those which were regarded as regalities or franchises is discussed. The lord of the manor, as such, had no right to market jurisdiction. He only obtained it by charter ; so that the market

was necessary for the holding of a market or fair, and these franchises were thenceforth treated on the same footing as the many other liberties the possession of which entitled the holder to a definite jurisdiction. It was laid down that where there was no attempt to exercise such jurisdiction the promotion of a gathering of buyers and sellers was not to be regarded as the assumption of a franchise. There are several cases in the *Placita de Quo Warranto* (a) which show that such gatherings at stated times were not considered to be necessarily markets. They were sometimes called Wakes, and were not usurpations of a franchise, at any rate when no toll was taken.

These cases were followed in the eighteenth century in the case of R. v. Marsden,(b) where it was decided that the mere promotion or encouragement of a concourse of buyers and sellers at stated times was not the usurpation of a franchise, there being no holding of a court of pie powder, nor taking of toll. In this case Wilmot, J., said that 'the reason why a fair or market cannot be otherwise claimed [than by grant or prescription] is not merely for the sake of promoting traffic and commerce, but also for the like reason as in Roman law, for the preservation of order and prevention of irregular behaviour : *ubi est multitudo, ibi debet esse rector.*'

It was, and is, an essential condition of holding a market or fair that it should be open for all persons to frequent it for the purpose of buying and selling. In consideration of the provision of land for the benefit of the public the crown frequently granted to lords of markets and fairs the right to take toll upon goods sold therein. But no toll could be taken without a grant. Toll was not incident to a market or fair, and many of them were toll-free. To take toll in a toll-free market, or to take excessive toll in any market, is unlawful and a ground of forfeiture of the franchise. The market must be kept open to all to buy and sell therein freely, subject only to

---

jurisdiction belongs rather to the class of franchise jurisdictions than to that of manorial or feudal jurisdictions.

(a) See pp. 115 (Crosthwaite), 801 (Ramesbury), 212 (Emmeseye), 321 (Canterbury). In the last case the place seems to have been open, not to the public, but only to the tenants of the manor. The judges said that this is '*non regale, nec libertas: immo potius debet dici liberum tenementum.*' See also Abbot of Abingdon's case (Trin. 14 John), Abb. Plac., p. 54.

(b) (1765) 3 Burr. 1812 ; see also R. v. —— (1682) 2 Show. 201.

Nature of Markets and Fairs

the payment of such tolls as have been duly authorised by the crown or parliament.

Where there is no market or fair there appears to be nothing illegal in demanding payments resembling toll from persons admitted to buy and sell upon one's land. A person may, as a rule, throw open a building to buyers and sellers, and may stipulate for what payments he pleases ; but if he holds a market or fair he is bound to admit the public free of charge, unless he has also a grant of toll. Such payments, when demanded without any franchise, cannot be recovered as toll. They cannot be distrained for or recovered by action without showing a contract ; whereas market-tolls are recoverable by action without proof of contract, and may be distrained for.

The taking of toll has been treated either as indicating that a gathering was in fact a market, or as being in itself the usurpation of a franchise.(a) Probably it should be regarded only as evidence that the person who takes the toll is assuming to exercise a franchise.

There are some gatherings which are often spoken of as fairs or markets, but which are not properly so called, and which must be distinguished from franchise fairs and markets.

In many parts of the country statute sessions are still held in the spring or autumn, at which labourers are hired for the ensuing season. These statute sessions go by the name of hiring fairs or statute fairs, or sometimes hiring mops, but they have nothing in common with franchise fairs for buying and selling. Their origin is derived from the Statutes of Labourers, the first of which was passed in the reign of Edward III.,(b) and was followed by several others in the same and subsequent reigns. These statutes either regulated the rate of wages for labourers or empowered the justices to do so by proclamation, and they imposed penalties on persons who took or gave higher wages. The last statute on the subject was the 5 Eliz. c. 4. This repealed all previous enactments, but at the same time provided (c) that it should be lawful ' for the high constables in every shire to hold and continue petty sessions, otherwise called statute sessions, in all shires wherein such sessions have

Statute sessions

(a) Lord Mansfield, in R. v. Marsden (1765) 3 Burr. 1812, said : ' There are no marks of a fair or market, no toll taken.' See also R. v. ——— (1682) 2 Show. 201 ; and the cases from the Plac. Quo Warr., cited in note (a). p. 4, ante.

(b) 23 Edw. III. (c) By s. 48.

Introduction

been used to be kept, in such manner as theretofore accustomed.' The origin, therefore, of these statute fairs was that, when the proclamations at the sessions were to be made, both masters and labourers were in the habit of attending, to hear what the rates of hiring were to be and to make bargains for hiring for the ensuing term.(*a*) Though stalls be put up and goods sold at these gatherings, that does not make them franchise fairs.(*b*)

Gatherings of costermongers There are in some towns certain streets in which costermongers and hawkers are accustomed to put up stalls and sell their goods. There are many of these so-called street markets in London. No tolls are taken, and they are not franchise markets. It is possible that in some cases they are held where markets formerly existed, but at the present day they appear to be simply gatherings of costermongers at places chosen by them for their own convenience.

As regards the metropolis, costermongers may now carry on their business in the streets in this way, provided that they comply with the regulations from time to time made by the Commissioner of Police with the approval of the Home Secretary.(*c*)

§ 2. *Courts of Pie Powder.*

There was formerly held in every fair a court of pie powder.(*d*) Such a court was incident to every fair and market granted by the crown,(*e*) and might exist by grant, prescription, or custom without a fair or market ;(*f*) but now nearly all these courts have ceased to be held.(*g*)

(*a*) See per Blackburn, J., in Simpson *v.* Wells (1872) L.R. 7 Q.B. 214.
(*b*) *Ibid.*
(*c*) See 30 & 31 Vict. c. 134, s. 6; 31 & 32 Vict. c. 5, s. 1; Keep *v.* Vestry of St. Mary's Newington [1894] 2 Q.B. 524; Summers *v.* Holborn District Board of Works [1893] 1 Q.B. 612. See also *post*, p. 45.
(*d*) 'Court of Pepoudres, vulgarly pipowders;' 4 Inst. 272. A corruption of O.F. 'pied pouldre,' Lat. 'curia pedis pulverisati'; so called from the dusty feet of the suitors; see Skeat, *Etymol. Dict.* In Wilkinson *v.* Nethersol (1597) Cro. Eliz. 530, Anderson, C.J., said that these courts had this name 'because they are there to hold pleas only of things *parvi ponderis*'!
(*e*) Stat. 17 Edw. IV. c. 2, preamble, and 1 Rich. III. c. 6; 4 Inst. 272; Howel *v.* Johns (1600) Cro. Eliz. 773; Goodson *v.* Duffield (1613) Cro. Jac. 313, 2 Bulstr. 21; Y.B. 8 Hen. VII. 4 b, 12 Hen. VII. 16 b.
(*f*) Goodson *v.* Duffield, *supra*; Y.B. 13 Edw. IV. 8 b; 4 Inst. 272.
(*g*) The Report of the Royal Commission, vol. iii., p. 102, refers to a pie powder court as still held at Hemel Hempstead. And such a court still exists at Bristol. With regard to the latter court see the Orders in

Courts of Pie Powder

The court was a court of record, held before the steward (seneschal) appointed by the lord,(*a*) or (by special custom) before the mayor or his deputy and two citizens.(*b*) At Stourbridge fair, which belonged to the corporation of Cambridge, it was held before the mayor and bailiffs of Cambridge.(*c*) The court, as a rule, had jurisdiction only in matters arising within, and during the time of, the fair or market, such as contracts, covenants, debts, deeds, trespasses, batteries, or disturbances made, done, or arising in the fair or market.(*d*) The court, perhaps, dealt with slanders spoken in the fair or market concerning wares exposed therein, but not with slanders of the person which did not touch any matter of contract made therein.(*e*) The court had no jurisdiction in penal matters.(*f*) The jurisdiction was contemporaneous with the holding of the market, and a court held at one fair could not decide questions arising on a contract made at a preceding fair.(*g*)

The County Courts Act, 1888,(*h*) enables the lord of any hundred, honour, manor, or liberty, having any court in right thereof in which debts or demands may be recovered, to surrender to the crown the right of holding such court for any such purpose, and provides that such surrender shall not be deemed to infer the surrender or loss of any other franchise incident to the lordship.(*i*) The same Act enables the crown, by order in council, to exclude from the jurisdiction of a court of local jurisdiction causes of which a county court has cognisance, if a petition, praying for such order, be presented to

Council dated May 16, 1871, June 26, 1873, July 19, 1883, and the orders and rules for that court, dated June 20, 1878.
 (*a*) Y.B. 6 Edw. IV. 3 b ; 3 Black. Comm. 32.
 (*b*) Goodson *v*. Duffield, *supra*; see also Com. Dig., Market, G 1 ; Bac. Abr., Court of Pipowders ; 4 Inst. 272.
 (*c*) Dyer, 132 b, pl. 80.
 (*d*) Goodson *v*. Duffield (1613) Cro. Jac. 313, 2 Bulstr. 21 ; Howel *v*. Johns (1600) Cro. Eliz. 773, 4 ; Statutes 17 Edw. IV. c. 2, and 1 Rich. III. c. 6 (still unrepealed).
 (*e*) Howel *v*. Johns, *supra*; see 10 Co. 73 b.
 (*f*) Wilkinson *v*. Nethersol (1597) Cro. Eliz. 530. The Record of the Court of the Fair of St. Ives (1275), extracts from which have been published by the Selden Society in vol. ii. of the *Select Pleas in Manorial Courts*, presents a vivid picture of the procedure in the court of a fair. It is not clear, however, that all the matters dealt with by the steward of the fair came before him in the exercise of his jurisdiction as judge of a Court of Pie Powder. (See Prof. Maitland's introduction.)
 (*g*) Goodson *v*. Duffield, *supra* ; Dyer, 132 b, pl. 80.
 (*h*) 51 & 52 Vict. c. 43.
 (*i*) s. 6. The repealed 9 & 10 Vict. c. 95, s. 14, was to the like effect.

the crown by the council of any city or borough, or a majority of the ratepayers of any parish, within which the local court is established.(*a*)

§ 3. *Correction of the Market.*

Notwithstanding some general statements which may be found to the contrary, lords of markets or fairs, as such, do not appear to have had any general jurisdiction therein over matters of a criminal nature. Offences in the market, such as the sale of unwholesome meat, or the use of false weights and measures, mentioned in the 'Judicium Pillorie,' (*b*) came more properly within the jurisdiction known as view of frankpledge (*visus franci plegii*) or court leet, or that of the sheriff's tourn ; and the records of courts leet furnish many examples of the punishment of offences of this nature.(*c*) The right to punish forestallers was either a separate franchise,(*d*) or part of the jurisdiction of frankpledge.(*e*)

Very often, however, the lord of a market or fair possessed also the view of frankpledge, and in such cases the same authority which had the market jurisdiction had also criminal jurisdiction over market offences.

Although, as we have just stated, the lord of a market, as such, had no general criminal jurisdiction, yet it seems fairly clear that he had the right and duty of enforcing the assize of bread and ale on market and fair days within the market, and that this right was incident to a market or fair, and followed from the grant.(*f*)

The 'Assize of Bread and Ale' (*g*) fixed the price of bread in relation to that of wheat, and the price of beer or ale in relation to that of wheat, barley, and oats. Bakers and brewers convicted of not observing the assize were to be fined for the first three offences, but if the offence were 'grievous

(*a*) S. 7.
(*b*) 51 Hen. III. st. 6, Ruff.
(*c*) See, for instance, *The Court-Leet Jurisdiction in Norwich*, Selden Soc. vol. v.
(*d*) See Plac. Quo. Warr., Northolm, p. 556.
(*e*) For the statute for View of Frankpledge, see 18 Edw. II. Ruff. (repealed by 50 & 51 Vict. c. 55, but without prejudice to any court leet, &c., then still held ; see s. 40.)
(*f*) See Plac. Quo Warr., Ormskirk (p. 370), Wigan (p. 371,) Hovingham (p. 219).
(*g*) Assiza Panis et Cervisiæ (51 Hen. III. st. 1, Ruff.); see also Judicium Pillorie (51 Hen. III., st. 6, Ruff.). These statutes were finally repealed by the St. Law Revision Act, 1863.

Correction of the Market 9

and often' they were to be sentenced, the baker to the pillory, and the brewer to the tumbrel. For the punishment of offenders against the assize, the market-owner was bound to have in the market-place his pillory and tumbrel, and to use them.(a) Many markets were forfeited because the lord took fines when he ought to have had recourse to these instruments. This administration was spoken of as the *correction* of the assize or the correction of the market,(b) and the lord's officers for enforcing it were called correctors. So far as the lord of a market or fair was concerned, this right did not, it seems, carry with it any general right of correcting the assize of bread and ale, but only extended to breaches in the market or fair.

Beyond what has now been stated, we have not been able to trace any general right in a market-owner to exercise criminal jurisdiction. In reading the records of fair courts, no safe conclusion as to the extent of market jurisdiction can be drawn, unless it be clear that the market-owner had not also view of frankpledge. Moreover, it would be dangerous to conclude that jurisdiction in fact exercised in any such court was always rightfully exercised.

§ 4. *Extraordinary Jurisdiction.*

In some cases lords of fairs claimed very extensive jurisdiction by special grant or prescription. An example of this claim will be found in the case of St. Giles' Fair at Winchester. There a charter of Edward III.(c) (confirming and enlarging previous charters) granted to the Bishop, who was lord of the fair, that the keys of the city should be given up to him before the fair ; 'and the Bishop from the time that the keys and custody of the gates have been delivered to him shall, by his justiciaries and other ministers, have the custody of the whole city and cognisance of all pleas between the men and tenants of the city, and all other persons within a circuit of seven leagues round the fair, regarding breaches of law, debts, and all contracts whatsoever. . . . And the said justiciaries shall hold all the pleas of the crown, whether by appeals or by indictments

(a) Stat. Judicium Pillorie (*supra*) ; see also Plac. Quo Warr., Northolm (pp. 551–7), Seton (p. 123), Wahull (p. 36), Ireby (p. 124), Ilkeston (p. 137), Suthyevele (p. 75).
(b) Y.B. 11 Hen. VI. f. 19; see also per Littledale, J., in R. v. Starkey, 7 A. & E. 95, 107.
(c) Edited by G. W. Kitchin, D.D., formerly Dean of Winchester, and printed in the Report of Royal Commission, vol. i. p. 91.

10   *Introduction*

arising out of the facts, within the aforesaid precinct, shall pass judgment thereon, and take execution during the fair, as our justiciaries do in like case elsewhere in our realm of England.'

Similarly, the Archbishop of York had a fair there by prescription, and at the time of the fair the city bailiffs handed their staves over to the Archbishop's bailiffs, 'who shall during the fair keep the peace of the city, and collect the tolls, and take all other profits, as the city bailiffs do at other times.' (a) Again, at Hereford, the Bishop claimed by charter 'the whole care and custody of the city at the time of the fair,' and 'to have all attachments and power over all merchandise, as well in houses as without; and that all plaints of all manner of forfeitures are to come before the bailiffs of the Bishop, and they are to do justice to all complainants, and are to receive the amercements thereon during the fair.'(b)

§ 5. *The Clerk of the Market.*

The franchise of a market or fair did not carry with it the right to keep standards and hold assizes of weights and measures. Where the lord of a market possessed this right, he had it as a separate and independent franchise.(c) Any general history of the law of weights and measures would be out of place here,(d) but it seems proper, on account of his name and office, to make some reference to the Clerk of the Market of the King's Household (*Clericus mercati hospitii regis*).

It has been said that the duties of this ancient officer of the crown originally consisted in the regulation of a continual market kept at the gate of the king's court.(e) But in the time of Edward I., and afterwards, when this method of supplying the royal table had been abandoned, his duties were somewhat different. He was entrusted with standards and samples of the king's weights and measures; and with these he travelled from place to place and held his courts at all

(a) Plac. Quo. Warr. 222-3; Drake's Hist. of the City of York (1736), pp. 218, 256.
(b) Abb. Plac. p. 113; Duncombe's Hist. of Hereford (1804), p. 293.
(c) See e.g. Plac. Quo. Warr., Stanford (p. 395), Catthorp (Id.), Stanewyg (p. 70).
(d) The present law on the subject, so far as it relates particularly to markets and fairs, is dealt with *post*, pp. 98-104.
(e) 4 Inst. 273; 2 Inst. 543.

The Clerk of the Market

markets within the verge.(a) He examined the weights and measures used in the market, burned such as were false, and amerced offenders.(b) The refusal of the bailiff of a market to submit to his jurisdiction was a ground for seizure of the franchise into the king's hands.(c) In some cases he may have had power to inquire into the jurisdiction of the lord of the market, and to ascertain whether the assize of bread and ale had been duly kept.(d)

By the retention of fines which ought to have been paid into the Exchequer (e) and the exaction of bribes and illegal fees, the office was made very profitable ; and in 1389 and 1392 the abuses of the office attracted the attention of parliament.(f) Another matter of complaint about the same period was that the officer acted outside his jurisdiction, and refused to recognise the charters which the crown from time to time granted to cities and other places exempting them from his control.(g) Such exemptions seem to have been granted freely down to the reign of Henry VIII. At any rate, two of

(a) The verge extended to within 12 miles from the place where the king was keeping his court.
(b) Fleta, bk. 2, c. 20; Britton, bk. 1, c. 31, ff. 75 b, *et seq.*; 4 Inst. 273.
(c) See Britton, loc. cit. *supra*; cf. per Brian, C.J., Y.B. 2 Hen. VII. f. 11.
(d) *Ibid.* In 1406 the clerk of the market was ordered 'to do his office as in the time of Edward 1st ordained and used'; see Rot. Parl. 8 Hen. IV. no. 82. The extent of his jurisdiction must have depended in each case upon the terms and validity of the letters patent appointing him ; see Burdett's Case (1710) 1 Salk. 327, which seems to be the latest reported case in which this officer's powers were considered in a court of law. This royal officer must not be confused with the clerk or bailiff of a market appointed by the lord to regulate it on the lord's behalf.
(e) The accounts of the clerks of the market from 25 Edw. I. to 36 Eliz. appear to be kept at the Record Office ; see 19th Rep. of the Deputy Keeper of the Public Records, p. 7 (1858), and 20th Id. p. xiii. (1859).
(f) See 13 Ric. II. st. 1, c. 4, and 16 Ric. II. c. 3. See also Rot. Parl. 18 Edw. III. no. 12 (4), and 50 Edw. III. nos. 87 and 152.
(g) See Rot. Parl. 51 Edw. III. no. 53 ; 1 Ric. II. nos. 75 and 128. Under the charters of 1327, 1462, and 1550, the exclusive right of performing all that appertained to the office within the city of London and the borough of Southwark was conferred upon the Lord Mayors and their deputies, who thus acquired authority to regulate the weights and measures used in the London markets (see Birch, *Hist. Charters of London*, 1887, pp. 55, 82, 122 ; Royal Commission, 1893, City of London, Statement by the Corporation, p. 272). In the Duchy of Lancaster the Duke acquired by charter the like exclusive right (see Hardy's *Charters of the Duchy*, 1845). The University of Oxford still appoints Clerks of the Market under its statutes. As to their duties, see *Corpus Stat. Univ. Oxon.* (1768), p. 168.

his statutes provided that, notwithstanding any grant to the contrary, the King's Clerk of the Market, and none other, should exercise the office within the verge in places where the king from time to time tarried in person.(*a*)

'The Description of England' in Holinshed's Chronicles contains an interesting chapter on Fairs and Markets.(*b*) The 'covetousness' of the clerks of the market is there bewailed, and it is stated that at each view of measures they had a trick of providing business for the next. By 1640 further abuses had arisen. The clerks were assuming to have jurisdiction both within and without the verge,(*c*) and the office was usually farmed out in each county at a sum which the lessee could make up only by extortion. To remedy this, the 16 Car. I., c. 19, was passed, which again confined the jurisdiction of the crown official within the verge of the king's court, and entrusted the execution of the office outside, in cities and boroughs, to the mayor or other head officer, and in liberties and franchises to the lord or his deputy. All these persons were subsequently empowered and required to seal or mark measures of corn and salt when brought to them for that purpose ;(*d*) and it was further provided (*e*) that in places where there was no clerk of the market this duty should be performed by 'the person having the benefit of the market.' These seem to be the latest statutes in which the Clerk of the Market of the King's Household is referred to by name.(*f*)

Blackstone says that 'the court of the clerk of the market is incident to every fair and market in the kingdom, to punish misdemeanors therein' ;(*g*) but at the time when he wrote the court of this officer of the king's household was, in all

---

(*a*) 27 Hen. VIII. c. 24, s. 12 ; 32 Hen. VIII. c. 20, s. 7. The franchise rights of London and certain other places were preserved.
(*b*) Bk. 2, ch. 18 (2nd edit., 1587.)
(*c*) Relying, possibly, on the 14 Edw. III. st. 1, c. 12 : 'And it is not the king's mind but that the clerk of the market shall do his office *where he will*, according as he was wont to do in times past.'
(*d*) 22 Car. II. c. 8, s. 4.
(*e*) 22 & 23 Car. II. c. 12, s. 4.
(*f*) The repeal of these statutes by the St. Law Revision Act, 1863, was without prejudice to established jurisdictions or existing franchises or offices, though derived therefrom. The Weights and Measures Act, 1878, preserved existing franchises to examine, and verify or destroy, weights and measures ; and the Weights and Measures (Purchase) Act, 1892, authorised county and borough councils to purchase such franchises by agreement.
(*g*) 4 Bl. Com. 275.

probability, almost obsolete.(*a*) Indeed, even in Coke's day there was 'no great need for him, for the justices of assize, the justices of oyer and terminer, the justices of the peace, the sheriffs in their tourns, and the lords in their leets, may so inquire of false weights and measures.'(*b*) It has been stated recently that one of the latest recorded instances of a clerk of the market exercising powers as a king's officer was in Middlesex, in 1738, when such an officer was authorised by letters patent to inspect all weights and measures within the 'little virge.'(*c*)

(*a*) Blackstone was misled by a passage in Nathaniel Bacon's *Law of English Government* (bk. I, c. 8) into stating that the court derived its jurisdiction from the bishop.

(*b*) See 4 Inst. 273. The sheriff's tourn was abolished by 50 & 51 Vict. c. 55, s. 18.

(*c*) See *Our Weights and Measures*, by H. J. Chaney (1897).

PART I

THE LAW OF MARKETS AND FAIRS GENERALLY

THE LAW OF MARKETS AND FAIRS GENERALLY

CHAPTER I

TITLE TO THE FRANCHISE

THE right of holding a market or fair is well known to the common law. It is an incorporeal hereditament, and is one of those incorporeal hereditaments which are called franchises.(*a*) A franchise is usually defined to be a royal privilege, or branch of the crown's prerogative, subsisting in the hands of a subject.(*b*) The right of creating a franchise to hold a market or fair has from time immemorial been annexed to the crown as part of the prerogative ;(*c*) and no market or fair in the hands of a subject can have a legal origin or legal existence unless established by the royal prerogative, or by the authority of an Act of Parliament.(*d*)

Franchises

The crown, indeed, may erect a market or fair 'by ordinance, without granting it unto any' ;(*e*) that is to say, the crown may, by virtue of the prerogative, establish a market or fair to subsist in the hands of the crown, and the formal instrument providing for its establishment is called an ordinance. The early records contain several references to markets and fairs subsisting in the hands of the crown,(*f*) and

Ordinances

(*a*) Finch, L. 164 ; 2 Blac. Comm. 37, 38.   (*b*) *Ibid.*
(*c*) Bracton, lib. 3, tract. 2, cap. 1, sect. 3, fol. 117 ; Bacon, Abr., Fairs and Markets (A. 1) ; notes to 2 Wms. Saund. 501 n (b).
(*d*) As to the rare case of the valid creation of a franchise by a subject having jura regalia, see Grant *on Corporations,* 11. Durham market seems to have originated in a grant in 1180 to the Corporation of Durham by the then Bishop of Durham ; see Report of Royal Commission, vol. xiii. part ii. p. 176 ; vol. iv. p. 384.
(*e*) Hob. 15, the source of the statements to the same effect in 2 Roll. Abr. 197, 17 Vin. Abr. 145, Chitty, Prerog. 193.
(*f*) See, for example, Rot. Hundred. vol. i. p. ii. (Sallingford fair) : Id. p. 13 (Wycombe fair) : Id. p. 18 (Windsor fair) : Id. p. 70 (Exeter fair, a moiety whereof was in the hands of the king and the citizens) : Abb.

C

also examples of ordinances for their erection.(a) It seems, however, that, at the present day, there are few, if any, markets or fairs which belong to the crown.(b) The 'king's markets' and 'king's fairs' of former times have been either granted away to subjects (c) or discontinued.

The franchise of holding markets and fairs was in early times usually granted to the lord of the manor within which they were to be held, or, where they were to be held within a city or borough, to the city or borough corporation. The charters whereby the inhabitants of towns were incorporated often contained grants of markets and fairs to the new corporations. Sometimes the inhabitants were incorporated for no other purpose than that the body corporate might hold a market or fair, as was the case at Hemel Hempstead under a charter of 1539.(d) Sometimes the inhabitants were not incorporated, but a body corporate was created to hold markets and fairs in trust for them. Thus at Hungerford the franchise was granted in 1432 to the then lords of the manor, and the grant incorporated them and made them trustees of the franchise for the inhabitants.(e) In the reign of Queen Anne we find instances of grants to individual persons in fee in trust for the inhabitants, in which neither the inhabitants nor their trustees were incorporated ;(f) and in one case the trust was for the poor of the parish.(g) Markets and fairs at one time existed at Skipsea and Withernsea under grants simply 'to the men of the vill their heirs and successors.'(h) The difficulties, both legal and practical, in the way of the

Plac. p. 206 b (Hereford fair) : Id. p. 246 (Marlborough market) ; Plac. Quo War. p. 185 (Bridport market).

(a) See, for example, Rot. Chart. p. 77 (2 John, Portsmouth) ; Id. p. 135 (6 John, Marlborough).

(b) See the Parliamentary Return on Market Rights and Tolls, 1886 ; the 74th Report of the Commissioners of Woods, 1896 ; and the Final Report of Royal Commission, on Market Rights and Tolls, pp. 18, et seq.

(c) Thus the crown sold Romford Market in 1829; see Report of Royal Commission, vol. iii. p. 53. See Id. p. 40, as to Hitchin.

(d) See Report of Royal Commission, vol. iii. p. 102.

(e) Id. vol. iv. p. 173.

(f) Pat. 8 Anne, p. 5, No. 13 (Chagford) : Pat. 5 Anne, p. 2, No. 18 (Wincalton). See Report of Royal Commission (1888) vol. i. pp. 133, 134.

(g) Pat. 4 Anne, p. 3, No. 9 (St. Udy). See same report, vol. i. p. 132.

(h) See Calend. Rot. Chart. p. 174, 12 Edw. III. Nos. 29, 30. Poulson (*Hist. of Holderness*, vol. i. p. 445) sets out the grant to the men of Skipsea.

franchise being exercised by the inhabitants of a place when not incorporated were probably met in these cases by the fact that the manors were in the hands of the king, whose bailiffs seem to have regulated these markets and fairs ;(a) and accordingly these grants should, perhaps, be described as ordinances. There is authority, however, for the view that a grant by the crown to the inhabitants of a particular parish or vill for such a specific purpose as the holding of a market has the effect of incorporating them so as to carry that purpose into effect.(b)

In more recent times markets and fairs have generally been erected by Acts of Parliament, and in such cases they are often owned by trustees or commissioners appointed under such Acts. Acts of Parliament have also frequently been passed for the purpose of regulating markets and fairs already in existence. Now, under the provisions of the Public Health Act, 1875,(c) urban district councils possess the power to establish markets in their districts. In such cases the markets are owned by the district councils which establish them. *Market authorities*

An individual grantee of a market or fair is generally called the lord or the owner of the market or fair. But this is, perhaps, not an altogether convenient expression where a market or fair is in the hands of a body of persons, such as trustees or a district council. 'The market authority' is a suitable phrase which is often used to include every kind of market-owner.

§ 1. *Acquisition by grant.*

The instruments whereby the sovereigns of England make grants and express their intentions to their subjects are called charters, letters patent, and letters close. From the end of the twelfth century to the year 1516 all grants of fairs and markets were made by charter.(d) Since that date all such grants have been made by letters patent.(e) Since 1846 *Charters and letters patent*

(a) See Poulson, *Hist. of Holderness*, vol. i. p. 398, vol. ii. p. 458.
(b) See Rivers v. Adams (1878) 3 Ex. D. 361, 366, per Kelly, C.B., who cites the early authorities; and Willingale v. Maitland (1866) L.R. 3 Eq. 103, 109.
(c) 38 & 39 Vict. c. 55.
(d) Introduction to *Rotuli Chartarum*, by Sir Thos. Duffus Hardy, vol. i. part. i. pp. i. ii.
(e) Introduction to *Rotuli Litterarum Patentium*, vol. i. part ii. p. ii.

few, if any, grants of market-rights have been made by the crown. The difference between charters and letters patent is mainly one of form, charters being documents of a more strictly formal nature. Many examples of grants of markets and fairs may be found in the Rotuli Chartarum. The following is given as an example :—

Johannes Dei gratia [rex Angliae, dominus Hiberniae, dux Normanniae, Aquitanniae, et comes Andegaviae, archiepiscopis, episcopis, abbatibus, comitibus, baronibus, justiciariis, vicecomitibus, praepositis, et omnibus ballivis et fidelibus suis, salutem.] Sciatis nos dedisse et concessisse, et hac carta nostra confirmasse, Roberto Corbet et heredibus suis unum mercatum singulis ebdomadis (*a*) una die, scilicet die Mercurii, apud Cocs.(*b*) Quare volumus et firmiter praecipimus quod idem Robertus et heredes sui post ipsum praedictum mercatum habeant et teneant in perpetuum cum omnibus libertatibus et liberis consuetudinibus ad hujusmodi mercata pertinentibus, ita tamen quod mercatum illud non sit ad nocumentum vicinorum mercatorum. Testibus Gaufrido filio Petri comite Essexae, W. Marescallo etc., Wilhelmo Briwerro. Data per manum S. Wellensis Archidiaconi et J. de Gray etc., apud Wigorniam, x die Aprilis anno regni nostri primo.(*c*)

A grant of a market or fair from the crown does not necessarily carry with it the right to hold the market or fair granted. For the law does not permit the crown to grant new market-rights which would be injurious to other market-rights already in existence. The crown may not derogate or detract by new grants from other grants which it has previously made, even though the new grants would be beneficial to the public at large.(*d*) An Act of Parliament is the only instrument which can infringe or detract from a previous grant. This rule is well recognised by the clause 'ita ut non sit ad nocumentum vicinarum nundinarum,' or 'alterius mercati,' or other clause with words to that effect, which is usually inserted in grants of markets and fairs. But the omission of such a clause from a grant does not benefit the grantee ; for the law always

---

(*a*) ' In every week.' *Septimana* is the word more commonly used for 'week' in Latin charters.
(*b*) Caux, Caus, Cause, Course, or Corze, Salop.
(*c*) Rot. Chart. 1 John, part ii. membr. 15.
(*d*) Bracton, lib. ii. c. 24, fol. 56 b ; Vin. Abr. ' Franchise' (G) 9 ; Islington Market Bill (1835) 3 Cl. & F. 513, 12 M. & W. 20 n.

Acquisition by Grant

implies such a clause whenever it is not expressed.(*a*) It is said, however, that a prior grantee loses the benefit of his priority by not making use of his grant.(*b*)

In order to guard against the making of improper grants, it has been the practice of the crown not to make a grant until an inquisition has been held under a writ of *ad quod damnum*, and a jury has found, by their return to the writ, that the proposed market or fair would not be to the damage of the crown or any subject.(*c*) But an invalid grant derives no validity from the fact that such an inquisition was held. If it should appear, after the grant has been made, that it works an injury to an earlier grant, or that the crown was otherwise deceived in making it,(*d*) that is a ground for its repeal by *scire facias*.(*e*) Moreover, the grantee or owner of a market or fair which is injured by the erection of a new market or fair under a later grant has a remedy by action for damages, which he can enforce at once, and without waiting until the later grant has been repealed.(*f*)

The procedure to obtain a grant from the crown appears to be as follows.(*g*) The fiat of the Attorney-General, authorising the issue of a writ of *ad quod damnum*, must first be obtained. The writ will then be issued upon production of the fiat. It was formerly issued by the clerk of the petty bag as cursitor.(*h*) It seems that it would now be issued by the senior clerk of the Crown Office Department of the Central Office of the Supreme Court of Judicature.(*i*) The writ is directed to the sheriff of the county in which the proposed market or fair would be held. On receiving the writ, the sheriff summons a jury, who try the question whether the grant would be to the detriment of the crown or any subject. If the

Writs of ad quod damnum

Obtaining a grant

(*a*) R. *v.* Butler (1685) 3 Lev. 222.
(*b*) Bracton, lib. ii. c. 24, ff. 56 b, 57.
(*c*) F.N.B. 225 F.
(*d*) Vin. Abr. 'Prerogative' (O.b.) 14.
(*e*) R. *v.* Aires (1714) 10 Mod. 258, 354 ; (*S.C.*) R. *v.* Eyre, 1 Stra. 43 ; R. *v.* Butler (1685) 3 Lev. 220, 2 Ventr. 344 ; Islington Market Bill (1835) 3 Cl. & F. 513, 12 M. & W. 20 n.
(*f*) 2 Inst. 406. See *post*, Ch. V.
(*g*) Second Report of the Deputy Keeper of the Public Records (1841), p. 28.
(*h*) As to the abolition of the office of Clerk of Petty Bag, see 42 & 43 Vict. c. 78, s. 14 (2) and sched. I., part ii.
(*i*) 37 & 38 Vict. c. 81, s. 5 ; R.S.C., Jan. 30, 1889. See Short and Mellor's *Crown Office Practice*, p. 10.

verdict or inquisition of the jury be to the effect that the grant would not be detrimental, it is returned to the Crown Office Department, and the party who desires the grant must then apply for it by petition to the crown, transmitting with the petition an office copy of the inquisition. After receiving the petition, the crown makes an order of reference to the Attorney-General as to the expediency of granting the market or fair. If his report be favourable, the royal warrant under the sign manual follows, and in due course the grant under the great seal is made and enrolled.(*a*)

Grants have generally been made in perpetuity, but occasionally they have been limited in time, as for a term of 40 or 95 years, or with a clause determining the grant upon a certain event.(*b*)

§ 2. *Acquisition by prescription or usage.*

A claim to hold a market or fair, as of right, can be supported at the common law only on the ground that the crown has granted a franchise to the claimant or his predecessors in title.(*c*) But it by no means follows that inability to produce such a grant is fatal to the claim. 'Prescription and antiquity of time fortifies all titles and supposeth the best beginnings the law can give them.'(*d*)

If the possessor of a market or fair can show that he and his predecessors in title have held it openly, uninterruptedly, and as of right,(*e*) from time immemorial, the law will presume that the market or fair had a lawful origin in an ancient grant, which in the lapse of time must have been lost.(*f*) In such case the owner of the market or fair is said to have a prescriptive title to the franchise, and his title to it is said to be a title by prescription.

A market or fair is said to have been held from time immemorial, or, to use the fuller phrase, from time whereof the memory of man runneth not to the contrary, whenever it has

---

(*a*) See Second Report of the Deputy Keeper of the Public Records, p. 26.
(*b*) See Pat. 6 Anne, p. 4, No. 8; 9 Anne, p. 3, No. 7; 4 Anne, p. 4, No. 21; Report of Royal Commission, vol. i. pp. 132–134.
(*c*) *Ante*, p. 17.
(*d*) Slade *v.* Drake (1618) Hob. 295.
(*e*) 'Nec per vim nec clam nec precario'; Bracton, fol. 222 b.
(*f*) Co. Litt. 114 b.

Acquisition by Prescription or Usage

been held down from the beginning of the reign of Richard I.(*a*) For legal memory runs back to that time, but extends no further back, in accordance with the limitation as regards writs of right imposed by the Statute of Westminster I.,(*b*) and also in accordance with the provisions of the statutes of *Quo Warranto*.(*c*)

Positive evidence, however, that the market or fair has been held ever since legal memory began is not essential to secure a title by prescription. It would seldom be possible to produce such evidence.

Long user

Whenever an uninterrupted modern usage to hold the market or fair be proved, the proper direction to a jury is that they ought to infer that the market or fair has existed from time immemorial, unless there be evidence that it has not done so ;(*d*) and a usage for twenty years, if uncontradicted and unexplained, is sufficient to justify a jury in inferring an immemorial right.(*e*) If, however, it be shown that the usage arose since 1189, then, however long the modern usage may have lasted, a claim to a title by prescription necessarily fails.(*f*)

But, if the usage has continued for any considerable length of time, the right to hold the market or fair may, nevertheless, be established. It is always possible that a franchise was granted within the time of legal memory, and that the instrument of grant has been lost ; and the law fully recognises this possibility. ' It is a maxim of the law of England to give effect to everything which appears to have been established for a considerable time, and to presume that what has been done has been done of right and not of wrong.'(*g*) ' It is a most convenient thing that every supposition, not wholly irrational, should be made in favour of long-continued enjoyment.'(*h*)

Accordingly, although it is shown that there was a time

(*a*) Co. Litt. 215 a ; 2 Roll. Abr. 268, 269.
(*b*) 3 Edw. I. c. 39 ; 2 Inst. 238.
(*c*) 18 Edw. I. st. 2, 3 ; 2 Inst. 494.
(*d*) Jenkins *v.* Harvey (1835) 1 C.M. & R. 877, 894 ; 2 Id. 393, 407, per Parke, B. ; Shephard *v.* Payne (1864) 16 C.B.N.S. 132, 135, per Blackburn, J.
(*e*) R. *v.* Jolliffe (1823) 2 B. & C. 54.
(*f*) Co. Litt. 115 a ; Mayor of Hull *v.* Horner (1774) 1 Cowp. 102, 108.
(*g*) Per Pollock, C.B., Gibson *v.* Doeg (1857) 2 H. & N. 623.
(*h*) Per Bramwell, B., Mayor of Penryn *v.* Best (1878) 3 Ex. D. 299.

within legal memory at which the market or fair did not exist, yet the fact that for a long time past it has been held, openly, uninterruptedly, and as of right, is always evidence from which a jury may infer that it had a lawful origin in a lost grant. The jury are not bound to draw the inference, but they are entitled to draw it, and the evidence must be left to their consideration to be credited or not, and for them to draw their inference one way or the other, according to all the circumstances of the case.(*a*) Markets and fairs are not easements or *profits à prendre* within the Prescription Act, 1832 ;(*b*) they must still be prescribed for at common law,(*c*) and no usage short of the time of legal memory does more than enable a jury to infer a legal origin, if they think that the circumstances justify it.(*d*)

In some cases the proper inference to be drawn from all the facts in evidence is that the origin of the usage was unlawful, so that claims founded on it cannot be supported. Thus, in Benjamin *v.* Andrews,(*e*) it was considered that a usage during twenty-five years to hold a market on Saturdays was merely an abuse of an existing grant to hold one on Fridays. Similarly, in A.-G. *v.* Horner (*f*) it was considered that a long usage to hold markets on certain week-days arose out of a grant from James II. which was subsequently made void by statute.(*g*) In both these cases, therefore, the claim failed.

To establish a claim to a market or fair by prescription or under a lost grant it is necessary to show a usage which, as regards such details as time and place, is in accordance with the right claimed. If the claim be to hold a market on Saturdays, it is useless to prove a usage to hold it sometimes on Saturdays and sometimes on Wednesdays; if it be to hold a fair in one place, it is useless to give evidence that it has sometimes been held elsewhere. Such evidence, as a rule, tends to defeat the claim set up. But a claim may be established by proving a larger right which includes the lesser right claimed.(*h*) A claim to hold a fair at a particular spot within a manor will be sustained by proving a right to hold it anywhere within the

---

(*a*) Mayor of Hull *v.* Horner (1774) 1 Cowp. 102.
(*b*) 2 & 3 Will. IV. c. 71.
(*c*) Benjamin *v.* Andrews (1858) 5 C.B.N.S. 299.
(*d*) Mayor of Hull *v.* Horner (1774) 1 Cowp. 102.
(*e*) (1858) 5 C.B.N.S. 299.
(*f*) (1884) 14 Q.B.D. 245.   (*g*) 2 W. & M. Sess. 1, c. 8.
(*h*) Per Coleridge, J., Bailey *v.* Appleyard (1838) 8 A. & E. 161.

manor: a claim to hold a market on Saturdays, by proving a right to hold markets on Wednesdays and Saturdays.

§ 3. *Acquisition by statute.*

An Act of Parliament is a better instrument whereby to obtain privileges than a mere charter from the crown; being made by the authority of parliament, it may 'cross and change the common law, which a charter alone cannot do';(*a*) and the powers which it confers are therefore much less disputable. The crown has no power to grant a market to the disturbance of another market previously granted,(*b*) nor can it authorise unreasonable tolls ;(*c*) but parliament is not bound to respect existing rights, and the reasonableness of tolls specifically authorised by parliament cannot be questioned.

In early times there was often no very great difference, as regards the general form of the instrument, between an Act of Parliament and a charter, and it may sometimes be difficult to say to which category a particular document belongs; but it is clear that a charter made by authority of Parliament is, and has the force of, an Act of Parliament.(*d*)

Since the beginning of this century many Acts of Parliament have been passed for the establishment or regulation of markets and fairs; and in 1847, in order to avoid the necessity of repeating provisions usually contained in such Acts, and to ensure greater uniformity therein, the Markets and Fairs Clauses Act, 1847,(*e*) was passed. This Act now affects all markets and fairs the construction or regulation whereof is authorised by any special Act of Parliament which declares that the Act shall be incorporated therewith.(*f*) Markets and Fairs Clauses Act

The special Act may incorporate the whole of this Act, or it may incorporate only a portion thereof, either by incorporating the Act with the exception of specified clauses or by incorporating specified clauses of the Act; and the Act, or the portion thereof so incorporated, forms part of the special Act

(*a*) The Prince's case (1606) 8 Co. Rep. 19 a.
(*b*) See *ante*, p. 20.   (*c*) See *post*, p. 58.
(*d*) The Prince's case (1606) 8 Co. Rep. 1 a, 20 a; G. E. R. Co. *v.* Goldsmid (1884) 9 App. Cas. 927, 25 Ch. D. 511.
(*e*) 10 & 11 Vict. c. 14, set out, *post*, Part II.
(*f*) Ss. 1, 2. As to the power of a municipal corporation to oppose a bill for establishing a market in the borough, see A.-G. *v.* Mayor of Brecon (1878) 9 Ch. D. 204.

as if the same were set forth therein at length, save in so far as the special Act expressly varies or excepts the same.(*a*)

At the date when the Markets and Fairs Clauses Act was passed it was probably thought that it would supply a complete code for market authorities; but experience has shown that the code is incomplete, and in modern practice special Acts for the establishment of markets usually contain more ample provisions for regulating the markets and keeping order therein.(*b*)

The law of statutory markets

When a market has been created by a special Act, the question may arise whether the whole law of the market must be sought for in that Act and such Acts as are incorporated therewith, or whether the statutory market can have any incidents of a common law market, in addition to the rights expressly attached to it by such Acts. The better opinion seems to be that all the incidents of a common law market are incidents of a statutory market, except in so far as they are expressly or impliedly varied or taken away by the statutes. There seems to be no reason to suppose that the word 'market' itself bears a different meaning or connotation, when used in an Act of Parliament, from that which it bears when used in a grant from the crown.(*c*)

Statutory modification of old markets

Similarly, when a special Act has been passed for the regulation of a common law market, the question may arise whether rights formerly enjoyed in connection with the market remain intact. When there is a franchise created by charter, and the legislature afterwards operates upon it, it is obvious that the legislature can do exactly what it pleases. It can either leave the old franchise standing, and place a new parliamentary right beside it, or it may leave the old franchise standing and incorporate certain statutory incidents into the old franchise, provided it makes its intention clear; or it may extinguish the old franchise, either expressly or by implication, and substitute in its place, not a franchise properly so called, but parliamentary rights and obligations as distinct from a franchise. It is necessary in each case to look at the Act itself

(*a*) Ss. 1, 5.
(*b*) See Clifford, *History of Private Bill Legislation*, p. 527.
(*c*) See *post*, pp. 87 and 121, where the application of this principle to actions for disturbance and to the law of sales in market overt is discussed, and some authorities are referred to.

Acquisition by Statute

to ascertain what the legislature has chosen to do.(a) And it is a question to be determined by a consideration of the whole of the Act whether the rights thereby given are intended to supersede the rights which previously existed.(b)

By the Local Government Act, 1858,(c) power was given to local boards to provide market-places, to construct market-houses and other conveniences for the purpose of holding markets, and to take stallages, rents, and tolls. That Act was repealed by the Public Health Act, 1875,(d) but its provisions were replaced by the similar provisions (e) of the repealing Act, which conferred the like powers upon urban sanitary authorities.

By ss. 166-168 of the Public Health Act, 1875, urban district councils (including borough councils acting as district councils) are now empowered to establish and hold markets in their districts. Markets established by local boards before the passing of the Public Health Act, 1875, or by urban sanitary authorities afterwards, or (since the Local Government Act, 1894,(f) came into force) by urban district councils, are all now governed by these provisions. The sections are set out and commented upon, *post*, p. 181.

Certain local authorities were empowered under the Contagious Diseases (Animals) Acts, and are now empowered under the Diseases of Animals Act, 1894, to provide wharves and markets for the landing and sale of foreign and other animals (see *post*, p. 189).

§ 4. *The devolution of market-rights.*

The transfer of market franchises is governed by the law relating to incorporeal hereditaments. Accordingly, a conveyance of the franchise can only be made by deed ;(g) and a deed is necessary to create a valid lease of the franchise for any term, however short.(h) This general rule, however, may be modified in particular instances by Act of Parliament; and a statutory provision that upon a lease of a market, or its site, and all

---

(a) Mayor of Manchester *v.* Lyons (1882) 22 Ch. D. 287, 310, per Bowen, L.J.
(b) *Ibid.* 307, per Cotton, L.J. See Taylor *v.* New Windsor Corporation [1898] 1 Q.B. 186.
(c) 21 & 22 Vict. c. 98, s. 50.   (d) 38 & 39 Vict. c. 55, s. 343.
(e) Ss. 166-168.   (f) 56 & 57 Vict. c. 73.
(g) Co. Litt. 9 a, 49 a, 169 a.
(h) *Ibid:* Duke of Somerset *v.* Fogwell (1826) 5 B. & C. 875, 882.

28   The Acquisition of the Right

or any of the buildings thereon, the lessee should be entitled to the tolls, has been construed as giving to a lessee under a parol demise of the market-place a right to the tolls, and not a mere licence to take them.(*a*)

Recovery of rent

Generally speaking, where rent is reserved upon a lease of a market for a term of years, arrears of rent cannot be recovered by distress, but only by action.(*b*)   But upon a lease by the crown the arrears may be distrained for upon any lands belonging to the lessee.(*c*)   If the lease be a lease of lands, as well as of the franchise, and one entire rent be reserved, it may be that the whole of the rent is recoverable by distress upon the lands, provided that such lease be valid as regards both lands and franchise ; but if it be invalid as regards the franchise, a distress for the entire rent would be wholly unlawful.(*d*)

It has been held that a covenant by the lessee to pay the rent reserved upon a lease of the tolls of a market or fair runs with the tenement and binds an assignee of the lessee, whether named in the covenant (*e*) or not.(*f*)

Escheat and forfeiture

. Formerly, if the owner in fee of a market or fair died without an heir and intestate, the franchise became extinct ;(*g*) but ' it now escheats by virtue of the Intestates' Estates Act, 1884.(*h*) Upon a forfeiture or surrender of the franchise to the crown, the franchise is not extinguished, but continues in esse in the crown, so that the crown can either hold the market or fair on its own behalf or again grant it out to a subject.(*i*)

Alienation and leasing by public body

Where market-rights, whether at common law or statutory, are vested in a public body, a question may sometimes arise as to the powers of such body to alienate such rights.   If a body of persons be invested by Act of Parliament with duties to be

---

(*a*) Bridgland *v.* Shapter (1839) 5 M. & W. 375.
(*b*) Co. Litt. 47 a : Jewel's case (1588) 5 Rep. 3 ; Gardiner *v.* Williamson (1831) 2 B. & Ad. 336.
(*c*) Lord Mountjoy's case (1589) 5 Rep. 4 a, b ; Knight's case (1588) Id. 56 a ; Chitty, Prerog. 208.
(*d*) 2 Roll. Abr. 451 ; Gardiner *v.* Williamson (1831) 2 B. & Ad. 336.
(*e*) Earl of Lucan *v.* Gildea (1831) 2 Hudson & Brooke, Ir. K.B. 635.
(*f*) Earl of Egremont *v.* Keene (1837) 2 Jones, Ir. Exch. 307. See notes to Spencer's case, 1 Smith, L.C. (10th ed.), p. 90.
(*g*) 3 Inst. 21 ; Chitty, Prerog. 233.
(*h*) 47 & 48 Vict. c. 71, s. 4.
(*i*) Heddy *v.* Wheelhouse (1597) Cro. Eliz. 591 ; case of Abbot of Strata Mercella (1591) 9 Co. Rep. 25 b ; Whistler's case (1613) 10 Co. Rep. 65 a. See further, *post*, p. 93.

The Devolution of Market-Rights 29

performed for the benefit of the public, and with property to enable them to perform those duties, such body cannot, unless authorised by parliament so to do, make over their duties to third persons,(a) or alienate their property so as to prejudice the performance of their duties.(b)

The Municipal Corporations Act, 1882,(c) now prohibits a municipal corporation from selling, mortgaging or alienating any franchise, forming part of their corporate land, without either the authority of an Act of Parliament or the approval of the Treasury.(d) Nor can a municipal corporation now lease or agree to lease any such franchise without the same authority or approval, except for a term not exceeding thirty-one years from the date of the lease or agreement, and with the reservation of a clear yearly rent without any fine.(e) The Act, however, reserves to a municipal corporation wide powers of renewing leases pursuant to a covenant made, or some ancient custom, usage or practice existing before June 5, 1835.(f)

Under s. 136 of this Act, trustees or commissioners acting under a local Act of Parliament for providing or maintaining a market in a borough have power to transfer to the municipal corporation of the borough, with the consent of the borough council, all their rights, powers, property and liabilities under the local Act; and upon such transfer being made the municipal corporation become the trustees for executing by the borough council the powers and provisions of the local Act.

Under ss. 213-218 of the same Act, whenever a new municipal corporation is created by charter, a scheme can be carried out for the adjustment of the rights, powers, privileges, franchises, duties, property and liabilities of the various local authorities, including trustees or commissioners, who, as a public body, and not for their own profit, act under any Act for providing or maintaining a market.

(a) See Gardner v. L. C. & D. R. Co. (1866) L.R. 2 Ch. 201, 212; A.-G. v. G. E. R. Co. (1880) 5 App. Cas. 473; and see the other cases on the *ultra vires* doctrine collected in 1 Smith's L.C. (10th ed.) 378 *et seq.*

(b) See Staffordshire, &c., Canal Navigation v. Birmingham Canal Navigations (1866) L.R. 1 H.L. 254; Mulliner v. Midland Ry. Co. (1879) 11 Ch. D. 611; Hobbs v. Midland Ry. Co. (1882) 20 Ch. D. 418.

(c) 45 & 46 Vict. c. 50.

(d) S. 108 (1). As to 'corporate land' including franchises, see s. 7 of the Act; s. 3 of the Interpretation Act, 1889; and G. W. R. Co. v. Swindon, &c., R. Co., 9 App. Cas. 787.

(e) S. 108 (2) (a). Clause (b) does not seem to apply to a franchise.

(f) S. 110.

The Public Health Act, 1875, contains no provisions enabling an urban district council to sell, mortgage or lease any rights in markets or tolls provided or acquired by them under ss. 166-168 of the Act. Unless, therefore, they be empowered to do so by some local Act, it seems that they are not entitled to make any such sale,(*a*) mortgage,(*b*) or lease.

The Public Health Act, 1875, s. 168, contains provisions under which market companies can transfer their rights, powers and privileges, and their property, to urban district councils.

Local authorities under the Diseases of Animals Act, 1894,(*c*) are expressly empowered,(*d*) when they exercise their powers of borrowing money for the purposes of the Act, to give as security (either with the local rate or separately therefrom) the charges or tolls which they are authorised to take for the use of a wharf or market provided by them under the Act. But they have no power to sell or mortgage or lease the market undertaking generally, or the land appropriated to and required for the purposes of the undertaking.(*e*)

Receiver of profits

If the undertakers of a statutory market have power under their statutes to mortgage the undertaking or the tolls, the High Court has jurisdiction, unless it be expressly taken away by the statutes, to appoint, at the instance of the mortgagee, a receiver of the rents and profits, or the tolls, and will do so whenever it be necessary or proper for the protection of the mortgagee's security.(*f*) The court, however, will not appoint a manager of an undertaking, the management of which has been entrusted by parliament to the undertakers alone.(*g*)

(*a*) As to their power to sell or let superfluous or spare lands, see ss. 175, 177 of the Public Health Act.
(*b*) As to their powers to borrow upon the credit of any fund or rate out of which they are authorised to defray their expenses, or of lands held by them for the purposes of the disposal of sewage, see Id. ss. 233, 236.
(*c*) 57 & 58 Vict. c. 57.　　　　(*d*) By s. 42 (5).
(*e*) As to the disposal of superfluous lands, see s. 33 (2.)
(*f*) De Winton *v.* Mayor of Brecon (1859) 26 Beav. 533 ; Hopkins *v.* Worcester, &c., Canal Co. (1868) L.R. 6 Eq. 437, 447 ; see also Drewry *v.* Barnes (1826) 3 Russ. 94, 104 ; Fripp *v.* Chard Ry. Co. (1854) 11 Hare, 241.
(*g*) Gardner *v.* L. C. & D. Rly. Co. (1867) L.R. 2 Ch. 201, 212 ; Blaker *v.* Herts, &c., Waterworks Co. (1889) 41 Ch. D. 399 ; De Winton *v.* Mayor of Brecon (1859) 26 Beav. 533, 542.

CHAPTER II

THE MARKET-PLACE AND THE PLACE FOR HOLDING FAIRS

§ 1. *The rights of the public therein.*

WHEREVER a market or fair be held, every member of the public has, of common right, the liberty of coming into the market-place and frequenting it for the purpose of buying and selling, and also the liberty of bringing his goods there and exposing them for sale.(*a*) The sole limitations on this public right appear to be that it may be exercised only whilst the market or fair is open, and that if the market or fair is not a general one the goods brought or exposed for sale there must be goods of the kind or kinds for which the market or fair is held. With regard to the former limitation, it may be observed that the approaches to a market or fair, and the ways over it, may be public highways (in which case the public may use them as such at all times), but they are not necessarily so.(*b*)

To frequent the market-place

Whilst the market or fair is proceeding, goods brought into the place for sale,(*c*) or goods in course of removal from the place after sale,(*d*) are not liable to distress damage feasant; and this is so, even though some toll be due in respect of the goods and payment of the toll be refused.(*e*)

To bring goods for sale

But, although every person has the right of frequenting the market or fair, and of bringing his goods there, no one has, of common right, the liberty of occupying exclusively any particular part of the soil on which it is held.(*f*) A member of the

Stalls

(*a*) Austin *v.* Whittred (1746) Willes, 623.
(*b*) A.-G. *v.* Horner (1885) 11 App. Cas. 66, 80.
(*c*) Austin *v.* Whittred (1746) Willes, 623 ; Wigley *v.* Peachy (1732) 2 Ld. Raym. 1589; Mayor of Lawson's (Launceston's) case (1588) Cro. Eliz. 75.
(*d*) Sawyer *v.* Wilkinson (1598) Cro. Eliz. 627.
(*e*) Wigley *v.* Peachy, *supra*. Non-payment does not constitute a trespass ; Six Carpenters' case (1610) 8 Rep. 146 a.
(*f*) See cases cited in notes (*a*) and (*b*), p. 32.

public has no general right to erect a stall,(a) or to place a table, chair, basket, or other article, or his goods,(b) upon the soil, in such a manner as to occupy the land to the exclusion of other persons. He may only do that if he has obtained the leave of the owner of the soil, or has in some way acquired a special right so to do.(c) If he do such an act without any such leave or right, he is a trespasser, and he is liable to an action of trespass at the suit of the owner of the soil.(d) Moreover, the latter is probably entitled to pursue after notice all the usual summary remedies in case of a trespass, and to pull down the stall,(e) put out the offender,(f) and remove the offending article or goods,(g) using and doing no unnecessary force and damage.

It is proper to add, however, that the mere placing upon the soil for some temporary purpose of goods, or of a basket or sack which contains goods, does not necessarily amount to an exclusive occupation; whether it does so or not is a question of fact, depending upon all the circumstances of the case.(h)

A person who erects a stall, or anything in the nature of a stall, with the express or implied consent of the owner of the soil, is liable for stallage.(i) The subject of stallage will be dealt with more fully later.(j)

Dangerous structures

An owner of a market or fair who charges a toll for the standing of cattle therein owes to the owners of the cattle a duty of providing a reasonably safe place for the standing ;(k) and it has been laid down that, inasmuch as the public come into the market as of right, and not merely by licence, the lord is under an obligation to every person who attends the market to maintain the market-place in a condition reasonably fit for the purposes of the market, or at any rate to abstain from erecting in it any dangerous structure.(l)

(a) Mayor of Northampton v. Ward (1746) 2 Stra. 1238.
(b) Mayor of Yarmouth v. Groom (1862) 1 H. & C. 102; Mayor of Norwich v. Swann (1777) 2 W. Bl. 111, 6.
(c) See *post*, p. 64.
(d) See cases cited in notes (a) and (b) *supra*.
(e) Cf. Davies v. Williams (1851) 16 Q.B. 546.
(f) Sturbridge Market case, 11 Hen. 6, fo. 23, pl. 20.
(g) The cases against distress damage feasant (*supra*, p. 31) are scarcely authorities against removal for misfeasance. The distinction between non-feasance and misfeasance is recognised in Northampton v. Ward, *supra*.
(h) Mayor of Yarmouth v. Groom (1862) 1 H. & C. 102; Townend v. Woodruff (1850) 5 Exch. 506.
(i) Mayor of Yarmouth v. Groom, *supra*.   (j) See *post*, p. 63.
(k) Lax v. Darlington Corporation (1879) 5 Ex. D. 28.
(l) *Ibid.* per Lush, J.

It may be mentioned here that cattle on their way to a market or fair, which are put into a ground with the consent of the occupier to graze for only one night, are not liable to the distress of the landlord of the ground for arrears of rent.(*a*) This privilege is apparently for the encouragement of persons frequenting markets and fairs from distances which their cattle cannot travel without being fed on the way.

<small>Distress for rent of cattle on the way to market</small>

It is a misdemeanour at common law to prevent or endeavour to prevent by force or threats any goods, wares, or merchandise being brought to any fair or market. Though all the general enactments with regard to the offences of forestalling and regrating were repealed by 7 & 8 Vict. c. 24, that Act provided by s. 2 that 'nothing in this Act shall be construed to apply to the offence of knowingly or fraudulently spreading or conspiring to spread any false rumour with intent to enhance or decry the price of any goods or merchandise, or to the offence of preventing or endeavouring to prevent by force or threats any goods, wares, or merchandise being brought to any fair or market, but that every such offence may be inquired of and tried and punished as if this Act had not been made.'(*b*)

<small>Forestalling and regrating</small>

The offender may be punished by fine and imprisonment.(*c*)

§ 2. *The rights and duties of the owner in providing a place.*

A grant of a market or fair usually specifies, more or less definitely, some area or district within which the market or fair is to be held; and whenever that is the case the market or fair must be held within the area or district specified, and not elsewhere.

<small>Where</small>

It is laid down in Dixon *v.* Robinson (*d*) that if the place for keeping a fair be not limited by the grant, the grantees 'may keep it where they please, or rather where they can most conveniently.' It would be incorrect, however, to suppose that the area was not limited by the grant then before the court. The grantees, the burgesses of Andover, were merely claiming to keep their fair at Weyhill in any one place where they

---

(*a*) Nugent *v.* Kirwan (1838) 1 Jebb & Symes 97; see per Parke, B., Muspratt *v.* Gregory (1836) 1 M. & W. 633, 647; Fowkes *v.* Joyce (1689) 3 Lev. 260, 2 Lutw. 1161.
(*b*) Repealed by S.L.R. Act, 1892. And see per Fry, L.J., in Mogul Steamship Co. *v.* McGregor, Gow & Co. (1889) 23 Q.B.D. 598, 629. See also *post*, p. 129.
(*c*) Russell *on Crimes*, vol. i. pp. 476 and 66; 3 Inst. 196.
(*d*) (1687) 3 Mod. 107, per Herbert, C.J.

D

pleased, and their grant in fact limited this fair to Weyhill.(*a*) There does not appear to be any instance of a grant imposing no limits whatever as to space; and it is difficult to see how, with a view to such a grant, any proper return could be made to a writ of ad quod damnum, or in what locality the inquisition could be held.

In A.-G. *v.* Horner (*b*) the question arose as to the effect of a charter which granted a market to be held 'in sive juxta' Spital Square. It was decided that the grant permitted the extension of the market, if the owner thought fit and had the means of extending it, beyond Spital Square into the surrounding area. Lord Blackburn, however, was not prepared to accept the view that the grant permitted any and every extension however great,(*c*) and it is submitted that a grant of a market to be held 'in or near' a specified place would not authorise an extension to a point which could not reasonably be said to be 'near' that place.

Grants have generally been for the holding of a market or fair in some city, borough, township, manor, or other like district. But they have sometimes required it to be held in a particular place in such district.(*d*) As an instance of a grant limiting a market to a fixed spot, defined by metes and bounds and containing a precise quantity of land, the grant may be mentioned which Charles II. made of Covent Garden Market.(*e*)

Where the grant merely specifies a district, such as a borough or manor, for the holding of the market or fair, the grantee has a general right, as between himself and the public, to hold it anywhere within that district,(*f*) and to determine in what place or places within that district it is to be held.(*g*) This general right is limited, however, by the rule that an obligation is cast upon the grantee by his acceptance of the grant to provide convenient accommodation for all who wish to buy and sell in his market or fair.(*h*) The grant is made for the benefit

(*a*) See Patent Roll. 41 Eliz. part 12.
(*b*) (1885) 11 App. Cas. 66; (1884) 14 Q.B.D. 245.
(*c*) 11 App. Cas. 81. See also per Cotton, L.J., 14 Q.B.D. 261.
(*d*) See, for example, the grant to Charles Hore and Richard Hore of markets to be held 'within a place inclosed with brick walls, called Vinegar Ground,' in the parish of St. James, Clerkenwell, Middlesex; Pat. Roll. 6 Anne, part 4, no. 8.
*(*e*) See Prince *v.* Lewis (1826) 5 B. & C. 363, 365.
(*f*) Islington Market Bill (1835) 3 Cl. & F. 518, 12 M. & W. 20 n.
(*g*) Mosley *v.* Walker (1827) 7 B. & C. 40, 54, per Bayley, J.
(*h*) Islington Market Bill (1835) 3 Cl. & F. 518, 12 M. & W. 20 n.

Rights and Duties of Owner in Providing a Place 35

of the public as well as for the benefit of the grantee, and if he confines his market or fair to particular places within the district he must fix it in such places as will from time to time yield to the public a reasonable accommodation.(a).

The grantee of a market to be held in a fixed spot defined by metes and bounds has a similar general right, limited by similar considerations of public convenience. If the space allotted by the grant is more than is necessary for the purposes of the market in ordinary times, he may lawfully appropriate a part of that space to other purposes, and he is not bound to extend the market over the whole of the soil.(b) But he is bound to leave sufficient room for the purposes for which the franchise was granted to him, and whenever the convenience of the public requires that the whole of the allotted space shall be devoted to the use of the market there is an obligation on the part of the grantee so to devote it.(c)

If the owner of a market fails in his duty by not providing sufficient accommodation for the public, there would be a good defence to an action brought by him against any person for selling out of the market to the prejudice of his right, provided such person had been prevented from selling in the market by the want of convenient room.(d)

Failure to provide

'A second consequence would be that this breach of public duty on the part of the grantee of the franchise might, unless these inconveniences were removed, and a sufficient space restored for the accommodation of the public, operate as a forfeiture, and furnish a ground for a *scire facias* to repeal the patent by which the market was granted. And thirdly, we are not prepared to say that such misconduct of the grantee would not render him liable to an indictment for a misdemeanour, in like manner as the grantee of a ferry is punishable for a default in providing proper boats and ferrymen ; though we are not aware of any instance in which such a proceeding against the owner of a market has been adopted. And if such an indictment would lie against him for his default, an action would also lie at the suit of any private individual who should have received any special injury thereby.'(e)

, (a) Mosley *v.* Walker (1827) 7 B. & C. 40, 50, per Bayley, J.
  (b) Prince *v.* Lewis (1826) 5 B. & C. 363. (c) *Ibid.*
  (d) Prince *v.* Lewis (1826) 5 B. & C. 363 ; Mosley *v.* Walker (1827) 7 B. & C. 40 ; Islington Market Bill (1835) 3 Cl. & F. 513, 519, 12 M. & W. 20, 23. (e) Islington Market Bill, *supra.*

In the case of a market held under a grant which confines it to a fixed place, limited by metes and bounds, the grantee fulfils his duty to the public of providing them with accommodation if he properly devotes the whole of that place to the purposes of the market; for the grant does not permit him to do more. If the accommodation be insufficient for the wants of the public, that can be no ground for the repeal of the grant, or for any proceedings against the grantee. It might be a sufficient ground for a new grant of a new market to be held elsewhere in the same neighbourhood; but such new grant would not be valid if it injuriously affected the existing grant, and the new market would not be legal if it did more than provide merely for the surplus wants of the public which the existing market was unable to meet.(a)

A like case to which the same principles would be applicable might possibly arise with regard to a market not confined to a fixed place, but granted to be held anywhere in a district. The district might be so narrow, and the residue of the district not appropriated to the market might be so occupied, that the grantee could not be held responsible for not providing all the accommodation required by the public.(b)

It must be observed that the owner of a market does not fail in his duty to the public merely because the market is sometimes very full. 'The very idea of a market is that it is a place which will on market-days be crowded.'(c)

Extent of market-place

In Mosley v. Walker,(d) Bayley, J., observes that, generally speaking, the grantee of a market may 'permit every place within the specified limits of the market to be the place where articles may be sold'; and on other occasions judges have recognised that the owner of a market or fair, granted to be held in a district, generally has a right, and sometimes owes a duty, to allow it to be held throughout the district.(e) Instances in which whole cities have been given over to fairs are supplied by St. Giles' Fair at Winchester and Lammas Fair at

(a) Islington Market Bill (1835) 3 Cl. & F. 518, 12 M. & W. 20 n.
(b) Ibid.
(c) Goldsmid v. G. E. R. Co. (1883) 25 Ch. D. 511, 543, per Cotton, L.J.
(d) (1827) 7 B. & C. 40, 54.
(e) See the Islington Market Bill (1835) 3 Cl. & F. 518, 12 M. & W. 20. In Kerby v. Wychelow (1700) 2 Lutw. 1498, Powell, J., said, apparently with regard to the pleadings, that 'the vill, in this case, shall be taken to be the market-place.'

Rights and Duties of Owner in Providing a Place 37

York ; and in this connection, perhaps, mention may be made of the custom which still prevails in the city of London, whereby every shop open to the public is market overt.(a) In early times, when a very great part of the trade of the country was conducted at markets and fairs, their extension over so large a district as a city or town was, no doubt, justified by the wants of the public ; and there may be cases in which it is, or would be, still quite justifiable. It is submitted, however, that if the owner of a market or fair were to extend it so unreasonably that the public lost the benefit of the concourse of buyers and sellers which the grant was intended to bring about, and other substantial inconveniences ensued, that would constitute a ground for the repeal of the grant by *scire facias*. The question, however, does not appear ever to have arisen, and it is hardly likely that it ever will arise.

§ 3. *The right of removal.*

Whenever a fair or market is granted to be held within an area, such as a city, borough, township, or manor, there is incident to such grant a right to remove the fair or market from time to time from one convenient place to another within that area ; and the right continues, although the fair or market has always been held in one particular place.(b) The right may be exercised not only with regard to the whole market or fair, but also with regard to particular parts of it.(c) Within the area

This right of removal is incident to every grant, unless the grantee be tied down by its terms to some particular spot ;(d) and it may be established even in the case of a prescriptive fair or market. Where a market has always been owned, or was originally owned, by the corporation of a borough, or the lord of a manor, a jury may infer that it was originally granted to be held anywhere within the borough, or manor, and if such an inference be drawn the right of removal within the limits of the borough or manor follows as incident to the grant.(e)

A removal to a situation outside the area defined by the grant is generally illegal, and it constitutes a ground of for- Outside the area

(a) See, further, as to this custom, *post*, p. 122.
(b) Curwen v. Salkeld (1803) 3 East, 538.
(c) Wortley v. Nottingham L. B. (1870) 21 L.T.N.S. 582; cf. per Bayley, J., Mosley v. Walker (1827) 7 B. & C. 40, 54.
(d) Curwen v. Salkeld, *supra*.
(e) R. v. Cotterill (1817) 1 B. and Ald. 67 ; De Rutzen v. Lloyd (1836) 5 A. and E. 456.

feiture.(a) But such a removal may be made legal by statute. In the case of a borough the boundaries of which were extended by the Municipal Corporations Act, 1835,(b) a market which might have been held, either by grant or prescription, in any part of the ancient borough, may now be held in any place within the extended boundaries, whether within or beyond the limits of the ancient borough.(c)

In exercising his power of removal, the owner of a fair or market must take care to accommodate the public.(d) The power must not be exercised to the prejudice of the object of the grant; and a removal to an inconvenient place would lay the foundation of a *scire facias* to repeal the grant.(e) An illegal removal is not a defence to an action for disturbance by setting up a rival market ;(f) but it would probably be a defence to an action for disturbance by selling outside the market ;(g) and it would certainly justify selling in the old market-place, for if a removal be bad the market continues in point of law in the old market-place.(h)

Bad removal

A removal is not good unless the new market-place be as unrestricted and free as the old.(i) Where a market in which no toll or stallage had ever been taken was removed to a close which belonged to the owner of the market, but which he had leased on terms which allowed the lessee to take stallage, it was held that the removal was illegal, and that no nuisance was committed by resorting to the old market-place.(j)

Where any persons other than the owner of the market possess prescriptive rights therein, a removal without their consent is bad, if it injuriously affects such rights.(k) Thus, where the occupiers of shops adjoining a market-place had a prescriptive right to erect stalls in the market-place opposite

(a) For an early case of an illegal removal, see Abb. Plac. p. 72, temp. John (Holland, Linc.).
(b) 5 & 6 Will. IV. c. 76, ss. 7, 8, schedules A and B, part i. ; 2 & 3 Will. IV. c. 64, s. 35, schedule O; see 45 & 46 Vict. c. 50, s. 228 (1).
(c) Mayor of Dorchester v. Ensor (1869) L.R. 4 Ex. 335.
(d) Curwen v. Salkeld (1803) 3 East, 538.
(e) R. v. Cotterill (1817) 1 B. & Ald. 67, 75, per Lord Ellenborough.
(f) Midleton v. Power (1886) 19 L.R. Ir. 1.
(g) See Prince v. Lewis (1826) 5 B. & C. 363; Mosley v. Walker (1827) 7 B. & C. 40, 53; and cf. Aiton v. Stephen (1876) 1 App. Cas. 456.
(h) R. v. Starkey (1837) 7 A. & E. 95; Ellis v. Mayor of Bridgenorth (1863) 15 C.B.N.S. 52, 79.
(i) R. v. Starkey, *supra*.   (j) *Ibid.*
(k) Ellis v. Mayor of Bridgenorth (1863) 15 C.B.N.S. 52.

The Right of Removal

their shops, it was held that the market-owner could not remove the market to a place where this right would become worthless.(a) Where the owner of a market does not own the soil on which it is held, a removal might deprive the owner of the soil of the right to stallage; but it seems that a removal which did so would not generally be bad on that account.(b)

It may become the duty of the owner to remove a market for the better accommodation of the public. 'I take it to be implied in the terms in which a market (c) is granted, that the grantee, if he confine it to particular parts within a town, shall fix it in such parts as will from time to time yield to the public reasonable accommodation; and that if the place once allotted ceases to give reasonable accommodation he is bound, if he has land of his own, to appropriate land on which to hold it; or, if not, to get land from other persons, in order that the market, which was originally granted for the benefit of the public, as well as for the benefit of the grantee, may be effectually held; and that the public may have the benefit which it was originally intended they should derive from it.'(d)

Duty to remove

The consequences which follow upon the owner of a market failing in his duty to provide reasonable accommodation for the public are stated elsewhere.(e)

After the market has been lawfully removed, the public have no longer a right to go into the old market-place as such.(f) It appears that the owner of a market who removes it ought to give a reasonable public notice of the removal.(g) Probably, public notices ought to be placed at the entrance or entrances to the old market-place.

Consequences of removal

§ 4. *Upon what lands a market or fair may be held.*

A market or fair must be held on land on which the lord of the market can properly perform his duties of correcting the market and protecting the rights of the public. Such duties can be most readily performed where the lord owns both the market or fair and the land on which it is held.

At no time, however, does it seem to have been thought

(a) Ellis v. Mayor of Bridgenorth (1863) 15 C.B.N.S. 52.
(b) De Rutzen v. Lloyd (1836) 5 A. & E. 456, 458 n.
(c) I.e. a market granted to be held in a town or other like district.
(d) Mosley v. Walker (1827) 7 B. & C. 40, 55, per Bayley, J.
(e) *Ante*, p. 35.
(f) Curwen v. Salkeld (1803) 3 East, 538.
(g) *Ibid.*

necessary that the market-owner should own the fee of the market-place. In 1433 the Corporation of Cambridge pleaded (a) that they had, by prescription, a fair at Stourbridge as part of the fee of the town of Cambridge; and the court held that they might so have it, although the land on which the fair was held was the fee of the Prior of Barnwell, because, as Paston, J., said,(b) the corporation might 'prescribe to have a fair in another's freehold well enough.' The case, however, shows that the corporation had sufficient control over the soil to have the regulation of the stalls in the market. The case of Stourbridge Fair came up again in 1747 ;(c) and then the plea was that the corporation were seised in fee of the fair, and 'of the sole and separate use of the ground and soil of the places at Barnwell and Stourbridge where' the fair was held, during the times of holding it, 'for pickage, stallage, and groundage there, and all other uses and purposes of the said fair.'

In Rex v. Starkey (d) the owner of a market removed it on to land held by his tenant under a lease which did not demise the franchise, but empowered the tenant to exact from vendors in the market certain novel tolls. To these tolls the market-owner himself had no right. The Court held that the removal was illegal because, 'when the lord removes, the new market must be as unrestricted and free as the old.' Littledale, J., however, was of opinion that the removal was also illegal, because 'the market must be held in the soil of the lord': 'the lord is to have the correction of the market, and how can he have that when he has not the soil?' But an opinion contrary to that of Littledale, J., was expressed in Lockwood v. Wood.(e) There one of the questions was whether any right to stallage could exist under a grant of a market to be held in lands in which neither the crown nor the grantee had any rights at the date of the grant. Lord Denman, C.J., in delivering the judgment of the Queen's Bench, laid it down that the grantee could not claim stallage unless he possessed land in which to hold the market, but could claim it at whatever time after the grant he became interested in the land. His lordship added that 'if he never was so interested, he might, nevertheless, hold the fairs and markets on land belonging to other persons by their mere

(a) Y.B. 11 Hen. VI. fol. 23, pl. 20.
(b) Ibid. (c) Austin v. Whittred (1747) Willes, 623.
(d) (1837) 7 A. & E. 95. (e) (1841) 6 Q.B. 31.

Upon What Lands a Market or Fair May be Held

sufferance and permission ; but unless he had the actual possession of it he could not claim stallage.' This judgment was afterwards affirmed in general terms in the Exchequer Chamber.(a)

The question whether a grant of a market could be made otherwise than in respect of lands held by the grantee at the date of the grant was fully considered in the more recent case of A.-G. v. Horner ;(b) and there the Court of Appeal (over-ruling Stephen, J.) held that it could. 'A grant,' said Lord Esher, M.R., 'of a franchise of a market has nothing to do with the ownership of the land by the person to whom it is granted.'(c) The judgment of the Court was affirmed in the House of Lords.(a)

From the above cases it seems clear that, apart from questions as to the right to stallage, the owner of a market need not own, or even have the possession of, the land upon which his market is held : he may hold the market on any land on which he has obtained a right or a licence to hold it. All that is necessary is that he hold it upon land in which he can exercise his duties of correcting the market and can secure to the public their rights and immunities.

It is perhaps hardly necessary to add that if he hold the market upon another's land under a mere licence from the landowner his power to hold it there may be determined at any time by the withdrawal of the licence. 'As against the owner of land the crown cannot by its grant enable anyone to take that land and use it, either for the purposes of a market or anything else.'(e)

It is said by the judges in Heddey v. Welhouse,(f) and repeated in several later cases,(g) that if the crown grant a market to one to be held in land that is Borough English, and the grantee die intestate, the market descends to the heir-at-law, but the soil of the market-place to the heir in Borough English, who will therefore be entitled to stallage. The books, however, do not furnish any instance of such an inconvenient occurrence. If an instance were to occur, questions might arise as to the right of the heir-at-law to

(a) (1841) 6 Q.B. 47. (b) (1884) 14 Q.B.D. 245.
(c) Ibid. p. 254. (d) (1885) 11 App. Cas. 66.
(e) Per Cotton, L.J., A.-G. v. Horner (1884) 14 Q.B.D. 245, 260.
(f) (1597) Moore, 474.
(g) E.g. in R. v. Starkey (1837) 7 A. & E. 95.

remove the market, or of the heir in Borough English to require its removal. Similar inconvenience might occur if an owner in fee of a market and the soil should die intestate as to the market, but having devised the soil away from his heir.

§ 5. *Markets and fairs in churchyards and highways.*

Churchyards

Prior to 1285 it was a common practice to hold fairs in churchyards, and the fair was usually held on the day of the festival of the saint to whom the church was dedicated. But the Statute of Winchester (*a*) enacted that 'henceforth neither fairs nor markets be kept in churchyards, for the honour of the church.'

Highways

It was also a common practice in early times to hold a market or fair either wholly or in part in public streets, leaving a sufficient portion of the streets open for public passage.(*b*) The prevalence of this practice has been recognised by the judicial statement that 'formerly all markets were holden in the public streets';(*c*) and in one case, in which it was held that a removal of a market from a public street to a private close was bad, the right to hold the market in the street was, apparently, not disputed.(*d*) There are many instances in which the practice still obtains.

Where the origin of both the highway and the market or fair is immemorial, the practice, if shown to be ancient, is justifiable, although it somewhat abridges the right of the public in the use of the highway as such. For the proper inference is that the grant of the market or fair preceded the dedication of the highway and that the highway was dedicated subject to the right to hold the market or fair on the soil. The law recognises that a highway may be dedicated subject to a right of partial interruption during a certain limited and not unreasonable period of time for the purposes of a market or fair as often as it may be lawfully held.(*e*) Accordingly an immemorial custom for victuallers to erect stalls in the high-

---

(*a*) 13 Edw. I. stat. 2, c. 6.
(*b*) Cheapside seems to have been used as a market-place until circ. 1667, when Honey Lane Market was opened; and Newgate Street until circ. 1681, when the market was removed to Newgate Market (replaced, circ. 1866, by the Meat and Poultry Market in Smithfield).
(*c*) Per Lord Tenterden, Mosley *v.* Walker (1827) 7 B. & C. 40, 52.
(*d*) R. *v.* Starkey (1837) 7 A. & E. 95, see *ante*, p. 38.
(*e*) Elwood *v.* Bullock (1844) 6 Q.B. 383.

way during a fair, sufficient room being left for public passage, has been upheld as reasonable and valid.(a)

The practice may also be justified although the market or fair was granted, and the highway was dedicated, within the time of legal memory. Upon proof that the market is older than the highway, and that, going as far back as living memory can go, the practice has always obtained, the proper inference, in the absence of evidence to the contrary, is that the highway was dedicated subject to the right to hold the market or fair therein.(b) The burden of proving that he is entitled to hold his market in the highway lies upon the market-owner, but, in considering whether he has discharged that burden, regard must be paid to the principle on which presumptions from usage are made,(c) and 'all reasonable presumptions should be made in support, and not in destruction, of long enjoyment.'(d) Evidence that the market-owner did not own the soil of the highway at the date of its dedication does not of itself make the practice unlawful, as the inference may reasonably be drawn, until the contrary be shown, that at that date he was exercising a right of holding the market on the soil with some consent or other from the landowner.(e)

It has been suggested by high authority that the practice might be upheld even though the market were shown to be of later origin than the highway, and that after proper inquiry the crown might grant a valid franchise to hold a market in public streets.(f) But there seem to be great difficulties in the way of accepting the latter proposition. During the argument in Elwood v. Bullock (g) Lord Denman observed that 'if the way was first, no grant of a fair could control it'; and the safer view, probably, is that where the market is of later origin than the highway the right to hold it there, so as to obstruct any part of the thoroughfare, could be created only by an Act of Parliament.

Cases may, perhaps, be found in which markets or fairs are

(a) Elwood v. Bullock (1844) 6 Q.B. 383.
(b) A.-G. v. Horner (1885) 11 App. Cas. 66, (1884) 14 Q.B.D. 245.
(c) Ibid., per Lord Selborne, 11 App. Cas. 77, 78.
(d) Per Lord Selborne, G. E. R. Co. v. Goldsmid (1884) 9 App. Cas. 927, 939.
(e) A.-G. v. Horner, supra.
(f) Per Lord Esher, A.-G. v. Horner (1884) 14 Q.B.D. p. 258. Lindley, L.J., however, expressed doubt upon the point, Id. p. 265.
(g) (1844) 6 Q.B. 383, 407.

44 The Market-Place and the Place for Holding Fairs

known to have been held from a very early date in public streets, whilst those streets are known to be older than the grants of the markets or fairs. It may be that such markets or fairs were originally held on narrow strips of land at the side of the highway, which have subsequently become part of the highway; and perhaps a presumption to this effect ought to be made, whenever necessary and possible, in order to support an ancient usage.

Highway Acts   Market rights in public streets are not taken away or affected by Acts of Parliament which prohibit the exposure for sale of marketable articles, or the placing of stalls in the streets, so as to incommode the passage thereof, if the statutes ought to be construed as being aimed merely against nuisances; for no acts lawfully done in the exercise of market-rights can be treated as nuisances.(a) For this reason it appears that valid rights and customs relating to markets and fairs lawfully held in highways are not affected by the provisions of the Highway Act, 1835,(b) which prohibit obstructions by tethering animals or pitching booths or stalls in highways.(c) But a custom to set up stalls on a highway at statute sessions cannot be immemorial, and therefore affords no justification for obstructing an ancient highway.(d)

The Metropolitan Police Act, 1839,(e) prohibits the commission of a variety of acts in any thoroughfare or public place within the limits of the metropolitan police district. And the Town Police Clauses Act, 1847,(f) contains like prohibitions with regard to any street (g) within the towns and districts to which the Act applies. In prohibiting the exposure for show or sale of any horse or other animal, these statutes expressly except

---

(a) G. E. R. Co. *v.* Goldsmid (1884) 9 App. Cas. 927, (1883) 25 Ch. D. 511; A.-G. *v.* Horner (1885) 11 App. Cas. 66, (1884) 14 Q.B.D. 245; where the effect of 12 Geo. III. c. xxxviii., 28 Geo. III. c. lx., and 57 Geo. III. c. xxix. was considered.
(b) 5 & 6 Will. IV. c. 50, s. 72.
(c) See Elwood *v.* Bullock (1844) 6 Q.B. 383; Gerring *v.* Barfield (1864) 16 C.B.N.S. 597; Mercer *v.* Woodgate (1869) L.R. 5 Q.B. 26.
(d) Simpson *v.* Wells (1872) L.R. 7 Q.B. 214, where the origin of statute sessions for hiring servants was considered. R. *v.* Smith (1802) 4 Esp. 109, seems of doubtful authority.
(e) 2 & 3 Vict. c. 47, ss. 54, 60.
(f) 10 & 11 Vict. c. 89, s. 28.
(g) Street here includes any road, square, court, alley, and thoroughfare, or public passage (s. 3); see Curtis *v.* Embery (1872) L.R. 7 Ex. 369.

Markets and Fairs in Churchyards and Highways 45

from the prohibition such an exposure in a market lawfully appointed for that purpose.(*a*) No such express exception is made with regard to certain other prohibited acts which, apart from the statutes, might be justified in some cases by some valid right or custom in connection with a market or fair, such as the causing of an obstruction in a public footpath or thoroughfare, or the placing of a stool or stall on a footway. It seems, however, that the statutes do not affect such acts if it can be proved that the thoroughfare or street, or the portion thereof upon which the acts are committed, was only dedicated subject to the right to commit them.(*b*)

An auctioneer who sells in an open market-place situate by the side of a street cannot be convicted under s. 28 of the Town Police Clauses Act of causing an obstruction in the street because a crowd collects in the street to listen to him.(*c*)

The Metropolitan Streets Act, 1867,(*d*) provides that no goods or other articles shall be allowed to rest on any footway or other part of a street within the general limits of the Act,(*e*) or be otherwise allowed to cause obstruction or inconvenience to the passage of the public, for a longer time than may be absolutely necessary for loading or unloading such goods or other articles. But, by reason of the Metropolitan Streets Amendment Act, 1867,(*f*) the above provision, prohibiting the deposit of goods in streets, does not apply to costermongers, street hawkers, or itinerant traders, so long as they carry on their business in accordance with the regulations from time to time made by the Commissioner of Police with the approval of the Home Secretary.(*g*) Under the

---

(*a*) The exception in 10 & 11 Vict. c. 89, s. 28, is 'in any market, market-place, or fair lawfully appointed for that purpose.'
(*b*) See Spice *v.* Peacock (1875) 39 J.P. 581; Jones *v.* Matthews (1885) 1 T.L.R. 482; Leicester Sanitary Authority *v.* Holland (1888) 57 L.J.M.C. 75; see also Curtis *v.* Embery (1872) L.R. 7 Ex. 369; and cf. Whittaker *v.* Rhodes (1881) 46 J.P. 182; R. *v.* Young (1883) 52 L.J.M.C. 55; Hitchman *v.* Watt (1894) 58 J.P. 720.
(*c*) Ball *v.* Ward (1875) 33 L.T. 170.
(*d*) 30 & 31 Vict. c. 134, s. 6.
(*e*) Viz. within six miles from Charing Cross; see 48 Vict. c. 18.
(*f*) 31 & 32 Vict. c. 5, s. 1.
(*g*) As to the effect of the amending Act upon the Act which it amends, and also upon the 57 Geo. III. c. xxix. s. 65, see Keep *v.* Vestry of St. Mary Newington [1894] 2 Q.B. 524, where Summers *v.* Holborn District Board of Works [1893] 1 Q.B. 612 was considered.

original Act (*a*) the surface of any space over which the public have the right of way that intervenes in any street between the footway and the carriage way was to be deemed to be part of the footway, notwithstanding any claim of any person by prescription or otherwise to the deposit or exposure for sale of any goods or other articles on such surface; but the amending Act (*b*) repealed this definition. It would seem that the provisions of the original Act, as now amended, cannot be construed as taking away actual market-rights in streets. This view appears to be supported by the speedy repeal, as already mentioned, of the definition given by the original Act to footways, which might certainly have been considered to interfere with rights subject to which streets had been dedicated.

With regard to the Metropolis Management Act 1855,(*c*) it has been decided that the provisions of this Act which relate to streets are subordinate to paramount rights reserved when the streets were dedicated.(*d*) S. 91 of the Act provides that 'nothing in the Act shall extend to or affect any rights, privileges, powers or authorities vested in any person in reference to a market.' This provision prevents other provisions of the Act from vesting the control of the markets in the vestries; and such bodies are not entitled to interfere with the rights of the market-owners or of persons frequenting the markets.(*e*)

The Municipal Corporations Act, 1882,(*f*) which authorises the making of by-laws for the good rule and government of any borough to which the Act applies, does not justify a by-law which prohibits or restricts the exercise of market-rights in streets.(*g*)

The owner of a market held in a street may, however, be answerable for a nuisance arising in the market-place. Thus, in Draper *v.* Sperring (*h*) it was held that the owner of such

---

(*a*) 30 & 31 Vict. c. 134, s. 6.
(*b*) 31 & 32 Vict. c. 5, s. 1.   (*c*) 18 & 19 Vict. c. 120.
(*d*) Le Neve *v.* Vestry of Mile End Old Town (1858) 8 E. & B. 1054; Vestry of St. Mary Newington *v.* Jacobs (1871) L.R. 7 Q.B. 47; Vestry of Chelsea *v.* Stoddard (1879) 43 J.P. 782.
(*e*) Horner *v.* Whitechapel B. of W. (1886) 53 L.T.N.S. 842.
(*f*) 45 & 46 Vict. c. 50, s. 23, which replaced 5 & 6 Will. IV. c. 76, s. 90, to the same effect.
(*g*) Elwood *v.* Bullock (1844) 6 Q.B. 383, a decision upon the earlier Act of 1835.
(*h*) (1861) 10 C.B.N.S. 131.

Markets and Fairs in Churchyards and Highways 47

a market in which sheep were penned so that their droppings created a nuisance was a person by whose 'act, default, permission or sufferance,' the nuisance arose, and was therefore liable to an order to remove the nuisance under the Nuisances Removal Act, 1852.(a) Such a case can now, no doubt, be dealt with under the provisions of the Public Health Act, 1875,(b) or the Public Health (London) Act, 1891.(c)

(a) 18 & 19 Vict. c. 121 ; repealed by 38 & 39 Vict. c. 55, s. 343;
54 & 55 Vict. c. 76, s. 142.
(b) 38 & 39 Vict. c. 55, ss. 91 *et seq.*
(c) 54 & 55 Vict. c. 76, ss. 2 *et seq.*

CHAPTER III

THE DAYS AND HOURS FOR HOLDING MARKETS AND FAIRS

§ 1. *The days.*

IN grants of markets and fairs, the days on which they are to be held are usually specified. Where a market or fair is held under a prescriptive title, it is presumed that it is held under a lost grant, and that such grant specified as the days for holding it the days upon which the evidence shows that it has in fact been held.

In most grants of fairs the specified days have reference to some saint's day, usually the day of the patron saint of the place where the fair is to be held.(*a*) For a three days' fair the grant generally provides for its being held on the eve, the day, and the morrow of such a saint. Grants allotting three days to a fair are common. But in some cases a greater number of days have been allotted. Thus, Westminster Fair was granted to be held from the eve of St. Edward for 15 days.(*b*)

Markets are usually granted to be held upon a particular day or particular days in every week. Instances can be found, however, of monthly (*c*) and fortnightly (*d*) markets. A grant of markets to be held on two days in the week is often treated as a grant of two separate franchises.

As a general rule, the grantee is bound to hold his fair or market upon the days for which it has been granted, and it is unlawful for him to hold it on other days. Holding a market

---

(*a*) The Latin 'feria' (fair) was the proper ecclesiastical term for a saint's day.
(*b*) See Chart. 29 Hen. III. part 1, memb. 3; and Plac. Quo. Warr. p. 480.
(*c*) E.g. at Chester, Okehampton, Aberdare, Lechlade, &c.
(*d*) E.g. at Cranbrook, Axminster, Gillingham, Stalbridge, &c. At Llangadock there is a market every third Tuesday.

or fair upon days other than those on which there is a right to hold it was, at one time, a common cause of forfeiture.(a)

There is, however, a distinction in this respect between fairs and markets. An entire change of day, whether for a fair or a market, being illegal, is a cause of forfeiture.(b) But whereas illegally to extend the time of holding a fair is a cause of forfeiture of the whole fair,(c) yet if a market be held on the proper day, and also on an additional and improper day, that does not lead to a forfeiture of the whole market, but only to a forfeiture of the market held on the improper day,(d) for the market held on the additional day is treated as an entire and separable market, wrongfully usurped, and not as a mere extension of the lawful market.

In the case of fairs, the duty of the lords to keep them open for a time neither longer nor shorter than that specified in the grants is enjoined by the Statute of Northampton.(e) That statute requires 'all the lords that have fairs' to hold the same 'for the time that they ought to hold them, and no longer; that is to say, such as have them by the king's charter granted to them, for the time limited by the said charter; and also they that have them without charter(f) for the time that they ought to hold them of right.' The statute also requires every lord at the beginning of his fair there to publish how long the fair shall endure.(g) The penalty imposed by the statute for holding a fair over the due time is seizure of the fair into the king's hands (after office found) (h) until payment of a fine for the offence.

This statute makes it unlawful for merchants to remain at fairs over the due time, but imposes no penalty upon them for the offence. That omission, however, is supplied by the 5 Edw. III. c. 5, which provides that any merchant who shall sell any ware or merchandise at a fair after the due time shall

(a) See Abb. Plac. p. 36 (4 John, Luton), p. 43 (5 John, Lichfield and Wolverhampton); Plac. Quo. Warr. p. 384 (temp. Edw. I. Lancaster): *Select Pleas of Crown* (Selden Soc.) vol. i. pl. 22, 44, 50.
(b) *Ibid.* See Y.B. 22 Ass. f. 93, pl. 34.
(c) Stat. of Northampton, 2 Edw. III. c. 15, *infra*; Y.B. 22 Ass. f. 93, pl. 34. As to the metropolis, see also *post*, p. 205.
(d) Y.B. 22 Ass. f. 93, pl. 34; Com. Dig., Market (I); A.-G. v. Horner (1884) 14 Q.B.D. 245.
(e) 2 Edw. III. c. 15. (f) See *ante*, p. 22.
(g) For a form of proclamation, see *First Report of Royal Commission*, vol i. appendix xiv.
(h) See Midleton v. Power (1886) 19 L.R. Ir. 1.

E

forfeit to the crown the double value of what he shall so sell, such double value to be recoverable at the suit of a common informer, who shall be entitled to a fourth part of the amount recovered.

§ 2. *Change of the days.*

In early times any change of the market-day was unlawful, including a change from Sunday to a week-day.(*a*) But in the thirteenth century it appears that the opinion began to prevail that Sunday marketing was wrong, and consequently changes of market-days from Sunday to week-days were often allowed without payment of a fine,(*b*) and at last they came to be regarded as lawful.(*c*) Finally, in 1448 a statute (*d*) was passed which made it illegal to show or expose any goods or merchandise (except necessary victual) for sale in any fair or market held upon any Sunday,(*e*) or upon Good Friday,(*f*) or upon certain 'principal feasts'; and permitted persons who had no day for holding their fair or market other than these days to hold it within three days later or three days earlier, after making proclamation of the change of day. The feast days mentioned in the statute are Ascension Day,(*g*) (*h*) Corpus Christi Day,(*i*) (*j*) Assumption Day,(*k*) (*j*) and All Saints' Day.(*l*) (*h*) With regard to Sundays, an exception was made of 'the four Sundays in harvest';(*m*) but this exception was abolished in 1850.(*n*) The penalty for exposing goods con-

(*a*) Plac. Quo. Warr., p. 710 (temp. Edw. I. Eccleshall); Abb. Plac. p. 43 (5 John, Litchfield and Newcastle-under-Lyme).
(*b*) Abb. Plac. p. 71 (temp. John, Edenham and Lafford); Maitland, *Pleas of the Crown for Gloucester*, p. 12, and note at p. 139.
(*c*) Bracton, fol. 117.
(*d*) Stat. 27 Hen. VI. c. 5, 'considering the abominable injuries and offences done to Almighty God, and to his saints, always aiders and singular assisters in our necessities.'
(*e*) At a much earlier date, Sunday markets had been forbidden; see the Laws of Athelstan (circ. 925 A.D.) and of Aethelred, Witan of 1014.
(*f*) 'Accustomably and miserably holden and used in the realm of England.'
(*g*) Moveable feast, falling on the Thursday which comes forty days after Easter.
(*h*) A holy day under 5 & 6 Edw. VI. c. 3, and a feast day according to the calendar of 1750 (24 Geo. II. c. 23).
(*i*) Thursday next after Trinity Sunday.
(*j*) Not a holy day under 5 & 6 Edw. VI. c. 3, nor recognised as a feast day in the calendar of 1750.
(*k*) Assumption B.V.M., August 15.
(*l*) November 1.   (*m*) Lat. 'in autumpno.'
(*n*) By Stat. 13 & 14 Vict. c. 23. (Repealed by S.L.R. Act, 1875.)

trary to the statute is forfeiture of the exposed goods to the lord of the fair or market.

This statute does not affect the prescriptive or charter rights of persons entitled to markets or fairs by making it unlawful to hold them on Sundays or the other specified days : it only imposes penalties on persons who expose goods for sale in markets and fairs held on such days.(*a*)

When the calendar was reformed by the Calendar (New Style) Act, 1750,(*b*) the nominal days for keeping the fixed feasts and fasts remained the same ;(*c*) and accordingly all fairs and markets the dates for holding which depended upon the dates of such feasts and fasts continued holdable on the same nominal days; and the Act provided (*b*) that any market, fair, or mart which had been held at a moveable time depending upon the fall of Easter, or any other moveable feast, should continue so to be held, the fall of Easter or such other moveable feast being computed in accordance with the new tables.

<small>Reformed Calendar</small>

But in the case of markets, fairs, and marts fixed to certain nominal days of a month, or depending upon the beginning or any certain day of a month, the nominal days for holding them were changed by the provisions of the Act ;(*d*) and such markets, fairs, and marts are now held eleven days later than their old nominal days. So that, for example, Dunstable Fair, which was originally granted to be held on August 1 and May 11, was afterwards properly held on August 12 and May 22.

The Fairs Act, 1873,(*e*) gives to a principal Secretary of State power to alter or increase or abridge the days of holding fairs in England and Wales. He may order that a fair shall be held (1) on some other day or days, or (2) on the same day or days and any preceding or subsequent day or days, or (3) on or during a less number of days than the fair is used to be held.(*f*) But he can only make such an order upon a representation duly made to him (*g*) that it would be 'for the convenience and advantage of the public' that the change should be made ; and the representation can only be made to him (*g*) either (1) by the owner of the fair or (2) by the

<small>Fairs Act, 1873</small>

(*a*) Comyns *v.* Boyer (1596) Cro. Eliz. 485 ; Corporation of Cork *v.* Shinkwin (1825) Smith and B., 395, 399. It is curious, therefore, that the penalty should go to the lord.
(*b*) 24 Geo. II. c. 23.   (*c*) s. 3.   (*d*) s. 4.
(*e*) 36 & 37 Vict. c. 37.   (*f*) s. 6.   (*g*) Ibid.

52 Days and Hours for Holding Markets and Fairs

district council of the district in which the fair is situate, or, if the fair be situate in the county of London, by the justices acting in and for the petty sessional division in which the fair is held.(*a*)

Before the Secretary of State takes the representation into consideration, the Act requires a notice of (1) the representation, and (2) the time when it will be considered by him, to be both given and published.(*b*) Where the representation is made by the owner of the fair, this notice must be given to the district council,(*c*) or, if the fair is situate in the county of London, to the clerk of the justices ;(*c*) and where the representation is made by the district council, or the justices, the notice must be given to the owner of the fair.(*b*) In every case, before the representation is considered, the notice must be published (1) once in the 'London Gazette,' and also (2) in three successive weeks in some one and the same newspaper published in the county, city, or borough in which the fair is held, or, if there be no newspaper published therein, then in the newspaper of some county adjoining or near thereto.(*d*)

As soon as the order has been made, notice of the making of the order must be similarly published ;(*e*) and the order has apparently no force until such publication has been completed. When the requirements of the Act with regard to publication have been complied with, the fair may only be held on the day or days mentioned in the order.(*e*) The Act expressly preserves all the rights of the owner of the fair, with regard to toll or otherwise, notwithstanding the change of day or days.(*e*)

For the purposes of the Act, 'owner' means 'any person or persons, or body of commissioners or body corporate, entitled to hold any fair, whether in respect of the ownership of any lands or tenements or under any charter, letters patent, or otherwise howsoever.'(*f*)

Presumed grant to change day

If a market or fair has been held for a long time past upon days other than the days specified in the grants which relate

---

(*a*) The Local Government Act, 1894 (56 & 57 Vict. c. 73, s. 27 (i.) (*e*), has substituted the district council for the justices, except as regards the County of London (see s. 35). If the fair be situate in a borough, including a county borough, the borough council may make the representation in its capacity of district council. See Id. ss. 21, 27, and 32.
(*b*) s. 6.   (*c*) *Ibid.*, and see note (*a*), *supra*.
(*d*) s. 6.   (*e*) s. 7.   (*f*) s. 3.

Change of the Days

to the market or fair, it may sometimes be presumed from the long user that there was a further grant or licence, which has since been lost, authorising the change of the days.(*a*)

§ 3. *The hours.*

With regard to the proper hours for holding fairs and markets, it has been said that *dies* in grants means *dies solaris* (i.e. from sunrise to sunset), and not *dies naturalis* (i.e. from midnight to midnight), so that fairs and markets can be lawfully held only by day.(*b*) It cannot be said that this doctrine has always been maintained in practice. It seems, however, to be recognised in the custom of the city of London whereby every shop open to the public is market overt only between sunrise and sunset.(*c*) In and near London, the hours for holding hay and straw markets through which there is a public carriage-way, and also for holding fairs, are regulated, to some extent, by statute.

The Hay and Straw Act, 1796,(*d*) enacts that every market for sale of hay and straw within the cities of London and Westminster, or the weekly bills of mortality, or within thirty miles thereof,(*e*) must end at 3 P.M. on every market-day between Lady Day and Michaelmas, and at 2 P.M. on every market-day between Michaelmas and Lady Day,(*f*) and the clerk or toll-gatherer, or his deputy, must give notice thereof on each market-day by ringing 'a large hand bell' round the market one hour before the time, and again at the time, when the market must end.(*f*) If the market be held *on* Michaelmas or Lady Day, it seems doubtful, from the wording of the Act, whether it ought to end at 2 P.M. or 3 P.M.

The Act imposes upon the person whose duty it is to ring the bell a fine of not more than ten nor less than five shillings for every offence in not ringing.(*f*) It also imposes upon every person who shall sell any hay or straw in the market after the market hours a fine of sixpence for every bundle or truss of

---

(*a*) See Mayor of Penryn *v*. Best (1878) 3 Ex. D. 292, as explained in Mayor of Manchester *v*. Lyons (1882) 22 Ch. D. 287, 300; Midleton *v*. Power (1886) 19 L.R. Ir. 1, 12.
(*b*) 2 Inst. 714.
(*c*) See Taylor *v*. Chambers (1604) Cro. Jac. 68; and, as to the custom generally, see *post*, p. 122.
(*d*) 36 Geo. III. c. 88. (*e*) s. 2. (*f*) s. 15.

hay, and of threepence for every bundle or truss of straw, so sold.(*a*)

The Act also provides that if any person having the care or direction of any waggon, wain or cart, used for the purpose of bringing hay and straw, shall suffer the same to remain in the market, on a market-day from Lady Day to Michaelmas after 5 P.M., or on a market-day from Michaelmas to Lady Day after 3 P.M., he shall forfeit for every such waggon, wain or cart, a sum not exceeding twenty and not less than five shillings.(*b*) The penalties imposed by the Act are recoverable summarily, under the Summary Jurisdiction Acts. When recovered, they are payable to the prosecutor.(*c*)

The Act does not now apply to any markets 'through which there does not exist by law any public right of way for carts and carriages,' as it was repealed, so far as regards those markets, by the Hay and Straw Act, 1834.(*d*) The latter Act expressly casts the burden of proving the public right of way upon a party suing for any penalty.

The business and amusements of fairs held within the metropolitan police district are required by the Metropolitan Police Act, 1839,(*e*) to cease at 11 P.M., and not to begin earlier than 6 A.M. If any house, room, booth, standing, tent, caravan, waggon, or other place, be 'open' between 11 P.M. and 6 A.M., for any purpose of business or amusement, in the place where the fair is held, a constable may take into custody the person having the care or management thereof, and also every person being therein who shall not quit the same forthwith upon being bidden by the constable so to do.(*e*) The former is liable to a penalty not exceeding five pounds, and the latter to a penalty not exceeding forty shillings, upon summary conviction.(*e*)

For the purposes of the Shop Hours Acts, 1892 to 1895,(*f*) 'shop' includes markets and stalls in which assistants are employed for hire.

(*a*) s. 15.   (*b*) s. 16.   (*c*) s. 30.
(*d*) 4 & 5 Will. IV. c. 21.   (*e*) 2 & 3 Vict. c. 47, s. 38.
(*f*) 55 & 56 Vict. c. 62 ; 56 & 57 Vict. c. 67 ; 58 Vict. c. 5; see s. 9 of the first mentioned Act.

CHAPTER IV

TOLL AND STALLAGE

§ 1. *The nature of tolls and stallage and other charges.*

THE usual payments made to the owners of markets and fairs are of toll and stallage. In some places, however, piccage, pennage, and other dues are payable. These terms require explanation.

The legal definition of *toll* (in connection with a fair or market) is 'a reasonable sum of money due to the owner of the fair or market upon the sale of things tollable within the fair or market, or for stallage, piccage or the like' ;(*a*) and it has been held that in grants,(*b*) Acts of Parliament,(*c*) as well as in pleading,(*d*) 'toll' may include stallage, as a general word for all such duties or payments.

It is, however, convenient and usual to limit the word toll, in this connection, to payments made on the sale within the market or fair of things tollable, as distinguished from stallage and other payments which are made in respect of some user of the soil beyond the mere entry thereon ;(*e*) and the word will generally be used in this book in this limited sense.

Stallage is a satisfaction to the owner of the soil on which a market or fair is held for the liberty of placing a stall upon it or for standing room for cattle or goods within the market or fair ; and if the soil be broken it is called *piccage*.(*f*) *Pennage* is payable for the erection of pens.(*g*)

(*a*) 2 Inst. 220.
(*b*) Lockwood *v.* Wood (1841) 6 Q.B. 31.
(*c*) Duke of Bedford *v.* Emmett (1820) 3 B. and Ald. 366, 371.
(*d*) Bennington *v.* Taylor (1701) 2 Lutw. 1517.
(*e*) Com. Dig., Market (F. 1); Duke of Bedford *v.* Overseers of St. Paul (1881) 51 L.J.M.C. 41, 45, per Bowen, J.
(*f*) Mayor of Northampton *v.* Ward (1746), 2 Stra. 1238; and see *Spelman's Glossary* and *Termes de la Ley*.
(*g*) R. *v.* Marsden (1765) 3 Burr. 1812.

56 Toll and Stallage

It may be convenient here to state very briefly the nature of certain other tolls—(some of them are now obsolete)—which are or have been more or less connected with markets and fairs.(*a*)

Lastage, or *Lestage*: a toll paid for liberty for persons to carry their goods up and down to markets and fairs.(*b*)

Pesage or *Poizage*: a duty paid for weighing commodities.(*c*)

Tronage: a duty paid for weighing wool, and other heavy commodities.(*d*)

Scavage, or *Shewage*: toll paid for a licence to show or expose wares.(*e*)

Sumage, or *Summage*: toll paid for carrying goods on horseback.(*f*)

Toll-turn: toll paid for cattle or goods on their return from a fair or market.(*g*)

Toll-traverse: toll paid for cattle or goods taken over private land.(*h*)

Toll-through: toll paid for passing through or into a town or over a public way, bridge or ferry.(*i*)

Special tolls
In particular markets or fairs tolls of a special kind may be payable by custom or prescription. Thus, at Lichfield market there was payable to a bell-man for sweeping out the market a toll on all corn brought into the market, whether sold or not.(*j*)

§ 2. The right to toll.

Grant of toll
The right of taking toll is not incident to a fair or market, and some markets and many fairs are toll-free. Every person has of common right the liberty of buying and selling in a public market or fair, and toll is not payable to the lord in

---

(*a*) It is difficult to say what meanings are to be attached to some of the terms, but to the best of the authors' judgment the definitions given are fairly accurate.

(*b*) See Birch's *Historical Charters, &c., of London* (1887) p. 328.
(*c*) *Ibid.* 331.   (*d*) *Ibid.* 336.   Lat. 'trutina' (scales).
(*e*) *Ibid.* 333; Jacob's *Law Dict.* The 'scavenger' collected it.
(*f*) Jacob's *Law Dict.* Cf. 'Sumpter,' a pack-horse.
(*g*) Com. Dig. Toll. (B.).
(*h*) Com. Dig. Toll (D. a); see Brecon Market Co. *v.* Neath R. Co. (1872) L.R. 7 C.P. 555.
(*i*) Com. Dig. Toll (C.).
(*j*) Hill *v.* Hawker (1615) Mo. 835; *S.C.* Hill *v.* Hank, 2 Bulstr. 201, 1 Roll. Rep. 44; and see Riley's *Memorials of London*, p. 366: Ordinance for the cleansing of Smithfield, 46 Edw. III.

respect of sales there unless he be entitled to it by special grant or prescription (*a*) or statute.

According to Moore's report of Heddy *v.* Weelhouse,(*b*) the judges there said that toll is payable of common right for live cattle, but not for victual or other wares ;(*c*) but this statement is not borne out by the decision in the case, which was that toll is not demandable for a heifer or cow, unless by grant from the king or by prescription. The case seems to be more correctly reported by Croke.(*d*)

A grant of a fair or market does not carry with it a grant of toll, unless there be special words appropriate to create a right to toll. It is not enough that a fair be granted 'cum omnibus libertatibus et liberis consuetudinibus ad hujusmodi feriam spectantibus vel pertinentibus,'(*e*) or 'with all profits, commodities, emoluments, liberties, and free customs appertaining to such a fair,'(*f*) or any similar general words, not peculiarly applicable to toll. For toll is not incident to a fair.

There is a distinction, however, between an original grant of a new market or fair and a confirmatory grant of an ancient one, or a re-grant of the latter after it has passed by forfeiture or otherwise into the hands of the crown. In the case of such a confirmatory grant, or of such a re-grant, general words may be sufficient to continue any right to toll, whether by grant or prescription, which had previously existed.(*g*) But the grant or re-grant must be of the ancient market or fair, and not merely a grant of a new franchise, as was the case in Holloway *v.* Smith,(*h*) where new fairs were granted, and it was held that

(*a*) R. *v.* Corporation of Maidenhead (1620) Palmer 76; Osbuston *v.* James (1688) 2 Lutw. 1377; Holloway *v.* Smith (1743) 2 Stra. 1171; Austin *v.* Whittred (1747) Willes, 623; Lowden *v.* Hierons (1818) 2 B. Mo. 102; Mayor of Stamford *v.* Pawlett (1830) 1 Cr. and J. 57; Earl of Egremont *v.* Saul (1837) 6 A. and E. 924.
(*b*) (1597) Mo. 474.
(*c*) Toll is not due by common usage 'for hens or geese, or for many other things of such nature,' per Clench, J., Escot *v.* Lanreny (1594) Owen, 109. Cf. 1 Rot. Hundred. p. 280 b. (Lafford, Linc.), and p. 239 b. (Lutterworth, Leic.).
(*d*) Heddy *v.* Weelhouse (1597) Cro. Eliz. 558, 591.
(*e*) Heddy *v.* Weelhouse (1597) Cro. Eliz. 558, 591; Earl of Egremont *v.* Saul (1837) 6 A. and E. 924.
(*f*) Holloway *v.* Smith (1743) 2 Stra. 1171
(*g*) Heddy *v.* Weelhouse (1597) Cro. Eliz. 591, per Popham, J.; Earl of Egremont *v.* Saul (1837) 6 A. and E. 924, 931.
(*h*) (1743) 2 Stra. 1171.

58   *Toll and Stallage*

a custom to take toll in an old fair, though recited in the grant, did not justify taking toll in the new fairs.

Toll-free markets

If the crown grant a market or fair without a special grant of toll, the market or fair is toll-free; and the crown has no power afterwards to grant toll for such market or fair 'without *quid pro quo,* some proportionable benefit to the subject.'(*a*) For a market or fair, when once established, exists for the benefit of the public, as well as for the benefit of its owner. In Lowden *v.* Hierons,(*b*) however, it appeared that there had been a usage to take toll in Covent Garden market for some 150 years before action brought, but that the market had been free down to 1670, when a further grant (*c*) was obtained of the market *cum tolnetis hujusmodi mercaturae aliquatinus spectantibus.* On these facts the court seem to have thought that it was open to a jury to presume from the usage that a valid grant of toll had been made since the original charter.(*d*)

Amount of toll

A grant of toll sometimes specifies the amount which may be taken, and such amount must be reasonable. A grant of an unreasonable toll is wholly void, and no portion of it whatever is payable.(*e*)

Reasonable toll

see p. 60

A grant of a toll which does not specify the amount to be taken is interpreted to be a grant of a reasonable toll ;(*f*) but if the language of the grant be ambiguous it may be void for uncertainty, as was held in the case of a grant of 'such toll as is used to be taken *ibi et alibi infra regnum Angliae.*'(*g*)

In Corporation of Stamford *v.* Pawlett,(*h*) it was argued that the grant of a reasonable toll without specifying the amount was void, on the ground that 'to permit the grantee to take whatever may appear to him to be a reasonable toll is to make the grantee a judge for himself, and to expose the subject to extortion.' But, as Alexander, C.B., said in delivering the judgment of the Court of Exchequer,(*i*) 'the grantee

---

(*a*) 2 Inst. 220; R. *v.* Mayor of London (1682) 2 Sho. 266; Lancum *v.* Lovell (1834) 6 C. and P. 437, 465.
(*b*) (1818) 2 B. Mo. 102.   (*c*) 22 Car. II.
(*d*) See per Dallas, J.
(*e*) 2 Inst. 220; Heddy *v.* Weelhouse (1597) Cro. Eliz. 558, 591, Mo. 474.
(*f*) R. *v.* Corporation of Maidenhead (1620) Palmer, 76; Corporation of Stamford *v.* Pawlett (1830) 1 Cr. & J. 57, 400.
(*g*) Lightfoot *v.* Lenet (1618) Cro. Jac. 421.
(*h*) (1830) 1 Cr. and J. 57, 400.
(*i*) At p. 81; affirmed in the Exchequer Chamber, Id. 400.

The Right to Toll

demands it at his peril, and at the hazard of a private as well as of a public prosecution ; of a private, at the suit of the party injured ; of a public, at the suit of the Attorney-General in the name of his Majesty. The inconvenience of raising such questions cannot be avoided by specifying the sum. The king cannot grant an unreasonable toll : and it is competent to every subject of the realm from whom the toll is demanded to question its being reasonable, even when the exact sum is specified in the charter. This question may always be brought under discussion, in whatever terms the grant may be expressed.' In that case the grant(a) was of two fairs or markets ' cum omnibus *tolnetis* et aliis proficuis predictis feriis sive nundinis pertinentibus et spectantibus,' and it was held that the grant passed the right to a reasonable toll.

Where the right to take toll is founded on prescription, it seems that a jury may find, if the evidence be adequate, either a lost grant of a reasonable toll, or a lost grant of a toll of specified amount.(b) The former finding is the more favourable for the lord of the market or fair, as such a grant does not prevent his varying the amount of his toll, provided that the amount taken is always reasonable, and the toll is not liable to be invalidated on the ground of rankness.(c) — Prescriptive toll

Where a reasonable toll is due, and excessive toll is taken, or where no toll at all is due and yet toll is unjustly usurped, the toll taken is said to be outrageous;(d) sometimes it is called excessive, or undue, or unjust.(e) Such toll is dealt with by the Statute of Westminster (the first).(f) In commenting upon the statute Lord Coke says (g) that toll is there used in the widest application, as including stallage, piccage and the like ; and that it includes toll to the fair as well as toll to the market. The statute(h) enacts that if outrageous — Outrageous toll

---

(a) 13 Anne.
(b) See Wright v. Bruister (1832) 4 B. and Ad. 116, Gunning *on Tolls*, 62; Lawrence v. Hitch (1868) L.R. 3 Q.B. 521. In the Worksop market and fair case, Plac. Quo. War. p. 627, the crown alleged as an abuse, and proved, that the lord had taken twice as much for tolls as he and his predecessors from time immemorial had before taken, and the market and fair were forfeited. The tolls were prescriptive. It does not appear whether the lord's claim was to tolls of specified or of reasonable amount; but the case is consistent with either view.
(c) Lawrence v. Hitch (1868) L.R. 3 Q.B. 521 ; and see *post*, p. 60.
(d) 2 Inst. 220. (e) *Ibid.* (f) 3 Edw. I. c. 31.
(g) 2 Inst. 220.
(h) 3 Edw. I., Stat. of Westm. (the first) c. 31.

60 Toll and Stallage

toll is taken by the lord, the crown may seize the franchise of the market or fair into its own hands; and that if it be taken by a bailiff, or any mean officer, without the authority of his lord, the bailiff or officer shall restore to the injured party as much more for the outrageous taking as he would have had of him if he had carried away his toll, and moreover shall have forty days' imprisonment.(*a*)

Lord Coke says that the statute authorises the crown to seize the franchise of the market or fair 'until it be redeemed by the owner'; but that the seizure can be had only upon an office found.(*b*) Apart from the statute, an abuse of the franchise of toll, by taking outrageous toll, renders that franchise liable to forfeiture, but does not, it seems, create a forfeiture of the market or fair.(*c*)

Reasonableness Reasonableness is a question of law. If a jury find that the sum demanded is due in accordance with the grant or prescription, it is the duty of the Court to support that verdict, unless the toll be unreasonable, and the onus of showing that it is such lies on the party disputing the toll.(*d*) A continuance of uniform payment and acquiescence therein is evidence of reasonableness.(*e*) The mere fact that a toll of particular amount has been taken for a long period of time will not, in the absence of all evidence on the subject, warrant the assumption that a toll of a larger amount is unreasonable.(*f*)

Recently an attempt was made to defeat a prescriptive toll by showing that the amount, though reasonable at the present time, would have been unreasonable in 1189, when the time of legal memory began, and for many years afterwards, from which it was argued that the toll could not have had a lawful origin. This principle, known as the doctrine of rankness, had some

---

(*a*) See *Revised Statutes*, 2nd. edit. vol. i. p. 13.
(*b*) 2 Inst. 221. 'Office found' seems to mean here a verdict in *quo warranto* proceedings.
(*c*) See Com. Dig. 'Market' (I.), citing Palmer, 82. Vin. Abr. Market (F.) 7, to the contrary, cites 2 Show. 265; but the passage in Shower is mere argument, on the false assumption that toll is incident to a market.
(*d*) Wright *v.* Bruister (1832) 4 B. and Ad. 116, where a toll of 1*d.* on every pig brought into a market was held to be not necessarily unreasonable.
(*e*) Gard *v.* Callard (1817) 6. M. & S. 69. As to slight variations from time to time, see Duke of Beaufort *v.* Smith (1849) 4 Exch. 450.
(*f*) See Mills *v.* Mayor of Colchester (1868) L.R. 3 C.P. 575.

place in the law of tithes,(a) but it has never been successfully applied to prescriptive tolls, though its application would have been fatal to many. The answer to the argument is that it may be presumed that the grant was of a reasonable toll, to vary in amount from time to time according to the varying value of money ;(b) and such a toll is valid in point of law.(c) Accordingly, a toll of 1s. on every cartload of vegetables brought into the market has been successfully prescribed for as a reasonable toll varying in amount, though a toll of that amount would have been unreasonable in the time of Richard I.(d) But if a toll were claimed by charter granting a toll of specified amount, which, though reasonable now, must have been unreasonable at the time of the grant, it might be successfully contended that on that ground the grant of toll was void.(e)

Many tolls which are now taken in ancient charter and prescriptive markets would have been unreasonable in the times when the charters were granted, or in the first year of Richard I.,(f) and would be bad unless they could be supported as tolls varying in amount.

It has been questioned whether toll is payable on articles not in use at the time of the grant, or not then known, which have subsequently become marketable articles. It is submitted that there can be no objection to taking toll on such articles if the terms of the charter by which the tolls were granted be sufficiently wide ;(g) and in the case of a prescriptive market,

(a) See Eagle *on Tithes*, p. 186.
(b) Lawrence v. Hitch (1868) L.R. 3 Q.B. 521.
(c) See R. v. Corporation of Maidenhead (1620) Palmer, at p. 86. Wright v. Brewster (1832) as reported in Gunning *on Tolls*, pp. 62, 63. This point does not appear from the report in 4 B and Ad. 116.
(d) Lawrence v. Hitch, *supra*.
(e) See Lawrence v. Hitch, *supra* ; and compare Bryant v. Foot (1868) L.R. 3 Q.B. 497.
(f) Thus, in the time of Edward III. the following tolls were held to be unreasonable, viz. one penny for each of the following when sold in market or fair : horse, ox, cow, eight sheep, four pigs over one year old, eight young pigs, and a cart laden with merchandise ; for a horse's load one halfpenny or farthing, and for a man's load one farthing. Plac. Quo. Warr. p. 146 (Meysham), and p. 140 (Bauquell). See also Id. p. 627 (Worksop). In 1832 a toll of a penny for a pig sold in market was held to be reasonable. (Wright v. Bruister, 4 B. and Ad. 116). See also Heddy v. Weelhouse (1598) Cro. Eliz. 558, Moore 474.
(g) See R. v. Corporation of Maidenhead (1620) Palmer 85 ; Brune v. Thompson (1843) 4 Q.B. 543, 552 ; Mayor of Carlisle v. Wilson (1804) 5 East 2 ; Waterhouse v. Keen (1825) 4 B. and C. 200.

or a market with prescriptive tolls, there might be evidence from which it could be inferred that the lost grant contained a clause which provided for such articles, as by granting a reasonable toll on all chattels and things brought into the market and there sold.

Toll is payable, as a general rule, by the buyer, and not by the seller.(*a*) Nevertheless, by statute it may be payable in particular markets by the seller, and not by the buyer ; and this is generally the case in modern statutory markets.(*b*) A custom or prescription for payment of toll by the seller would probably be good.(*c*) In a very early case,(*d*) the lord claimed a prescriptive right to take toll from both buyer and seller : the amount taken was held unreasonable, but if the total amount taken were not excessive, perhaps such a right might be successfully prescribed for.

Toll is usually payable only on tollable articles actually brought into the market and there sold.(*e*) If goods are sold by sample in a market, and the bulk is never brought into the market, toll is not payable on the bulk ;(*f*) and there cannot be a grant or prescription to take toll on goods not actually brought into the market and there sold.(*g*) ' Fairs were invented that contracts might have good testimony and be made openly, and that the seller might know what to ask and the buyer what to give. . . . The goods should be sold publicly. This sale by sample is directly contrary to the origin and purpose of markets ; and it would be a strange thing that toll should be taken by the owners of the market on that very transaction which is contrary to the intention of the market.'(*h*)

(*a*) Leight *v.* Pym (1687) 2 Lutw. 1336 ; Y.B. 9 Hen. VI. f. 45, pl. 28 ; 2 Inst. 221.
(*b*) See *Final Report of Royal Commission*, p. 45.
(*c*) See Leight *v.* Pym (1687) 2 Lutw. 1336 ; Hill *v.* Smith (1809) 10 East 476, overruled on another point (1812) 4 Taunt. 502.
(*d*) Case of Bauquell, Plac. Quo Warr. p. 140.
(*e*) Wells *v.* Miles (1821) 4 B. and Ald. 559 ; Kerby *v.* Whichelow (1701) 2 Lutw. 1498 ; Leight *v.* Pym (1687) 2 Lutw. 1336 ; Bennington *v.* Taylor (1701) 2 Lutw. 1517 ; Swindon Central Market Co. *v.* Panting (1872) 27 L.T.N.S. 578 ; Viner *v.* Mayor of Reading (1826) 12 B. Mo. 201 ; 2 Inst. 221 ; Y.B. 9 Hen. VI. f. 45, pl. 28.
(*f*) Bailiffs of Tewkesbury *v.* Diston (1805) 6 East 438 ; Moseley *v.* Piersjn (1790) 4 T.R. 104. But an action lies for the injury done to the market ; see Bailiffs of Tewkesbury *v.* Bricknell (1809) 2 Taunt. 120, and *infra*, p. 83.
(*g*) Hill *v.* Smith (1812) 4 Taunt. 520 ; Wells *v.* Miles (1821) 4 B. and A. 559 ; Kerby *v.* Whichelow (1701) Lutw. 1498.
(*h*) Per Mansfield, C.J., 4 Taunt. 532.

By special custom, however, toll may perhaps be payable for goods brought into the market for sale and not sold.(*a*) On goods/not sold

§ 3. *The right to stallage.*

For taking stallage, piccage or pennage, no grant or prescription need be shown. It may be demanded in the case of a newly erected market.(*b*) The soil of the market or fair is no further appropriated to the public use than that every man has a legal right to enter into the market or fair to buy and sell. Stallage and the like payments are made in respect of some user of the soil beyond the mere entry into the market; for no one has a right to erect a stall, or appropriate part of the market-place as a standing, without making a satisfaction for it to the owner of the soil ;(*c*) and such satisfaction may always be demanded by implied, if not by express, agreement. It is not necessary to show a special contract to pay it. An action for stallage is analogous to an action for use and occupation of land ;(*d*) and where there is no express agreement, or no special sum fixed by custom or prescription, a reasonable sum is demandable.(*e*)

Stallage can never be claimed unless there is some exclusive occupation of the soil. Where a cattle market was held in the streets, and no stalls or pens were erected, but the cattle stood or were driven on the public street, a claim for stallage failed.(*f*)

Persons using a market may rest their baskets or goods on the ground for a time without being liable for stallage ;(*g*) but

(*a*) Leight *v.* Pym (1687) 2 Lutw. 1336; Hill *v.* Hawker (about 1616) Moore 835.
(*b*) Per Lee, C.J., Mayor of Northampton *v.* Ward (1746) 2 Stra. 1238; Mayor of Yarmouth *v.* Groom (1862) 1 H. and C. 102; and see per Lord Denman, Lockwood *v.* Wood (1841) 6 Q.B. 31.
(*c*) *Ibid.* But though he is liable in trespass, it seems that ejectment will not lie for a stall erected in a public street; Doe *v.* Cowley (1823) 1 C. and P. 123; Cole *on Ejectment*, p. 92. Nor probably, for a stall erected in a close to which the public had admission for market purposes; see Mayor of Northampton *v.* Ward (1746) 2 Stra. 1238.
(*d*) 1 Roll Abr. 106; Mayor of Newport *v.* Saunders (1832) 3 B. and Ad. 411; Taunton Market *v.* Kimberley (1777) 2 W. Bl. 1120.
(*e*) Mayor of Newport *v.* Saunders (1832) 3 B. and Ad. 411; and see pp. 59 and 64.
(*f*) Swindon Central Market Co. Ld. *v.* Panting (1872) 27 L.T.N.S. 578.
(*g*) Townend *v.* Woodruff (1850) 5 Exch. 506; and see R. *v.* Bell (1816) 5 M. & S. 221; Wigley *v.* Peachy (1732) 2 Lord Raym. 1589;

where there is an exclusive occupation of a particular portion of the market-place by tables or baskets placed upon the ground, then stallage is due, and it is always a question of fact whether a basket is so used as to amount to a stall.(*a*)

Stallage may take the form of a rent payable weekly or at other intervals for the continuous hire of a stall ; or a payment may be made for the use of a stall during the whole course of a single fair or market day.

Sometimes stallages are paid upon goods pitched in the market, and are then not at first sight distinguishable from tolls. Thus, in Covent Garden market, beside the rents paid for stalls, payments are made upon articles pitched for sale in the market. These payments are called tolls, but are stallages, as they are paid upon articles placed or pitched in the market in respect of the space occupied by them, and not upon sales.(*b*)

The amount due for stallage may be a matter of express or implied agreement ;(*c*) but must in all cases be reasonable ;(*d*) and a market-owner who extorts an unreasonable stallage by compelling people to take stalls and running up their price may be indictable for so doing.(*e*) The amount due may be fixed by custom or prescription, and in such cases the customary amount cannot be exceeded.(*f*)

Customary stallage

Though generally no one has a right to occupy a stall without the leave of the owner of the soil, and anyone so doing will be a trespasser,(*g*) nevertheless there may be a custom for a particular class of persons to erect stalls in a market or fair

Mayor of Launceston's case (1587) Cro. Eliz. 75; Sawyer *v.* Wilkinson (1598) Cro. Eliz. 627, where the owner of the soil was held not justified in distraining damage-feasant goods brought into the market-place and laid down for sale.

In Spelman's *Glossary*, stallage is defined as 'Jus stationis, Jus erigendæ officinæ vel *exponendarum* mercium in foris et nundinis, Etiam nummus hoc nomine datus.' But this is not consistent with the cases here quoted.

(*a*) Mayor of Norwich *v.* Swann (1777) 2 W. Black. 1116 ; Mayor of Yarmouth *v.* Groom (1862) 1 H. and C. 102.
(*b*) Duke of Bedford *v.* Overseers of St. Paul (1881) 51 L.J.M.C. 41 ; Duke of Bedford *v.* Emmett (1820) 3 B. and Ald. 366.
(*c*) Mayor of Northampton *v.* Ward (1746) 2 Stra. 1238 ; 1 Wils. 114.
(*d*) 3 Ed. I. c. 31, *vide supra*, p. 59.
(*e*) R. *v.* Burdett (1697) 1 Lord Raym. 149 ; Russell *on Crimes*, pp. 425-428.
(*f*) Bennington *v.* Taylor (1701) 2 Lutw. 1517 ; Hickman's case, 2 Rol. Abr. 123, ' Market,' B. 2.
(*g*) Mayor of Northampton *v.* Ward (1746) 2 Stra. 1238 ; Mayor of Norwich *v.* Swann (1777) 2 W. Black. 1116.

The Right to Stallage

paying a certain, or a reasonable, sum as stallage. And such a custom will be an answer in an action of trespass.(*a*) Thus in Tyson *v.* Smith (*b*) a custom that victuallers should erect stalls on a common at the times of fairs, and continue the same for a reasonable time, paying 2d. to the lord of the manor, was held a good justification in an action for trespass. Tindal, C.J., said : 'At the early time at which this custom originated it may have been a profit to the lord, and at all events it may have been an object to him, with respect to the profits of his fair, to give encouragement to those who would erect booths and stalls for the entertainment of strangers coming to the fair. It is clear that a prescription for a certain toll by way of stallage is good notwithstanding toll and stallage are different things ; as was held in the case of Bennington *v.* Taylor ;(*c*) and if the lord of a fair can justify distraining for such toll under a prescription there seems no reason why the person who uses the stall on payment of the toll, and who cannot prescribe either in a *que estate* or in himself and his ancestors, being a stranger, should not justify under such a custom as the present. The custom, in fact, comes at last to an agreement, which has been evidenced by such repeated acts of assent on both sides from the earliest times, beginning before time of memory and continuing down to our own times, that it has become the law of the particular place.'

§ 4. *Tolls and stallage in kind.*

Tolls, stallage, and the like, are usually paid in money ; but by custom or prescription they may be payable in kind, as by taking a pint of every bushel of wheat exposed for sale.(*d*)

In cases of a custom to take in kind, the custom must be closely followed. At Cockermouth market the custom was for the collector to 'lift' a handful of corn out of every sack ; he varied from the regular mode by 'sweeping' the corn out,

---

(*a*) Tyson *v.* Smith (1838) 9 A. & E. 406 ; Elwood *v.* Bullock (1844) 6 Q. B. 383 ; Chasin *v.* Betsworth (1684) 3 Lev. 190.
(*b*) (1838) 9 A. & E. 406.
(*c*) (1701) 2 Lutw. 1517.
(*d*) Specot *v.* Carpenter (1681) Thos. Jones, 207 ; Norman *v.* Bell (1831) 2 B. & Ad. 190; Hickman's case (1599) Noy, 37 ; Roll. Abr. Market, B. 2 ; Hill *v.* Hawker (circ. 1616) Moore, 835 ; Abb. Plac. (4 John) p. 41, (8 Edw. I.) p. 321 ; Plac. Quo Warr. (Twywell) p. 569 ; *Final Report of Royal Commission*, p. 101.

and by so doing took more than a handful; and he was held liable in trover.(a)

§ 5. *Variable and differential tolls.*

Toll, being a payment on the sale of goods, is clearly distinguishable from stallage, which is a payment for the use of part of the soil, and which is generally payable whether a sale is effected or not. The amount of toll payable thereon depends on the goods sold, not the part of the market in which they are sold; and it is perhaps impossible to sustain at common law a different toll for the same article in different parts of the same market.(b) But payments in the nature of stallage, though taken in the name of toll, may vary according to the part of the market-place in which the goods are pitched; for one part may be so much more convenient than another for exposing wares for sale as to justify a different payment for the privilege of erecting stalls there.(b)

In some markets differential tolls are taken, according as the person charged is or is not one of a particular class. Sometimes inhabitants or freemen of a borough, or copyholders of a manor, are charged less for toll or stallage than outsiders, and sometimes persons of a particular calling, such as auctioneers, pay more or less than others when buying or selling the same goods. There is a great variety of differential tolls in fact taken in markets ;(c) and there appears to be nothing unlawful at common law in taking differential tolls, provided that the highest do not exceed the maximum which may be taken in the particular market.(d) There seems no reason why a partial remission of toll should not be valid to the same extent as a total exemption.

§ 6. *The recovery of toll and stallage.*

By action Toll and stallage may be recovered by action without proof of a special contract.(e) A form of statement of

(a) Norman v. Bell (1831) 2 B. & Ad. 190.
(b) Duke of Bedford v. Emmett (1820) 3 B. & Ald. 366.
(c) See *Final Report of Royal Commission*, pp. 95-98.
(d) Hungerford Market Co. v. City Steamboat Co. (1860) 3 E. & F. 365. See also, Plac. Quo Warr. (Derby) p. 158 Rot. Hund. (Wallingford) p. 2; Abb. Plac. (Faversham) p. 140.
(e) For forms of action and declarations before the Judicature Acts, see Bullen & Leake, 3rd edit. p. 227; Seward v. Baker (1787) 1 T.R. 616; Duke of Bedford v. Emmett (1820) 3 B. & A. 366; Mayor of Reading v.

The Recovery of Toll and Stallage

claim for tolls is given in 'Allen's Forms of Pleading,' p. 105.(a)

In an action for toll the facts to be proved are usually as follows:—(1) That the plaintiff was in possession (as owner or lessee) of the market or fair and the tolls : (2) The due holding of the market or fair at the time and place in question : (3) That the toll claimed is reasonable; and that it was payable (either by charter, prescription, or otherwise) by the buyer or seller 'as the case may be) on any sale in the market or fair of the articles in respect of which it is claimed : (4) That tollable goods were brought into the market, and were there bought or sold (as the case may be) by the defendant : (5) That the toll has not been paid.

And in an action for stallage, or piccage, the facts to be proved are usually as follows :—(1) That the plaintiff was in possession (as owner or lessee) of the soil of the market or fair : (2) The due holding of the market or fair at the time and place in question : (3) That the defendant erected therein a stall, or took a standing, and, if piccage be claimed, that in so doing he broke the soil : (4) That the sum claimed is a reasonable sum, and if it be claimed by special agreement, or by custom or prescription, that the agreement was made, or the custom or prescription exists : (5) That the defendant has not paid the amount due.

No action for toll (or stallage) can be maintained in a county court if the title to the toll, or the fair or market, be in question, unless the parties consent to the jurisdiction.(b)

After demand and refusal of toll due in respect of any particular goods, the owner of a market or fair may seize those goods, or a reasonable part thereof, by way of distress, and detain the same until the toll be paid or the goods replevied.(c) In some of the cases on this subject the right to distrain was

By distress

Clarke (1821) 4 B. & Ald. 268; Corporation of Stamford v. Pawlett (1830) 1 Cr. & J. 57; Mayor of Newport v. Saunders (1832) 3 B. & Ad. 411; Lockwood v. Wood (1844) 6 Q.B. 31; Mayor of Yarmouth v. Groom (1862) 1 H. & C. 102. See also Chitty on *Pleadings*, 7th edit., vol. ii., pp. 41-44 ; Wentworth's *System of Pleading*, vol. i., pp. 153 and 156.

As to the recovery of statutory tolls and stallage, see the Markets and Fairs Clauses Act, 1847, ss. 31-41, *post*, pp. 160-164.

(a) For Indorsement on Writ, see R.S.C. 1883, Appendix A. sect. ii.
(b) County Courts Act, 1888 (51 & 52 Vict. c. 43), ss. 56, 61 and 64.
(c) Heddy v. Weelhouse (1596) Cro. Eliz. 558, Moore 474; Agar v. Lisle (1674) Hob. 187 ; Roll. Abr. 666; see Smith v. Shepherd (1599)

claimed by prescription ;(a) and possibly it cannot be claimed except by prescription, toll not being due of common right.(b) It has been said, however, that distress is incident to every toll ;(c) and this seems to be the sounder view. The distress must be made, it seems, while the goods are still in the market or fair.(d) The goods may not be sold under the distress.(e) No distress for toll can be made on goods sold outside the market, though such sale amounts to a disturbance of the market.(f) The proper remedy for that is an action for damages for the disturbance.(g)

With regard to stallage, a claim to distrain after demand and refusal was upheld in Bennington v. Taylor, (h) when the owners of a fair prescribed for a reasonable stallage of ascertainable amount, and also for the right to distrain therefor during the fair upon the goods exposed for sale in the stall.

§ 7. *The remedies for toll wrongfully taken.*

An action on the case lies against anyone who takes toll when none is due, or takes more than is due, or takes from one who is exempt.(i) If the toll-taker improperly takes too much by way of toll in kind, or wrongfully distrains for any toll, he is liable in an action of trespass (j) or trover.(k) Money improperly exacted as a toll may be recovered as money had and received to the plaintiff's use.(l)

Cro. Eliz. 710; Hickman's case (1599) Noy, 37 ; Harris v. Hawkins (1674) 1 Keb. 342; Leight v. Pym (1687) 2 Lutw. 1329.
(a) See Agar v. Lisle (1674) Hob. 187 ; Smith v. Shepherd (1599) Cro. Eliz. 710; Bennington v. Taylor (1701) 2 Lutw. 1517.
(b) See Com. Dig. Distress (A. 1), citing 11 Co. 44 b; Harris v. Hawkins (1674) 1 Keb. 342.
(c) Hickman's case (1599) Noy, 37 ; Viner, Ab. Toll (I.); Gunning *on Tolls*, 216 ; see also Heddy v. Weelhouse (1596) Cro. Eliz. 558, where the right apparently was not prescribed for ; Gilbert, Distress, 19.
(d) Hickman's case (1599) Noy, 37 ; Viner, Ab. Toll (I.).
(e) Gunning *on Tolls*, 217 ; Gilbert, Distress, 19.
(f) Blakey v. Dimsdale (1777) 2 Cowp. 661.
(g) See *post*, p. 82.
(h) (1701) 2 Lutw. 1517; see Tyson v. Smith (1838) 9 A. & E. 406, 425.
(i) Com. Dig. Toll (H. 2), Market (F. 1); Wood v. Hankshead (1602) Yel. 13 ; F.N.B. 94 F. For the remedy under the Statute of Westminster I., see *ante*, p. 60.
(j) Leight v. Pym (1687) 2 Lutw. 1329; Wigley v. Peachey (1732) 2 Ld. Raym. 1589 ; F.N.B. 94 F.
(k) Norman v. Bell (1831) 2 B. & Ad. 190.
(l) Waterhouse v. Keen (1825) 4 B. & C. 200 ; see Lewis v. Hammond (1818) 2 B. & Ald. 206.

§ 8. *Exemptions from toll.*

The subject of exemptions from toll is now of less importance than it formerly was. But as some persons still claim exemption,(*a*) the subject cannot be omitted. Certain persons are entitled to exemption from toll by the common law. Other persons may be entitled to it by grant from the crown, by grant from the owner of the fair or market in which exemption is claimed, or by prescription.

(i.) *In favour of the king.* The king is not liable to pay toll for any of his goods ;(*b*) and it has been said(*c*) that to take toll for them is punishable under the Statute of Westminster I., c. 31.(*d*) The queen consort is likewise not liable to pay toll.(*e*) But other members of the royal family are not exempt from toll at common law, though they may be exempt from particular tolls by statute.(*f*)

Exemptions by the common law

(ii.) *In favour of ecclesiastical persons.* Ecclesiastical persons are at common law quit of toll for their ecclesiastical goods, and for goods bought by them for their sustenance, but not for merchandise.(*g*) This privilege extends to all ecclesiastical persons within the realm, of what quality or order soever.(*h*)

(iii.) *In favour of the lord of a manor which is ancient demesne*, and his tenants therein, whether free tenants or tenants for lives, or years, or at will. These persons are quit of toll in all markets and fairs by the custom of the realm.(*i*) Manors which were in possession of Edward the Confessor and after-

---

(*a*) Thus the commoners of the manor of Hungerford appear to claim exemption in Hungerford Market ; see *Report of Royal Commission*, vol. 4. p. 173 (1888). The men of the Duchy of Lancaster appear to be quit of toll under various charters ; see Hardy's *Charters of the Duchy f Lancaster* (1845). For a form of certificate of exemption given by the steward of the Duchy in 1828, see *Report of Royal Commission*, vol. Appendix, xiii.

(*b*) 2 Inst. 221; Com. Dig. Market (F. 1) ; Chitty, Prerog. 195, 377.

(*c*) 2 Inst. 221.

(*d*) See *ante*, p. 60.

(*e*) Co. Lit. 133 b ; Chitty, Prerog. 402.

(*f*) Chitty, Prerog. 405 n. (c).

(*g*) F.N.B. 227 F. ; 2 Inst. 4 ; Com. Dig. Ecclesiastical Persons (D), p. 549 (5th. ed.) ; Rot. Parl. 8 Edw. II., m. 4 ; Y.B. 30 Edw. III. 15 b.

(*h*) 2 Inst. 3. See Com. Dig. Ecclesiastical Persons, as to what persons are such ; see also Lord Middleton *v*. Lambert, 1 A. & E. 401, 421.

(*i*) Savery *v*. Smith (1687) 2 Lutw. 1144 ; F.N.B. 14 E., 228 A. D. ; Y.B. 9 Hen. VI. f. 25 b, pl. 20.

wards came to William the Conqueror, and were described in
'Domesday' as Terra Regis, are ancient demesne.(a) No
lands are ancient demesne but those described as such in
'Domesday.'(a)

Tenants in ancient demesne have 'many and divers
liberties, gifts and grants by law: as to be quit of toll and
passage, and such impositions which men shall demand of
them for the goods or chattels sold or bought by them in fairs
or markets.'(b) The reason for the exemption is stated by
Coke to be, 'because at the beginning of their tenure they
applied themselves to the manurance and husbandry of the
king's demesnes, and therefore, for those lands so holden, and
all that came or renewed thereupon, they had the said
privilege.'(c) This privilege of exemption still remains, and it
may be claimed even though the tenants have been paying
toll time out of mind.(d) ?

The better opinion appears to be that the exemption does
not extend to every purchase or sale by tenants in ancient
demesne ;(e) but there has been a difference of opinion on the
subject. It is clear that it extends to sales by them of the
produce of their tenements and to purchases by them of goods to
maintain their tenements, or themselves, or their households
there ;(f) and that consequently it extends to their buying and
re-selling of beasts bought to stock the land, and to be fatted
and resold when fatted.(g) These are transactions arising
out of the cultivation of tenements, and are not merchandisings.
FitzHerbert says :(h) 'I conceive that they shall be quit of toll
generally, although they merchandise with their goods.' But
Hale (i) and Coke (j) are of a different opinion; and Coke says,
'if such a tenant be a common merchant for buying and selling
of wares or merchandise that rise not upon the manurance or
husbandry of those lands, he shall not have the privilege for
them, because they are out of the privilege of ancient demesne,

(a) F.N.B. 14 D., 16 D.; Hob. 118; Hunt v. Burn (1701) 1 Salk. 57.
(b) F.N.B. 14 D. (c) 2 Inst. 221.
(d) 2 Inst. 654.
(e) Ward v. Knight (1588) Cro. Eliz., 227.
(f) Y.B. 9 Hen. VI. 25 b, pl. 20; 19 Hen. VI., 66 b, pl. 9.
(g) Y.B. 7 Hen. IV. 44 b, pl. 11.
(h) F.N.B. 228 E., citing Y.B. 7 Hen. IV.
(i) F.N.B. 228 E., note b. (j 2 Inst. 221.

and the tenant in ancient demesne ought rather to be a husbandman than a merchant by his tenure, and so are the books to be intended.'(a)

In Ward v. Knight (b) it was expressly decided that 'the tenants in ancient demesne should pay toll for their merchandises.'

In early times the crown frequently gave charters of exemption from toll in one or more market towns in England to the corporations of favoured cities or boroughs, such right of exemption to be exercised and enjoyed by the corporators of the corporation in whom it was vested. Thus, the corporation of London obtained the liberty or privilege, granted and confirmed by various charters and statutes, that the citizens of London and all their goods should be quit and free of and from toll, and passage, and lastage,(c) and other customs, throughout the whole kingdom of England, and the ports of the seas, except only the due and ancient customs of the crown, and the prisage of wines.(d) And to claim the exemption a citizen of London need not reside within the city.(e)

Exemptions by grant or prescription

Grants of exemption by the crown are either general or special; and they are good except in so far as they derogate from previous grants. A grant of exemption may exempt the grantees from payment of toll in a market or fair which belongs to the crown at the date of the grant, or in which toll is claimed under a later grant; but a grant of exemption does not avail against a toll claimed under an earlier grant, for the former cannot detract from the latter, nor against a prescriptive toll, for that is presumed to have existed from time immemorial under a lost grant.

After the crown has granted a market or fair with the right to take toll, the crown cannot grant any exemption from such toll; but, as a general rule, the grantee or owner of the market or fair can do so, and, in this way, rights to exemption, founded upon grant or prescription, may arise after the market or fair has

(a) See the subject discussed in Lord Middleton v. Lambert (1834) 1 A. & E. 401.
(b) (1588) Cro. Eliz. 227, 1 Leon. 231; see also the case of the town of Leicester (1586) 2 Leon. 190; Savery v. Smith (1687) 2 Lutw. 1144.
(c) See *ante*, p. 56.
(d) A duty payable to the crown on the importation of wines.
(e) Mayor of London v. Mayor of Lynn (1796) 1 H. Bla. 206; 1 B. & P. 487; 7 Bro. P.C. 120.

been established.(*a*) Exemption may be claimed by prescription or by long usage from which a lost grant will be presumed.(*b*) A grant of exemption from toll may include exemption from stallage.(*c*) If the grantee of a franchise grant any immunity thereout, and the franchise afterwards comes into the hands of the crown, the crown can only re-grant the franchise subject to the immunity.(*d*)

A lord of a manor may prescribe that his tenants therein ought to be free of toll; and it has been said that if he can establish such a prescriptive right he can maintain an action against any person who takes or claims toll from his tenants. (*e*)

Statutory abolition of exemptions

All exemptions from toll are liable to be taken away by Act of Parliament. Where a market or fair has been established, or is now regulated, by some statute, the question whether any exemption from toll is abolished or preserved must depend upon the words of the statute and the proper construction to be put upon them.

Where a claim is made to exemption from any toll or due 'levied wholly or in part by or for the use or benefit of any borough (*f*) or body corporate,' it is now necessary to consider the provisions of the Municipal Corporations Act, 1882.(*g*)

That Act provides (*h*) that no person shall have any exemption from any such toll or due 'except a person who, on the 5th of June, 1835, was an inhabitant, or was admitted or entitled to be admitted a freeman,(*i*) or was the wife, widow, son or daughter of a freeman, or was bound an apprentice.' The Act, however, does not affect the right of any person claiming exemption from toll 'otherwise than as an inhabitant, or freeman, or member of a municipal corporation,(*j*) or widow

(*a*) See F.N.B. 226 I., 227 B., note *c*; 2 Inst. 221; Bracton, lib. 2, c. 24, f. 56 b; Viner, 'Prerogative,' I. c. 2, K. c. 1; Archbishop of York's case (1574) 4 Leon. 168; Lockwood *v.* Wood (1841) 6 Q.B. 31. Other cases which may be consulted on the construction of grants of exemption are Mayor of Truro *v.* Reynolds (1832) 8 Bing. 275; Hill *v.* Priour (1679) 2 Show. 34; Lord Middleton *v.* Lambert (1834) A. & E. 401.
(*b*) See *ante*, p. 22.
(*c*) Lockwood *v.* Wood (1841) 6 Q.B. 31.
(*d*) Bailiffs of Tewkesbury *v.* Bricknell (1809) 2 Taunt. 120.
(*e*) Viner, 'Actions' [Case] N.C. 8, M.C. 2; Y.B. 43 Edw. III. 30.
(*f*) I.e. a city or town to which the Municipal Corporations Act, 1882, applies; see s. 7 (1).
(*g*) 45 & 46 Vict. c. 50, s. 208.
(*h*) s. 208 (2). (*i*) See s. 201.
(*j*) I.e. the body corporate constituted by the incorporation of the inhabitants of a city or town to which the Act applies; s. 7 (1).

or kin of such an inhabitant, freeman, or member.'(*a*) Accordingly, the Act would not affect any right of a person claiming exemption as tenant in ancient demesne, or as freeholder of the Duchy of Lancaster; nor would it affect any right of a person claiming exemption as a citizen of London, for the City of London is not a municipal corporation within the meaning of the Act.(*b*)

(*a*) s. 208 (3).   (*b*) See note (*j*), p. 72, *ante*.

CHAPTER V

DISTURBANCE OF THE FRANCHISE

The owner of a market or fair is entitled to the peaceable enjoyment of his franchise, and for the disturbance thereof he has remedies both at common law and in equity. The common law will give him damages, formerly recoverable in an action on the case for a nuisance; and equity will grant an injunction.(a) Both remedies are now obtainable in one action.

Disturbance of a market may be either by unlawfully setting up a rival market, or by doing some other wrongful act or acts whereby the market-owner is deprived, either wholly or in part, of the benefit of his franchise.

§ 1. *Disturbance by levying a rival market or fair.*

If a new market or fair be set up within the common law distance (i.e. seven miles) (b) of an old market or fair, and be held on the same day, the new market or fair is presumed to be a nuisance to the old. The early writers seem to have treated it as a rule of law that the new market in such circumstances is necessarily injurious to the old, though there be no damage in fact. Thus Bracton says, 'when, therefore, a market has been obtained within such a limit it will have to be levelled, since it is a hurtful and tortious nuisance because it is so near.'(c)

Agreeably with that view the law is thus stated by Channell, B., in delivering the considered judgment of the Court of

---

(a) An interlocutory injunction is not usually granted if the defendant undertakes to keep an account; Elwes *v.* Payne (1879) 12 Ch. D. 468.
(b) See *post*, p. 77.
(c) Bracton, Bk. iv. c. 46, f. 235b, and to the same effect are Britton, ii. c. 32, s. 8, f. 159; Fleta, iv. c. 28, s. 13.

Disturbance by Levying a Rival Market or Fair 75

Exchequer in Mayor of Dorchester *v.* Ensor :(*a*) 'We take the rule of law to be as laid down in the notes to Yard *v.* Ford,(*b*) that is, that where a new market is held on the same day as the old it shall be *intended* to be a nuisance, that where it is held upon a different day it shall be put in issue whether it be a nuisance or not.'

On the other hand, the nine judges who gave their opinion on the Islington Market Bill stated the rule as amounting only to a rebuttable presumption, throwing the burden of proof on the party who denies the nuisance, but not necessarily excluding the issue altogether. They thus stated the rule: 'The establishment of a new market to be holden at the same times within the common law distance of an old market, *prima facie* is injurious to the old market, and therefore void.'(*c*) Two of the judges (*d*) also suggested facts the proof of which would be sufficient to rebut the presumption.

Beyond these dicta there is very little authority. In Clinton's case (*e*) an issue was left to the jury whether a market alleged to have been set up within two miles of an old market, and held on the same day, was a nuisance or not. This seems to support the proposition laid down in the Islington Market case, rather than that laid down in Mayor of Dorchester *v.* Ensor.(*f*)

If a new market or fair be levied within the common law distance of an older market or fair, and held on different days, it cannot be presumed that the new market is a nuisance to the old, and actual damage must be proved in order to establish that an injury is done to the old market.(*g*) In

(*a*) (1869) L.R. 4 Ex. 343. See also to the same effect, Elwes *v.* Payne (1879) 12 Ch. D. 468, per Jessel, M.R., p. 472; and Corporation of Cork *v.* Shinkwin (1825) Sm. & B. 395, per Chatterton, V.C., at p. 398.

(*b*) 2 Wms. Saunders, at p. 174, citing F.N.B. 184a, note (*b*), where Hale cites Weston's case, Y.B. 11 Hen. IV. f. 5, in support of the above proposition; but Weston's case seems to be a direct authority only upon the second part of this proposition. Hale also refers to Clinton's case, Y.B. Pasch. 13 Ed. III. pl. 20, referred to in the text.

(*c*) Islington Market Bill (1835) 3 Cl. & Fin. 513; 12 M. & W. 20 n.
(*d*) Parke, B., and Littledale, J.
(*e*) Y.B. Pasch. 13 Edw. III. pl. 20. See Pike's edition of Y.B. 12 and 13 Edw. III. p. 208.
(*f*) The Newton case, P.Q.W. p. 184, and the Lyme case, P.Q.W. p. 185, may also be considered.
(*g*) Weston's case, Y.B. 11 Hen. IV. ff. 5, 6; Yard *v.* Ford (1670) 2 Wms. Saunders, 172; R. *v.* Aires (1761) 10 Mod. 354; Mayor of Dorchester *v.* Ensor (1869) L.R. 4 Ex. 335; Elwes *v.* Payne (1879) 12 Ch. D. 468, 472; Corporation of Cork *v.* Shinkwin (1825) Sm. & B. 395; Downshire *v.* O'Brien (1887) 19 L.R. Ir. 380, 387.

Disturbance of the Franchise

deciding that question, account may be taken of the facilities of traffic and communication, by railway or otherwise, existing at the time when the new market is set up.(a)

To prove actual damage, it is not necessary to show loss of tolls—to show loss of stallage is enough; and, even though no such pecuniary loss can be shown, it has been said that the exclusive privilege of holding a market, with the authority and jurisdiction incident thereto, may perhaps have a value which will render an encroachment upon the privilege the subject of an action for damages.(b)

It is said by Bracton (c) that a new market held on the second or third day *after* the old market *may be* advantageous to the old market, but that, if held on the second or third day *before* it, it *will be* injuriosum quia damnosum. In either case, however, the effect of the new market seems now to be a question of fact for the jury.(d)

It seems that a new market or fair levied more than the common law distance from an older cannot be injurious in law to the latter. Bracton (e) and Blackstone (f) both say expressly that it cannot be; and there appears to be no modern reported case in which an action has been brought for disturbance by erecting a new market or fair more than seven miles from an old.(g)

The common law distance

Accordingly a new market, though it is to be held on the same days, will not be a disturbance of an old if the former be set up at a greater distance from the latter than what is known as 'the common law distance.' Bracton (h) lays it down that the distance within which it may be a disturbance of an old market to set up a new one is 6⅔

(a) See per Jessel, M.R., Elwes v. Payne (1879) 12 Ch. D. 468, 472.

(b) Corporation of Cork v. Shinkwin (1825) Sm. & B. 395, 402. For an early case of disturbance by setting up a rival market, see Selden Society's Publications, vol. v. (*Leet Jurisdiction of Norwich*) p. 17.

(c) Bk. iv. c. 46, f. 235 b; cf. Fleta, lib. 4, c. 28, f. 14; Com. Dig. Market (C. 2).

(d) Reg. v. Aires (1761) 10 Mod. 258, 351.

(e) Bk. iv. c. 46, f. 235 b.

(f) Bk. iii. c. 13, p. 218, citing Hale on F.N.B. 184. Blackstone also explains the reason for the rule.

(g) See, however, to the contrary, for what they are worth, the Leominster Fair case (1285) Abb. Plac. 206, and the Bath Market case (1377) Rot. Parl. 50 Edw. III. vol. ii. p. 347.

(h) Bk. iv. c. 46, f. 235 b; cf. Britton, lib. ii. c. 32. s. 8, f. 159; Fleta, bk. iv. c. 28, s. 13.

Disturbance by Levying a Rival Market or Fair 77

miles :(a) 'because (he says) every reasonable day's journey consists of 20 miles. The day's journey is divided into three parts. The first part, that of the morning, is to be given to those who are going to the market. The second is to be given to buying and selling, which ought to be sufficient to all, unless they be merchants who have stalls, who have deposited their goods and exposed them for sale, to whom a longer delay in the market may be necessary. But the third part is left for those returning from the market to their homes. And all these things it will be necessary (b) to do by day and not by night, on account of the snares and attacks of robbers,(c) that all things may be in safety. When, therefore, a market has been obtained within such a limit, it will have to be levelled, since it is a nuisance, doing damage and injury because it is so near.'

The common law distance, however, is generally considered to be 7 miles, as stated in the declaration in Yard v. Ford.(d) That is the distance expressly mentioned in the charter granted by Edward III.(e) to the corporation of London, which contained a clause providing that no grant of markets should be made to others within 7 miles (f) of the city.

Markets and fairs are usually granted to be held at any

(a) ' Infra sex leucas et dimidiam et tertiam partem dimidiae.' Leuca, in this passage, has been generally translated by lawyers as ' mile ' ; see F.N.B. 184 n (a) ; 3 Bl. Comm. 218 ; and cf. 2 Inst. 567. As to some of the various distances from time to time denoted by the word, see Spelman's *Glossary*. Mr. Stuart Moore, in his Introd. to the Domesday Book for Northamptonshire (p. 13), says ' the leuca consisted of 12 furlongs, and (computing the perch at 16½ feet) contained about 2640 yards, or a mile and a half of our present measure.'

(b) Sir T. Twiss translated this passage somewhat differently (ed. 1880, vol. 3, p. 585) ; but cf. the corresponding passage in Fleta, loc. cit. *supra*.

(c) The danger was so great that the St. of Winchester, 13 Edw. I. c. 5 (repealed by 7 & 8 Geo. IV. c. 27) required the clearance of underwood and bush, whereby a man might lurk to do hurt, to be made for 200 feet on either side of highways leading from one market-town to another.

(d) (1670) 2 Wms. Saund. 173. See 3 Black. Comm. 218. In the Newton case (Plac. Quo Warr, p. 184) it was alleged for the crown that every market ought to be distant from another 5 miles (quinque miliaria). In the Lyme case (Id. p. 185), however, Lyme market was held to be a nuisance to Bridport market, which was more than 5 (but under 6) miles off.

(e) 1 Edw. III., confirmed by the charter of 7 Rich. II. Both charters were granted with the consent of parliament.

(f) Leucae, which is translated as ' miles ' in G .E. R. Co. v. Goldsmid (1884) 9 App. Cas. 927 ; as also in Birch's *Historical Charters of the City of London*, p. 58 ; cf. Nichol's Britton, vol. i. p. 413 n. (L). The use of

place within a town or manor, and not at some defined spot within such town or manor, and may be moved at the will of the grantee from one place to any other place therein.(*a*) It seems that where the grant is in that form the circuit of protection must be measured from the boundaries of such town or manor, and not from the particular place where the market is for the time being held.(*b*)

There appears to be no authority as to whether the seven miles should be measured by the nearest road or in a straight line. In view of the reason for fixing the distance at 6⅔ or 7 miles, viz. that it is one-third of a day's journey of 20 miles,(*c*) it might be thought that the proper way to measure the distance is by the nearest road. More probably, however, the distance should be measured as the crow flies.(*d*)

What is a rival market To sustain an action for disturbance by setting up a rival market, it is not necessary to show that the defendant has set up what purports to be a legal market, or has usurped a franchise upon the crown by taking toll or holding a court of pie powder.(*e*) It is enough that he has erected stalls on his own soil and taken rents in the nature of stallage for their use by persons bringing their goods thither for sale,(*f*) or has so used his land as to encourage and provide for a concourse thereon of buyers and sellers: for instance, by establishing a depôt with conveniences for the benefit of buyers and sellers,(*f*) or by holding public auctions or sales whereby persons are provided with a means of selling their goods without bringing them to the market.(*g*) It is not necessary that the defendant

the word 'league' as an equivalent in the Islington Market case (1835) 3 Cl. & F. 513, 12 M. & W. 20 n, was probably due to the desire to avoid a definite translation. The judges there expressed the opinion that such clause in a *grant* is void, *if* it adds, without any consideration therefor, 'any prohibition other than that which is attached by the common law to the grant of a market.'

(*a*) See *ante*, Ch. 2.
(*b*) Cf. the terms of the charter to the City of London, and the judges' observations thereon; Islington Market Bill (1835) 12 M. and W. 20 n; 3 Cl. & Fin. 513. See also 9 App. Cas. 936.
(*c*) See Bracton, Bk. iv. c. 46, f. 235 b.; 3 Black. Com. 219.
(*d*) See Mouflet *v.* Cole (1872) L.R. 7 Ex. 70, 8 id. 32, and Jewel *v.* Stead (1856) 6 E. & B. 350.
(*e*) Yard *v.* Ford (1670) 2 Wms. Saund. 172.
(*f*) G. E. R. Co. *v.* Goldsmid (1884) 9 App. Cas. 927.
(*g*) Mayor of Dorchester *v.* Ensor (1869) L.R. 4 Ex. 335; Elwes *v.* Payne (1879) 12 Ch. D. 468; Mayor of London *v.* Low (1879) 49 L.J. Q.B. 144.

Disturbance by Levying a Rival Market or Fair

should have actually sold or conducted sales in the rival market. Any active interference by him in the conduct of the market, or his participation in its profits or risks, is sufficient: for instance, if he provides land for sales by auction, and, in consequence of the use to which the land is put, takes an increased rent above that which would otherwise be obtainable.(*a*)

Nevertheless, every sale in a shop or private house near a market is not necessarily a disturbance. There is a substantial difference between the case of a man who sells his own goods on his own premises and that of a man who provides premises upon which others may sell their goods without taking them into the market. From a misunderstanding of an early case,(*b*) it was once supposed that a grant of a market carried with it a right to prevent persons from selling their goods on market days in their own private shops or houses. But it is now settled that such a right is not incident to a grant of a market. The mere selling of marketable articles on a market-day in a private shop, not within the limits of the market-place, is not, as a rule, an injury to the market.(*c*) Though, if the shop be in or next to the market-place, and the owner opens his shop for selling in the market, he may be liable to stallage.(*d*)

Private shops

A right to exclude sales in private houses or shops within the limits of the franchise on market-days may, however, exist by immemorial custom, or by prescription. Such a right would appear to have been reasonable in former times, for, while it secured to the lord a more certain profit in return for his holding the market, it benefited the public by securing the lord's supervision over all articles for sale on market-days.(*e*) It is probable, however, that in a modern grant of a market a

---

(*a*) Mayor of Dorchester *v.* Ensor (1869) L.R. 4 Ex. 335.
(*b*) Prior of Dunstable's case, Y.B. 11 Hen. VI., f. 19, pl. 13, f. 25, pl. 2; see Mayor of Macclesfield *v.* Chapman (1843) 12 M. & W. 18, 20, per Parke, B.
(*c*) Mayor of Macclesfield *v.* Chapman (1843) 12 M. & W. 18; The Same *v.* Pedley (1833) 4 B. & Ad. 397. See Mayor of Penryn *v.* Best, (1878) 3 Ex. D. 292; Mayor of Manchester *v.* Lyons (1882) 22 Ch. D. 287, 311.
(*d*) Newington Fair case (1608) 2 Roll. Abr. 123, B. 1; Com. Dig. Market (F.) 2.
(*e*) See the argument in Mosley *v.* Walker (1827) 7 B. & C. 40. See also Abb. Plac. p. 113, where the Bishop of Hereford claimed to prevent persons selling marketable goods in their own houses in Hereford during the fair. The townsmen, on the other hand, claimed to sell in their own shops, but admitted the right of the bishop to toll.

clause purporting to confer such a right would be void.(a) The only cases in which the right has been established have been cases of ancient markets in which the lord claimed the right as from time immemorial, and the evidence supported that claim. If the market be an ancient market, and the lord at all times appears to have prevented a sale in private houses, the exercise of such control is evidence of the right.(b)

It is impossible to lay down a precise definition by which sales in a private shop may be distinguished from such a system of selling as amounts to establishing a rival market. The mere fact that the sale in a shop attracts some persons who would otherwise buy in the market is not enough to constitute a disturbance, nor is the character or name of the building in which the sale is conducted. All the circumstances of the case must be taken into consideration, the nature and method of the business done,(c) and the character and management of the building, whether it be let out in stalls or entirely occupied by the proprietor for his own purposes.(d)

Grant, no defence

To an action for disturbance by erecting a rival market it is no defence to plead a grant from the crown. For the crown has no power to grant a new market to the injury of an existing market.(e) But it would be a good defence that the new market was established under a private Act of Parliament,(f) or pursuant to the Public Health Act, 1875, s. 166,(g) or the Diseases of Animals Act, 1894, s. 32,(h) or any other like enactment.

(a) See Mosley v. Walker, supra, per Holroyd, J.; Mayor of Penryn v. Best (1878) 3 Ex. D. p. 295.
(b) Mosley v. Walker (1827) 7 B. & C. 40 (where Bayley, J., justifies the right in a somewhat different manner); Mayor of Macclesfield v. Chapman (1843) 12 M. & W. 18; The Same v. Pedley (1833) 4 B. & Ad. 397; Mayor of Devizes v. Clark (1835) 3 A. & E. 506; Mayor of Penryn v. Best (1878) 3 Ex. D. 292; Prior of Dunstable's case, Y.B. 11 Hen. VI. ff. 19, 25.
(c) G. E. R. Co. v. Goldsmid (1884) 9 App. Cas. 927, 947; McHole v. Davies (1875) 1 Q.B.D. 59; Fearon v. Mitchell (1872) L.R. 7 Q.B. 690; Mayor of Dorchester v. Ensor (1869) L.R. 4 Ex. 335.
(d) Corporation of Cork v. Shinkwin (1825) Sm. & B. 395, 400; G. E. R. Co. v. Goldsmid, supra. See also the cases under the Markets and Fairs Clauses Act, 1847, s. 13, post, Part II.
(e) 2 Inst. 406; Islington Market Bill (1835) 3 Cl. & F. 513, 520. See also ante, p. 20. If the crown grants a market which turns out to be injurious to an older market belonging to the crown, the crown may repeal the new market by scire facias, and recover damages for disturbance; Weston's case, Y.B. 11 Hen. IV. ff. 5 & 6.
(f) Hammersmith Ry. Co. v. Brand (1869) L.R. 4 H.L. 171.
(g) 38 & 39 Vict. c. 55.   (h) 57 & 58 Vict. c. 57.

Disturbance by Levying a Rival Market or Fair

It is not a good defence to an action for disturbance by unlawfully levying a rival market that there was not room for all who wished to buy and sell in the plaintiff's market.(*a*) Want of room in a market may justify an individual in selling his goods outside it,(*b*) but cannot excuse the levying of a rival market without lawful authority.(*a*) The insufficiency of the public accommodation provided in a market may be given in evidence in mitigation of the damage claimed for setting up a rival market,(*c*) but is not of itself a good answer to the action. An abuse or misuse of the franchise, though it may entitle the crown to take proceedings against the owner, does not entitle third persons to usurp the market or fair rights, and thereby disturb the franchise.(*d*)

Insufficiency of accommodation

That a defence grounded on the impossibility of sufficient accommodation being provided in the old market might be good was suggested by two judges(*e*) in answer to questions proposed to them by the House of Lords when considering the Islington Market Bill.(*f*) The judges were of opinion that in the case of a market granted to be held in a fixed place, defined by metes and bounds, 'if those limits are not sufficient for the accommodation of the buyers and sellers at the market, and the market-owner has no power to enlarge the limits, that circumstance, coupled with the fact that it would be for the advantage of the public that a new market should be erected, would be a sufficient ground for the crown to take such steps as, according to law, would have the effect of erecting a new market to such an extent as would remedy the inconvenience without affecting the rights of the owner of the old market'; that is to say, 'to such an extent as to provide for what may be called the surplus accommodation of the public beyond what the old market can afford, and that the old market is not to be affected by the new. For instance, if the public require twenty acres of market accommodation, and the old market could only furnish ten, the new market could

---

(*a*) G. E. R. Co. *v.* Goldsmid (1884) 9 App. Cas. 927, (1883) 25 Ch. D. 511; Islington Market case (1835) 3 Cl. & F. 513. As to the duty of the lord to supply sufficient accommodation for the public, see *ante*, p. 33.
(*b*) Prince *v.* Lewis (1826) 5 B. & C. 363; Mosley *v.* Walker (1827) 7 B. & C. 40; see *post*, p. 83.
(*c*) Corporation of Cork *v.* Shinkwin (1825) Sm. & B. 395.
(*d*) Midleton *v.* Power (1886) 19 L.R. Ir. 1.
(*e*) Littledale, J., and Parke, B.
(*f*) (1835) 3 Cl. & F. 513, and 12 M. & W. 20 n.

not be granted for the whole twenty acres, but only for the additional ten acres, so as, upon the whole, the twenty should be capable of being used by the public.' 'For if a new market were granted for twenty acres, that would be to the damage of the old market, and it might have the effect of totally ruining it, when there was no default in the owner, but the necessity for a new market arose from the increase of population.'

The judges further suggested that the same principle would apply to the case of a market to be held in a district (and not in a place therein defined with metes and bounds), supposing that the district were so narrow, or the residue thereof not appropriated to the purposes of the market were so occupied, that further space could not be acquired by the market-owner to meet the increased wants of the public.

These opinions of the judges, however, though carefully considered, were delivered with some diffidence, as they had not had an opportunity of hearing argument on the matter, or of conferring with the other judges.

§ 2. *Disturbance by acts other than levying a rival market or fair.*

There may be an actionable disturbance of a market without levying a rival market.

Selling outside the market

Whenever a person seeks to take, and takes, the benefit of a market without payment of the market toll, that is a fraud upon the market, for which an action on the case will lie. A person who has goods for sale commits an actionable wrong against a market-owner if he takes advantage of the concourse of persons assembled in the market, but yet sells outside the market in order to evade the toll. Thus, in Bridgland *v.* Shapter,(*a*) it was held that an action lay against a cattle-jobber, who left his sheep at a public-house, but went himself into the market in quest of customers, whom he brought thence to the public-house, and there sold to them the sheep, refusing to pay toll.

Such acts, however, in order to be actionable, must be done designedly, and with an intention to obtain the benefit of the market without payment of toll. If a person in the ordinary course of his business comes to a town to sell goods there, and

(*a*) (1839) 5 M. & W. 375; cf. Blakey *v.* Dimsdale (1777) 2 Cowp. 661.

Disturbance by Evading Toll

sells them outside the market on a day which happens to be market day, without any design or trick whereby he may get the benefit of the market without paying toll, that does not constitute a disturbance of the market.(a)

In the Prior of Dunstable's case (b) the allegation was that the defendant sold in his shop, adjoining the market-place, secretly (occulte); and this raised the question of fraud, upon which issue alone the case was tried. The mere selling in a shop, unless done secretly to evade toll, would not have been actionable.

In an action for selling near to a market, but outside its limits, to the prejudice of the lord's rights, it is a good defence to show that there was not sufficient room within the market for the defendant to sell therein.(c) And if at ordinary times there is not sufficient room within the market, a person is not bound to attend day by day for the purpose of seeing whether there be room or not, but he may sell outside the market, though there be room within it, unless the lord give him notice that there is room.(d) This defence may be raised where the want of room in the market arises from the lord's neglect of his duty to provide sufficient accommodation for the public,(e) whether the market be limited by metes and bounds (f) or not.(g) And it seems, on principle, that it can be raised, although the want of room arises without any default in the lord, provided that the defendant has done nothing which amounts to the unlawful levying of a rival market.

In markets where toll is payable by the seller, it is an actionable disturbance to sell by sample in the market goods which are kept out of the market in order to evade the toll.(h)

No room in the market

Selling by sample

(a) Mayor of Brecon v. Edwards (1862) 1 H. & C. 51 ; Bailiffs of Tewkesbury v. Diston (1805) 6 East, 438; Blakey v. Dimsdale (1777) 2 Cowp. 661 ; Sprosley v. Evans, 1 Roll. Abr. 103.
(b) Y.B. 11 Hen. VI. f. 19 b ; 11 Hen. VI. f. 25.
(c) Prince v. Lewis (1826) 5 B. & C. 363 : see Islington Market case (1835) 12 M. & W. p. 23 ; G. E. R. Co. v. Goldsmid (1884) 9 App. Cas. p. 960, per Lord Blackburn ; 25 Ch. D. p. 542, per Cotton, L.J.
(d) Prince v. Lewis, supra, per Bayley and Littledale, J.J. See per Cotton, L.J., G. E. R. Co. v. Goldsmid, loc. cit. supra.
(e) See ante, p. 33.
(f) Prince v. Lewis (1826) 5 B. & C. 363.
(g) Islington Market Bill (1835) 12 M. & W. p. 23.
(h) Bailiffs of Tewkesbury v. Bricknell (1809) 2 Taunt. 120. See Mayor of Brecon v. Edwards (1862) 1 H. & C. 51 ; Mosley v. Pierson, (1790) 4 T.R. 104.

The seller, by going into the market, takes the benefit thereof, while the lord is deprived of his toll by reason of the goods not being brought into the market.(a) The gist of the action is the seller's intention to take the benefit of the market without payment of toll.(b) To sell by sample *near* the market is not of itself a disturbance.(c) In some circumstances it might be such ; but it is necessary to prove that the defendant by some device or other in fact obtained the benefit of the market, and designedly evaded the toll ; otherwise no action will lie.(d)

Bailiffs of Tewkesbury v. Diston (e) was an action brought against a *buyer* of corn by sample in Tewkesbury market, where toll was payable in kind. It was alleged that the defendant intentionally deprived the plaintiffs of their toll by buying corn in the market by sample. It was proved that he bought by sample in the market, knowing of the claim to toll, and refused to pay toll on the subsequent delivery of corn outside the market. It was held that no cause of action was disclosed, on the ground that it did not appear that the buyer induced the seller to keep the corn out of the market, or that the seller would have brought the corn into the market if the buyer had not bought by sample.

In Bailiffs of Tewkesbury v. Bricknell (f) an action was successfully brought against the *seller* of corn by sample in the same market. The toll seems to have been treated as payable by and was demanded of the seller, who had clearly evaded toll by keeping the bulk out of the market.(g) It seems probable that an action might lie against the seller who sold by sample in the market although the toll were payable by the buyer ; for instance, if it was the seller's intention to take the benefit of the market and deprive the lord of the benefit of the toll.

In some circumstances a buyer who buys by sample in a market would perhaps be liable in an action of disturbance— for instance, if he conspired with the seller to evade the toll by some trick or fraud.(h) But to buy by sample in a market is

(a) See note (h), p. 83.   (b) *Ibid.*
(c) Mayor of Brecon v. Edwards (1862) 1 H. & C. 51.   (d) *Ibid.*
(e) (1805) 6 East, 438.   (f) (1809) 2 Taunt. 120.
(g) In the earlier case of Bailiffs of Tewkesbury v. Diston (1805) 6 East, 438, the toll was treated as payable by the buyer ; see Id. p. 440 n. In Mayor of Brecon v. Edwards, *supra*, the toll was payable by the seller.
(h) See 6 East, 460.

Disturbance by Evading Toll

not of itself actionable; (a) and it may be observed that the buyer's case is very different from that of the seller. The seller has a choice whether he will sell by sample or bring the bulk into the market; the buyer has usually no such choice. Moreover, the buyer does not get the benefit of the market unless the whole of the goods are in the market; he has not the benefit of a view of the whole bulk; he has not the advantage in reduction of price which often results to the buyer from the seller's dread of being obliged to carry back his commodity in bulk unsold; and he does not acquire a title as by sale in market overt. All these circumstances make it more difficult to establish a case of designedly buying by sample in order to evade toll; they rather give countenance to the view that the buyer has bought by sample because he had not the opportunity of buying in bulk.(b)

An action for disturbance will lie for wrongfully hindering or stopping cattle or goods from being brought to the market,(c) or wrongfully disturbing or beating persons who are coming to the market, whereby the lord may lose his toll,(d) or for wrongfully assaulting and disturbing the lord or his servants in taking toll.(e) In more recent times an action of nuisance was successfully maintained by the owner of a market against persons who wrongfully erected a building which excluded the public from part of the space on which the market was used to be held.(f)

Other acts of disturbance

(a) Bailiffs of Tewkesbury v. Diston, *supra*.
(b) *Ibid.* per Lord Ellenborough.
(c) Per Wylde, J., Turner v. Sterling (1671) 2 Ventr. 26, citing Y.B. 41 Ed. III. f. 24, pl. 17, an observation by Belknap, counsel, in argument (cf. 2 Ventr. 28, per Vaughan, J.); per Powell, J., Ashby v. White (1704) 6 Mod. 49.
(d) Abbot of Denesham's case, Y.B. 29 Ed. III. f. 18; Viner, 'Actions [Case],' (N. c.) 3, citing Y.B. 11 Hen. IV. f. 47b (*infra*), 9 Hen. VI. f. 46, 41 Ed. III. f. 24b (*supra*), F.N.B. 124e; Fitzh., Actions sur le case, pl. 28, citing Y.B. 11 Hen. IV. f. 47b, where Skrene, counsel, states in argument that such is the law.
(e) Dent v. Oliver (1607) Cro. Jac. 122; Barton's case, Y.B. 9 Hen. VI. f. 45; Viner, 'Toll,' I. 4, and 'Actions [Case],' (N. c.) 4; F.N.B. 91 G. II.; Abbot of Ramsey's case, Abb. Plac. p. 151b; de Kenedon's case, Id. p. 233. In the Rot. Parl. (Temp. Ed. I.) there is a quaint complaint by the Prior of St. Freswide in Oxford that the Chancellor and Scholars of Oxford made an affray and riot in his fair, 'to the perpetual and final destruction of it,' Rot. Parl. vol. iii. p. 176b.
(f) Thompson v. Gibson (1841) 7 M. & W. 456.

§ 3. *Disturbance of market-rights vested in persons other than the lord.*

It seems that actions for disturbance may be brought, not only by the market-owner, but by any person who has a prescriptive or other well-established right in the market, such as a person who has a prescriptive right to place a stall in the market in front of his shop. He has a right in the market for injury to which he may maintain an action against the wrong-doer. Thus, he may maintain an action against the market-owner if the latter disturb him in the enjoyment of his right by wrongfully removing the market to another place.(*a*)

§ 4. *Nature of action for disturbance.*

Possessory action

The action for disturbance is a possessory action.(*b*) The plaintiff must prove the existence of the franchise, and that at the time of the disturbance he was in possession thereof; but he need not regularly deduce his title thereto, for, as against a stranger and wrong-doer possession is sufficient.(*c*)

The owner of a fair who has been compelled to discontinue it, owing to the absence of buyers and sellers, may nevertheless be in possession of the franchise for the purpose of an action for disturbance.(*d*) But if the owner of several markets has voluntarily discontinued to hold some of them, he will be unable to recover in an action of disturbance, except in respect of the markets which he continues to hold; and that will be so, although he may be entitled to revive the markets which he has discontinued.(*e*)

Limitation of actions

It has been suggested that the undisturbed possession of a rival market for twenty years is a bar to an action for disturbance.(*f*) But the better opinion is that the uninterrupted user of a rival market for twenty years is merely evidence from

(*a*) Ellis *v.* Mayor of Bridgenorth (1863) 15 C.B.N.S. 52.
(*b*) Yard *v.* Ford, 2 Wms. Saund. 171 n (1); Fitzgerald *v.* Connors (1871) 5 Ir. Rep. C.L. 191.
(*c*) Dent *v.* Oliver (1607) Cro. Jac. 122; De Rutzen *v.* Lloyd (1836) 5 A. & E. 456.
(*d*) Downshire *v.* O'Brien (1887) 19 L.R. Ir. 380, 389.
(*e*) See per Channell, B., Mayor of Dorchester *v.* Ensor (1869) L.R. 4 Ex. 335, 339.
(*f*) Holcroft *v.* Heel (1799) 1 B. & P. 400, as explained in notes to Yard *v.* Ford, 2 Wms. Saund. 175.

Nature of Action for Disturbance

which a jury may infer that the rival market has had a lawful origin in a grant from the crown,(a) supported by a grant from the owner of the older market, without which the grant from the crown would not be effectual.(b) In an action of disturbance the period of limitation for the recovery of damages is six years ;(c) but it seems that no length of adverse user creates a positive bar to the action. The Prescription Act, 1832,(d) has no application to market rights ;(e) nor have the Real Property Limitation Acts, 1833 and 1874.(f) And it may be added that franchises are expressly excepted from the provisions of the Crown Suits Acts, 1769 and 1861.(g)

§ 5. *Remedies for disturbance of statutory markets and fairs.*

Acts which would amount to a disturbance of a market established by royal grant may also constitute a disturbance of a market established by statute, and persons disturbing a statutory market may be liable to an action for damages or an injunction. But this is not necessarily the case, inasmuch as the statutes under which a market is established may contain provisions rendering the rights and liabilities between the market-owners and other persons different from what they would be at common law. The law with regard to disturbance is not altered, in the case of any particular market, by the mere fact that the charters of the market were granted with the consent of parliament, or that the market was originally established under an Act of Parliament, or has subsequently become merely statutory.(h) But it may nevertheless be altered by the express or implied terms of the provisions which parliament has inserted in the charters or statutes regulating the market.

Local Acts regulating statutory markets often incorporate

(a) Holcroft v. Heel, *supra*, as explained by Le Blanc, J., in Campbell v. Wilson (1803) 3 East, 294, 298.
(b) See *ante*, p. 20.   (e) 21 Jac. I. c. 16, s. 3.
(d) 2 & 3 Will. IV. c. 71.
(e) See *ante*, p. 24.
(f) 3 & 4 Will IV. c. 27 ; 37 & 38 Vict. c. 57 ; see s. 1 of the earlier Act.
(g) 9 Geo. III. c. 16 (Nullum Tempus Act) ; 24 & 25 Vict. c. 62.
(h) See G. E. R. Co. v. Goldsmid (1884) 9 App. Cas. 927 ; Mayor of Birmingham v. Foster (1894) 70 L.T. 371 ; Mayor of Manchester v. Lyons (1882) 22 Ch. D. 287 ; Newtownards Town Commissioners v. Wood (1877) 11 Ir.R.C.L. 506, 509, per Morris, C.J.

section 13 of the Markets and Fairs Clauses Act, 1847,(a) or contain sections to the like effect.

This section 13 of the Markets and Fairs Clauses Act is also incorporated by the Public Health Act, 1875, s. 167.(b) It is dealt with more fully elsewhere.(c) The section makes it an offence, punishable by fine on summary conviction, for any person, other than a licensed hawker, to 'sell or expose for sale in any place within the prescribed limits,(d) except in his own dwelling-place or shop, any articles in respect of which tolls are by the special Act authorised to be taken.'

It is not altogether clear what are the rights of a market-owner, with regard to bringing actions for disturbance, if his market-rights, including his right to toll, depend upon an Act which incorporates the above section, or contains a section to the like effect. But the position appears to be as follows :—

1. It cannot be said that the market-rights are infringed, or that the market is disturbed, merely because a person sells tollable articles in his own dwelling-place or shop, although it be within the prescribed limits.(e) A *fortiori*, it is not a ground of complaint that a person sells such articles in his own dwelling-place or shop outside the prescribed limits.

2. If an offence be committed against the section, the penalty thereby imposed may be recovered in a court of summary jurisdiction. Probably, in a proper case, an injunction to prevent a commission of the offence or its repetition will be granted by a court of competent jurisdiction.(f) But it seems probable also that for a mere offence against the section no action for damages lies. The section appears to create a liability not existing at common law,(g) and, as it prescribes the particular remedy for enforcing it, that remedy must be adopted.(h)

3. If the market be disturbed by the unlawful levying of a

(a) 10 & 11 Vict. c. 14.   (b) 38 & 39 Vict. c. 55, s. 167.
(c) See *post*, p. 150.
(d) I.e. 'prescribed for that purpose in the special Act ;' see s. 2, *post*, p. 142.
(e) See per Romer, J., Mayor of Birmingham v. Foster (1894) 70 L.T. 371, 372.
(f) See Cooper v. Whittingham (1880) 15 Ch. D. 501, 506.
(g) The offence created by the section appears to differ in several respects from the common law wrong of *intentionally* taking the benefit of the market without payment of toll, which is dealt with *ante*, p. 82.
(h) See the third rule stated by Willes, J., in Wolverhampton New Waterworks Co. v. Hawkesford, 28 L.J.C.P. 242, 246 ; 1 Smith L.C. (10th ed.) 285.

Remedies for Disturbance of Statutory Markets 89

rival market in a manner which does not constitute any offence against the section, an action lies for damages, as well as for an injunction.(*a*) It will be observed that a person may set up a rival market without committing an offence under the section, for the section only prohibits selling and exposing for sale, acts which a person who sets up a market does not necessarily commit.(*b*) Consequently, if the remedy by action did not exist, the market-owner might be without remedy against very serious infringements of his rights.

4. It is probable that, on similar grounds, an action is maintainable against persons who disturb the market by wrongful acts other than that of setting up a rival market, provided that the wrongful acts complained of amount to more than the commission of an offence under the section. But there seems to be no authority directly on this point.(*c*)

The effect of the section on the market-owner's rights of action is in some cases complicated by the fact that the section has to be read in conjunction with other sections of the special Act which incorporates it, and when so read its effect may be considerably altered.(*d*)

In the foregoing observations it has been assumed that the protection given by s. 13 of the Markets and Fairs Clauses Act is given, not in substitution for, but by way of addition to, the protection against disturbance by levying a rival market, which a market enjoys at common law. It cannot, however, be regarded as finally determined whether this assumption is correct.(*e*)

(*a*) Mayor of Birmingham *v.* Foster (1894) 70 L.T. 371. An inquiry as to damages was there granted.
(*b*) See *ante*, pp. 78, 79.
(*c*) See, however, the dictum of Morris, C.J., Newtownards Town Commissioners *v.* Wood (1877) 11 Ir. R.C.L. 506, 509.
(*d*) See Abergavenny Imp. Commrs. *v.* Straker (1889) 42 Ch. D. 83.
(*e*) See the judgments of Blackburn, J., in Pope *v.* Whalley (1865) 34 L.J.M.C. 76; and in Fearon *v.* Mitchell (1872) L.R. 7 Q.B. 690; and cf. Mayor of Birmingham *v.* Foster, *supra*.

CHAPTER VI

HOW THE FRANCHISE MAY BE LOST

§ 1. *Forfeiture.*

Abuse and non-user

THE owner of a market or fair is liable to be deprived of his franchise if he misuse or abuse it, or if he neglect to use it.(*a*) Such a franchise is granted on the implied condition that it be duly exercised according to the grant, and if this condition be broken the grant is liable to be repealed.(*b*)

The non-user of a franchise which is merely to the profit or pleasure of the owner is no ground for its loss or forfeiture ; but a fair or market is held, not merely for the profit of the owner, but also for the benefit of the public, who suffer a loss if the fair or market be not duly held ; and accordingly the non-user of a fair or market, or the neglect to hold it, is a good ground for the crown taking the necessary steps to seize the franchise.(*c*) The non-user or neglect of the franchise, or its abuse, does not of itself destroy the right, but it entitles the crown to obtain a repeal of the grant by *scire facias* or *quo warranto.*(*d*) An abuse of the franchise may entitle the crown to take proceedings for its forfeiture, but it does not entitle third persons to usurp market or fair rights, and thereby disturb the franchise.(*e*) Notwithstanding that he himself is in default, the owner of the franchise has a remedy against such wrong-doers.(*f*)

(*a*) 'Retinet possessionem per usum . . . donec amiserit per abusum vel non usum'; Bracton, lib. 2, c. 24, fol. 56, cited 2 Inst. 222. See also Cru. Dig. 4th ed. vol. iii. p. 268.
(*b*) See per Holt, C.J., City of London *v.* Vanacre (1700) 12 Mod. 270; Y.B. 20 Edw. IV. ff. 5, 6.
(*c*) See per Sir Edward Coke, case of Leicester Forest (1608) Cro. Jac. 155.
(*d*) See per Bayley, J., Peter *v.* Kendal (1827) 6 B. & C. 703; Midleton *v.* Power (1886) 19 L.R. Ir. 1. As to the result of long acquiescence in disturbance, see *ante*, pp. 86, 87.
(*e*) Midleton *v.* Power, *supra*.   (*f*) *Ibid.*

Forfeiture

Prescriptive markets are liable to forfeiture for non-user or abuse, as well as markets created by grant. But the crown cannot take proceedings to forfeit statutory markets. If abuses arise in connection with statutory markets, and the remedies provided by the statutes regulating them prove to be inadequate, recourse must be had to parliament to pass further statutes which will provide adequate remedies.

The printed volume of the 'Placita de Quo Warranto' contains many instances of forfeiture for non-user.(a) But the franchise was generally re-granted on payment of a fine. In one case the defendants produced a charter containing a clause that 'although they have not used any liberty, yet they may lawfully use it,' and so justified a market which they had been holding, since the date of this charter, by virtue of an earlier market-charter upon which they had not acted until that date.(b) In several cases the defendant pleaded successfully that he had held his fair or market as far as he could if any chose to attend it, but that it often happened that there was no access of buyers and sellers.(c) If a fair become unfrequented and useless, and to that extent be discontinued, the franchise right nevertheless remains unimpaired.(d)

Amongst abuses which entitle the crown to take proceedings to forfeit the franchise may be mentioned that of holding a fair on additional days beyond those authorised by the grant,(e) or of holding a market on a day other than the authorised day.(f) But to hold a market on an additional day, as well as on the authorised day, seems to be treated, not as an abuse of the franchise granted, but as an usurpation of another and separate franchise.(g)

Abuse may be of negative character, consisting in the neglect of something which ought of necessity to be done, or non-user of an essential part of the franchise.(h)

Non-user

Abuse

(a) E.g. Leamington (pp. 128, 129); Sandiacre (pp. 162, 163); Orlandston (p. 329).
(b) Melcheburne (pp. 6, 7).
(c) P.Q.W., Wardon (p. 64), Ilkeston (p. 137), Aston-in-Weston (pp. 143, 144), Hovingham (pp. 218, 219), Fiskarton (pp. 635, 636), Lib. Rad'i de Berners (p. 742), Lib. Prioris de Novo Loco (p. 747), Lib. Joh'is de Sc'o Joh'e (748).
(d) Downshire v. O'Brien (1887) 19 L.R. Ir. 380, 389.
(e) See *ante*, p. 49.   (f) See *ante*, p. 48.
(g) See *ante*, p. 49.
(h) Y.B. 2 Hen. VII. f. 11, per Brian, C.J., who refers, as an example, to 'an office of clerk of the market'; see *ante*, p. 11.

One of the grounds of forfeiture of frequent occurrence in the printed volume of the 'Placita de Quo Warranto' is the neglect to keep judicial instruments of pillory or tumbrel for the punishment of persons breaking the assize of bread and ale, or the neglect to use those instruments and the substitution of fines in cases where corporal punishment is due.(a) The pillory, however, was abolished by statute in 1816 ;(b) and in 1844 the statute called 'Judicium Pillorie,' or the 'Statute of the pillory and tumbrel and of the assize of bread and ale '(c), was entirely repealed.(d) In the case of a market not confined by metes and bounds, neglect to provide sufficient accommodation for the public may be an abuse on account of which the grant may be repealed.(e)

It seems that a market or fair cannot be forfeited for non-user of a part of the franchise which is not necessary to the due holding of the market or fair. If a market be granted with a right to take toll, the grant of the market cannot be repealed on the ground that no toll is taken. Toll is not an incident of the market,(f) and the grant of toll benefits the lord, and not the public.

Neglect to take toll

There remains the question, however, whether the right to toll can be lost by non-user. It seems that non-user does not of itself destroy the right.(g) But it may be that if the public have been using a market or fair for a great number of years without any demand of toll being made, this fact may, in the absence of any other explanation, warrant the inference that the right to toll has been at some time or other surrendered to the crown, or otherwise become extinguished, or, at any rate, that it has become severed from the ownership of the market or fair. Probably a forfeiture ought not to be presumed if there be no evidence that there was at any time any ground of forfeiture ; for a forfeiture implies a wrong done by the owner of the franchise, and, as a general rule, the presumption is against wrong.(h) But this objection does not apply to a presumption of a voluntary surrender.

(a) E.g. Wahull (p. 36), Hegham (p. 133), Lilleburn (pp. 536, 537). See *ante*, p. 9.
(b) 56 Geo. III. c. 138. (c) 51 Hen. III. st. 6 (Ruff).
(d) By 7 & 8 Vict. c. 24, s. 2. (e) See *ante*, p. 35.
(f) See *ante*, p. 56.
(g) See per Sir E. Coke, case of Leicester Forest (1608) Cro. Jac. 155.
(h) See Doe v. Catomore (1851) 16 Q.B. 745.

Forfeiture

It has been laid down that if a franchise become liable to forfeiture the crown may waive the forfeiture by any act, such as the receipt of rent, which recognises a continuance of the right to the franchise, and that the crown cannot take advantage of any forfeiture which has been so waived.(a)

Waiver of forfeiture

Markets and fairs, when forfeited to the crown, are not extinguished, but continue to exist in the crown's hands,(b) and unless re-granted are placed under the management of the Commissioners of Woods,(c) who are entitled to collect the tolls and other dues. But the Commissioners have the power at any time, with the consent of the Treasury, to abandon or discontinue, either permanently or for any limited time, the collection of any tolls or profits of any markets or fairs belonging to the crown which it may be considered inexpedient to collect, and also, with the consent of the Treasury, by deed, absolutely to relinquish any such tolls or profits.(d)

Effect of forfeiture

§ 2. Surrender.

Prescriptive and charter markets and fairs may be lost by their surrender to the crown.(e) It has been said that if the owner of prescriptive franchises accepts from the crown a grant of the *same* liberties, he cannot afterwards claim them by prescription, but he must rely upon the grant.(f)

§ 3. Extinction by Act of Parliament.

All franchises are liable to be extinguished by Act of Parliament. The statute of 25 Henry VI. expressly annulled all grants of markets and fairs in North Wales which had been made at any time to Welshmen.(g) Express words, however, are not necessary to cause an extinguishment; and a statute may abolish a franchise by implication. Where the owners of a pre-

---

(a) Midleton v. Power (1886) 19 L.R. Ir. 1. As to waiver of forfeiture, see notes to Dumpor's case, 1 Sm. L.C. 10th ed. 31.
(b) See *ante*, p. 28.
(c) 10 Geo. IV. c. 50, s. 8 ; 48 & 49 Vict. c. 79, s. 2.
(d) 15 & 16 Vict. c. 62, s. 6.
(e) Cru. Dig. 4th ed. vol. iii. p. 267.
(f) Com. Dig. 'Prescription,' G ; cited by A. L. Smith, L.J., in Taylor v. New Windsor Corporation [1898] 1 Q.B. 196 ; Cru. Dig. 4th ed. vol. iii. p. 428, citing Finch, Bk. 1, c. 3, s. 23, who in turn cites Y.B. 21 Hen. VII. f. 5 ; but the decision in the Year Book supports the contrary proposition ; and see also Goodson v. Duffield (1613) Cro. Jac. 313. The effect of the grant is probably a matter of construction in each case.
(g) 25 Hen. VI., repealed by 21 Jac. 1. c. 28, s. 11.

scriptive Saturday market obtained an Act of Parliament which empowered them to hold markets on every week-day, over an extended area, and with higher tolls, it was decided that the prescriptive rights were superseded by the parliamentary rights, and that the statute, on its true construction, conferred the latter in substitution for, and not by way of addition to, the former.(a)   The intervention of parliament for some subordinate purpose which presupposes the continuance of the old rights does not necessarily merge or extinguish the tenure of the old rights ;(b) but in each case the effect of the statute is a question of construction.(c)

§ 4. *The Fairs Act*, 1871.

By the Fairs Act, 1871,(d) special powers are given to the Home Secretary which enable him, under certain circumstances, to make an order abolishing any fair held in England or Wales.

The Secretary of State cannot make such an order without the previous consent in writing of the owner for the time being of the fair or of the tolls or dues payable in respect thereof ;(e) and he can only make the order in cases where he has received a representation that it will be for the convenience and advantage of the public that the fair be abolished, and where it appears to him that such is the fact.(f)   The representation, to entitle him to act upon it, must be made either (1) by the owner of a fair, or (2) by the district council of the district in which the fair is held, or, if it be within the county of London, by the justices of the petty sessional district within which it is held.(g)   Before the representation is considered by the Home Secretary, notice of the representation, and of the time when he will take it into consideration, must be published once in the 'London Gazette,' and in three successive weeks in some one

(a) Mayor of Manchester *v.* Lyons (1882) 22 Ch. D. 287 ; Mayor of Manchester *v.* Pedley (1876) 22 Ch. D. 294 n ; cf. Taylor *v.* New Windsor Corporation [1898] 1 Q. B. 186.
(b) Mayor of Manchester *v.* Pedley (1876) 22 Ch. D. 296 n.
(c) See *ante*, pp. 26, 27.   (d) 34 Vict. c. 12.
(e) s. 3.   (f) *Ibid.*
(g) s. 3, as amended by the Local Government Act, 1894 (56 & 57 Vict. c. 73) s. 27 (1) e, which substituted the district council for the justices, except as regards the county of London (see s. 35). If the fair be held in a borough, including a county borough, the borough council may make the representation in its capacity of district council; see the same Act, ss. 21, 27, 32.

and the same newspaper published in the county, city or borough in which the fair is held, or, if there be no newspaper published therein, then in the newspaper of some county adjoining or near thereto.(a) As soon as the order that the fair be abolished has been made, notice of the making of the order must be similarly published, and thereupon the fair becomes abolished ;(b) but the order appears to have no force until such publication has been completed.

For the purposes of the Act 'owner' means 'any person, or persons, or body of commissioners, or body corporate, entitled to hold any fair, whether in respect of the ownership of any lands or tenements, or under any charter, letters patent, or Act of Parliament, or otherwise howsoever.'(c)

(a) s. 3.   (b) s. 4.   c) s. 2.

CHAPTER VII

THE ADMINISTRATION OF MARKETS AND FAIRS

§ 1. *Regulation and by-laws.*

Regulation

THE lord of a market or fair had at common law extensive powers for regulating it. Thus he had a court of pie-powder for the determination of disputes arising therein ;(*a*) and he was bound to keep in the market-place pillory and tumbrel for the punishment of offenders.(*b*) How far the duties in connection with these and other matters belonged to the owner of a fair or market as such, or how far they properly belonged to other jurisdictions usually held along with that franchise, is a somewhat obscure subject, and not now of much practical importance. The question is referred to somewhat more fully in the Introduction.(*c*)

As owner or occupier of the market-place, he may be criminally liable if he keeps it so filthy as to be a public nuisance.(*d*) And if he keep it in a dangerous condition he may be liable in damages to one lawfully using the market-place and suffering thereby.(*e*)

By-laws

The private owner of a common law market or fair has, as such, no power to make by-laws. His regulations with regard to the use of the market or fair cannot be enforced either by fine or imprisonment. A municipal corporation, however, had at common law,(*f*) and now those corporations to which the Municipal Corporations Act, 1882, applies have, by that Act,(*g*) power to make by-laws 'for the good rule and

(*a*) See *ante*, p. 6.   (*b*) See *ante*, p. 8.
(*c*) See *ante*, p. 8.
(*d*) Draper *v.* Sperring (1861) 10 C.B.N.S. 131 ; see *ante*, p. 46.
(*e*) Lax *v.* Mayor of Darlington (1879) 5 Ex. D. 28 ; see *ante*, p. 32.
(*f*) 2 Selwyn, N.P. 1129 ; City of London *v.* Vanacre (1700) 12 Mod. 270 ; 1 Salk. 142 ; Carth. 482 (per Holt, C.J.) ; Chamberlain of London's case (1590) 5 Rep. 62 b ; Norris *v.* Staps (1611) Hob. 211.
(*g*) 45 & 46 Vict. c. 50, s. 23 ; cf. the repealed 5 & 6 Will. IV. c. 76, s. 90. The Act does not apply to the Corporation of London.

government of the borough'; and therefore a municipal corporation which, as such, owns a market or fair within the borough, can make by-laws for its regulation.

When a municipal corporation, acting as such, makes by-laws for the regulation of its markets or fairs, under the powers conferred by the Municipal Corporations Act, 1882,(*a*) it must make them in the manner prescribed by that Act.(*b*)

A municipal corporation, however, in its capacity of urban district council, has power, under the Public Health Act, 1875, ss. 166-168, to establish new markets and acquire existing markets, and to make by-laws with respect to such markets for the purposes mentioned in s. 42 of the Markets and Fairs Clauses Act, 1847.(*c*) When it makes such by-laws in its capacity of district council, it must make them in the manner prescribed by the Public Health Act.(*d*)

When, in pursuance of s. 136 of the Municipal Corporations Act, 1882, a transfer has been made to a municipal corporation of a market provided by trustees acting under a local Act, it seems that the municipal corporation may, for the purpose of making by-laws with respect to such market, rely upon the powers, if any, contained in the local Act.(*e*)

Urban district councils may, under s. 167 of the Public Health Act, make by-laws, for the purposes mentioned in s. 42 of the Markets and Fairs Clauses Act, with respect to any markets belonging to them as such. S. 32 of the Diseases of Animals Act, 1894,(*f*) enables a local authority to make by-laws for the same purposes with respect to any market provided by them under that section. Undertakers of statutory markets and fairs usually possess power, under their Acts, of making by-laws. In all these cases the by-laws must be made in the manner prescribed by the Act which confers the power.

All by-laws, by whatever authority made, are invalid and of no effect if not made in the manner (if any) directed by the statute, charter, or other authority under which they purport to

Validity of by-laws

(*a*) 45 & 46 Vict. c. 50, s. 23.
(*b*) See Ellis *v*. Bridgenorth (1861) 2 J. & H. 67. S. 187 of the Public Health Act, 1875 (as amended by s. 23 (6) of the Municipal Corporations Act, 1882), seems not to affect by-laws ' for the good rule and government of the borough.'
(*c*) See *post*, Part II. (*d*) See 38 & 39 Vict. c. 55, ss. 182 *et seq.*
(*e*) See s. 136 (3). (*f*) 57 & 58 Vict. c. 57.

be made,(*a*) or if they be inconsistent therewith, or if they be unreasonable,(*b*) or inconsistent with the law of the land,(*c*) or in restraint of trade ;(*d*) but a by-law may regulate, and to that end be in *partial* restraint of trade.(*e*) So by-laws for the following purposes have been held good—viz. for regulating the times at which sales by auction may take place in a market,(*f*) for setting aside a certain part of a market for sale by wholesale and forbidding sale by retail in that part,(*g*) and for confining sales of particular articles to special parts of the market.(*h*) But a by-law which prevents all dealing in a particular article in a market without permission is bad, if the article is one of those for which the market was established.(*i*)

§ 2. *Weights and measures.*

The general law with regard to weights and measures is to be found in the Weights and Measures Acts, 1878 to 1897.(*j*) These Acts provide for the use of the same weights and measures throughout the United Kingdom.(*k*) County councils (*l*) and borough councils (*m*) are now the local authorities to execute the Acts and appoint inspectors of

(*a*) Parry *v.* Berry (1718) 1 Comyns, 269.
(*b*) Ellwood *v.* Bullock (1844) 6 Q.B. 383; see also Kruse *v.* Johnson [1898] 2 Q.B. 91.
(*c*) Dyson *v.* L. & N. W. R. Co. (1881) 7 Q.B.D. 32.
(*d*) Parry *v.* Berry (1718) 1 Comyns, 269. Bacon Abr. ' By-laws,' B. ; see Corporation of Toronto *v.* Vigo [1896] A.C. 88.
(*e*) Collins *v.* Corporation of Wells (1885) 1 T.L.R. 328. Fazerkerly *v.* Wiltshire (1721) 1 Stra. 462.
(*f*) Collins *v.* Corporation of Wells (1885) 1 T.L.R. 328.
(*g*) Strike *v.* Collins (1886) 55 L.T.N.S. 182.
(*h*) Wortley *v.* Nottingham Local Board (1870) 21 L.T.N.S. 582; Savage *v.* Brook (1863) 15 C.B.N.S. 264; Player *v.* Jenkens (1666) 1 Sid. 284.
(*i*) Wortley *v.* Nottingham Local Board (1870) 21 L.T.N.S. 582. For more information on the subject of by-laws at common law, see Com. Dig. tit. ' By-law ;' Selw. N.P. pp. 1129-1133; and Grant *on Corporations*.
(*j*) 41 & 42 Vict. c. 49 (1878), which consolidated and amended the provisions of the earlier Acts thereby repealed; 52 & 53 Vict. c. 21 (1889) ; 55 & 56 Vict. c. 18 (1892); 56 & 57 Vict. c. 19 (1893); 60 & 61 Vict. c. 46 (1897).
(*k*) See the Act of 1878, s. 3. The Act of 1897 permits the metric system.
(*l*) 51 & 52 Vict. c. 41, ss. 3 (xiii.) and 39.
(*m*) 41 & 42 Vict. c. 49, ss. 40, 43, and Sched. IV. As to boroughs which, according to the census of 1881, had less than 10,000 inhabitants, see 51 & 52 Vict. c. 41, s. 39. In the city of London the common council is now the local authority; see 51 & 52 Vict. c. 41, ss. 41 (1) (*a*) and 100 ; 41 & 42 Vict. c. 49, s. 40, and Sched. IV.

weights and measures. It is proposed here to consider the enactments which more particularly relate to the weighing or measuring of goods or cattle or other things in markets or fairs.

Under the Weights and Measures Act, 1878,(a) it is the duty of the owner or manager of every public market in which goods are exposed or kept for sale to provide proper scales and balances and weights and measures or other machines for the purpose of weighing or measuring all goods sold, offered, or exposed for sale in the market: to deposit the same at the office of the clerk or toll-collector of the market, or some other convenient place: and to have their accuracy tested at least twice a year by the local inspector of weights and measures. The expenses of so doing are to be paid out of the moneys collected for tolls in the market.

Goods in markets

It is the duty (b) of the clerk or toll-collector at all reasonable times, whenever called upon to do so, to weigh or measure all goods which have been sold, offered or exposed for sale in the market, upon payment of such reasonable sum as may from time to time be decided upon by the owner or manager, subject to the approval and revision of the justices at general or quarter sessions.(c)

For a breach of any of the above duties, the offender is liable, on summary conviction, to a fine not exceeding £5.(d)

In addition to his duty to weigh and measure when required to do so, the clerk or toll-collector may, at all reasonable times, of his own accord, weigh or measure any goods sold, offered, or exposed for sale in the market; and if, upon such weighing or measuring, any such goods are found deficient in weight or measure, or otherwise contrary to the provisions of the Weights and Measures Act, 1878, he must take the necèssary proceedings for recovering any fine to which the person selling, offering, or exposing the goods is liable; and the court convicting the offender may award out of the fine a reasonable

---

(a) 41 & 42 Vict. c. 49, s. 86, and Sched. VI. pt. 2, whereby the provisions of the repealed Act, 22 & 23 Vict. c. 56, ss. 6-8, 12, are re-enacted.
(b) Ibid.
(c) This jurisdiction of the justices seems not to be affected by 51 & 52 Vict. c. 41, s. 3 (xiii.), which makes the County Council the 'local authority' of the Acts relating to weights and measures; see the Weights and Measures Act, 1878, s. 40, and Sched. IV.
(d) Authorities cited note (a) supra.

remuneration to the clerk or toll-collector. For any offence against, or disobedience to, these provisions the offender is liable on summary conviction to a fine not exceeding £5.

These provisions of the Act of 1878 do not apply to fairs, unless the word 'market' can be construed as including 'fair.'(*a*) The provision for the payment of the expenses out of the tolls in the market suggests that the Act does not apply to a toll-free market. The Act provides only for the weighing of 'goods.' It is doubtful whether 'cattle' are included in this expression.(*b*)

Cattle in markets and fairs
Markets and fairs in which, for the time being, tolls are authorised to be taken, and actually are taken, in respect of cattle, are subject to the provisions of the Markets and Fairs (Weighing of Cattle) Acts, 1887 and 1891.(*c*) 'Cattle' here includes ram, ewe, wether, lamb, and swine,(*d*) as well as such animals as would ordinarily be described as cattle. The company, corporation or person authorised to take the tolls is called 'the market authority.'(*e*)

Under these Acts it is the duty of the market authority to provide and maintain, in or near the market or fair, 'sufficient and proper buildings or places for weighing cattle brought for sale within the market or fair.'(*f*) The market authority is also bound, unless exempted by order of the Board of Agriculture, to 'provide and maintain, to the satisfaction of the Board, sufficient and suitable accommodation for weighing cattle.'(*g*) It is suggested that the object of this additional requirement is to provide facilities for weighing any cattle, whether brought for sale or not. The market authority is also required to keep in or near the market or fair weighing machines and weights for the purpose of weighing cattle : to

---

(*a*) It is so construed by Coke in Stat. Westm. II. c. 24 ; '*de mercato* . . . note that fairs are taken within this law, for every fair is a market, but every market is not a fair '(2 Inst. 406) ; and in Stat. Westm. I. c. 31 : '*marche* : this word doth here include a fair, as well as a market ' (2 Inst. 221). But in many modern Acts of Parliament, and usually in grants, markets and fairs are distinguished, and ' market ' does not include ' fair.'

(*b*) Compare the provisions of the Act with the preamble and provisions of 50 & 51 Vict. c. 27 ; see also 2 Blac. Com. 389.

(*c*) 50 & 51 Vict. c. 27 (see s. 2) ; 54 & 55 Vict. c. 70. These Acts may affect markets and fairs to which the Markets and Fairs Clauses Act, 1847, applies. As to the special provisions to which such markets and fairs are subject, see *post*, pp. 103 and 156-160.

(*d*) 50 & 51 Vict. c. 27, s. 3.   (*e*) *Ibid.* s. 2.
(*f*) *Ibid.* s. 4.   (*g*) 54 & 55 Vict. c. 70, s. 2.

appoint proper persons to have charge of the machines and weights : to afford the use of the machines and weights to the public for weighing cattle : and to have the accuracy of the machines and weights tested at least twice a year by the local inspector of weights and measures, at the cost of the market authority.(a) Failure to fulfil these duties renders it unlawful for the market authority, so long as such failure continues, to demand or take any tolls whatever, in respect of any cattle brought to the market or fair for sale ; and any person who demands or takes any such toll while the market authority is in default is liable, on summary conviction, to a fine not exceeding £5.(b)

Every person selling, offering for sale, or buying cattle in a market or fair provided with accommodation for weighing cattle may require such cattle to be weighed ;(c) and the person appointed to weigh cattle sold in the market or fair is liable on summary conviction to a fine not exceeding 40s., and not less than 2s. 6d., (i.) if he refuse or neglect to weigh such cattle when required, or (ii.) if he refuse or neglect to deliver to the seller or buyer a ticket specifying the true weight of the cattle weighed, or (iii.) if he give to any person a false ticket or account of any cattle weighed.(d) Every person who knowingly acts or assists in committing any fraud respecting the weighing of any cattle is liable, on summary conviction, to a fine not exceeding £5 for each offence.(e)

Unless it be otherwise expressly provided by any Act, the market authority may demand and receive in respect of the weighing of cattle tolls not exceeding 2d. for every head of cattle other than sheep or swine, or 1d. for every five or less number of sheep or swine, or such other amounts as the Local Government Board may authorise.(f) These tolls for weighing must be paid by the person requiring the cattle to be weighed to the person authorised by the market authority to receive them ;(g) and ss. 36 to 41 of the Markets and Fairs Clauses Act, 1847, apply to such tolls as if the Act of 1887 were the

(a) 50 & 51 Vict. c. 27, s. 4.
(b) Ibid. and 54 & 55 Vict. c. 70, s. 2.
(c) 50 & 51 Vict. c. 27, s. 5.
(d) Ibid. s. 6.   (e) Ibid. s. 7.
(f) 50 & 51 Vict. c. 27, s. 8. The duties of the Local Governmen Board under s. 8 are not affected by the Act of 1891 (54 & 55 Vict. c. 70) s. 1, which only substitutes the Board of Agriculture in s. 9.
(g) 50 & 51 Vict. c. 27, s. 5.

special Act, and the market authority were the undertakers.(*a*) The principal provisions of these sections are (i.) that the tolls may be recovered by distress or in any court having competent jurisdiction : (ii.) that disputes respecting tolls are to be settled by a justice : and (iii.) that lists of tolls are to be conspicuously set up in the fair or market, and in each weighing house.(*b*)

Certain market authorities (*c*) are required to send to the Board of Agriculture, at such intervals and in such form and with such particulars as the Board may order, returns showing so far as can be ascertained, the number of cattle entering the market or fair, the number and weight of cattle weighed, and the price of the cattle sold, thereat. These market authorities may, for the purpose of making such returns, cause cattle sold at the market to be weighed without fee. The Board has power to publish these returns. Wilful default in respect of these returns renders the market authority liable on summary conviction to a fine not exceeding £20 for each offence, or in case of a continuing offence to a fine not exceeding £10 a day. It is a misdemeanour to make a false and fraudulent statement in any return.(*d*)

Upon the application of any market authority, the Board of Agriculture has power to make an order exempting the market or fair from the provisions of the Acts, on the ground that the sale of cattle thereat is, or is likely to be, so small as to render it inexpedient to enforce the provision and maintenance of a place for weighing cattle and of a weighing machine ; but the order must limit the time, not to exceed three years, during which it is to be in force ; and it may be wholly or partially rescinded, altered or extended by any subsequent order.(*e*)

The Acts apply to a cattle market held on a highway dedicated subject to the right to hold the market thereon ; and the highway authorities cannot prevent the market authority from setting up, in pursuance of the Acts, a proper weighing

---

(*a*) 50 & 51 Vict. c. 27, s. 8.
(*b*) The sections are set out *post*, Part II.
(*c*) These are the market authorities of every market or fair held at Ashford, Birmingham, Bristol, Leicester, Leeds, Lincoln, Liverpool (Stanley Market), London (Metropolitan Cattle Market), Newcastle-on-Tyne, Norwich, Salford, Shrewsbury, Wakefield, York ; but the Board of Agriculture may from time to time vary or add to this list of places ; 54 & 55 Vict. c. 70. s. 3 (1) and (5), and Sched.
(*d*) 54 & 55 Vict. c. 70, s. 3.
(*e*) 50 & 51 Vict. c. 27, s. 9 ; 54 & 55 Vict. c. 70, s. 1.

Weights and Measures

machine in the market-place.(*a*) The Acts contemplate a permanent, and not merely a moveable, weighing-machine.(*b*)

The Acts which have hitherto been dealt with apply, so far as they are applicable to markets and fairs, whether they were established under the common law or under or by the authority of a statute. But further provisions with regard to weighing and measuring are contained in the Markets and Fairs Clauses Act, 1847,(*c*) and these apply to all markets and fairs established under a private Act which incorporates those provisions, and to all markets established in accordance with the Public Health Act, 1875,(*d*) or the Diseases of Animals Act, 1894,(*e*) or any of the earlier Acts which are now superseded by either of these two Acts. The provisions are set out in full elsewhere.(*f*)

Commodities, articles, and carts, under the Markets and Fairs Clauses Act, 1847

The buying and selling of hay and straw in markets and other places in or within thirty miles of the cities of London and Westminster are regulated by the Hay and Straw Acts, 1796, 1834 and 1856.(*g*)

Hay and straw in markets in and near the metropolis

Under the Act of 1796 the hay and straw may be sold only in trusses,(*h*) which must be of the prescribed weight,(*i*) and must be made up of only one quality of hay or straw.(*j*) Penalties may be incurred through non-compliance with these requirements of the Act.(*k*)

For the purpose of settling disputes as to the weight of any hay or straw sold within the limits within which the Act applies, the Act casts certain duties upon the clerk or toll-gatherer of every market which is held within those limits. He must provide and keep at his office proper scales and weights or engines for the weighing of all hay and straw which shall be required to be weighed; and he or his deputy must act as one of the public 'hay weighers' appointed by the Act.(*l*) The buyer of any hay or straw sold within the above-mentioned

---

(*a*) McIntosh *v.* Romford Local Board (1889) 61 L.T. 185.
(*b*) *Ibid.*
(*c*) 10 & 11 Vict. c. 14, ss. 21–30, 34, 42.   (*d*) 38 & 39 Vict. c. 55.
(*e*) 57 & 58 Vict. c. 57.   (*f*) See *post*, Part II.
(*g*) 36 Geo. III. c. 88; 4 & 5 Will. IV. c. 21; 19 & 20 Vict. c. 114.
(*h*) s. 2.
(*i*) s. 3. A truss of straw must weigh 36 lbs.; of new hay, 60 lbs.; of old hay, 56 lbs. Hay ceases to be new by September 1. Under s. 6 the bands with which the truss is bound must not weigh over 5 lbs.
(*j*) s. 5.   (*k*) ss. 2–7; but see also ss. 14, 25.
(*l*) s. 13.

limits, or his agent, may cause it to be weighed in the presence of the seller or his agent at the agreed place of delivery ; and if either party be dissatisfied with this weighing the buyer or his agent may send for a hay-weigher. In parishes containing a hay market he must send for the clerk or toll-gatherer of the market, or his deputy, but elsewhere for the nearest hay-weigher. The hay-weigher, upon a weighing-fee at the rate of three shillings per load (*a*) being paid or tendered to him, is bound to go with all convenient speed to the place where the hay or straw in question may be, and there weigh it ; and the weight as ascertained by him is conclusive to all parties.(*b*) A clerk or toll-gatherer incurs a penalty by neglecting the duties imposed upon him by the Act.(*c*)

Both the Act of 1796(*d*) and the Act of 1856(*e*) make it an offence fraudulently to increase the weight of a truss by mixing water, sand, or other matter therewith. The latter Act empowers and requires the clerk of any hay-market within the limits to which the Acts apply to weigh or examine any hay or straw exposed for sale in the market, if he has received a complaint that it is deficient in weight, or has been mixed or packed contrary to the provisions of the Acts.(*f*) If his weighing, or examination, discloses an offence, the clerk is empowered to prosecute the offender.(*f*)

§ 3. *Sale of unwholesome meat and provisions.*

It is a misdemeanour at the common law knowingly to send to market or expose for sale therein as fit for human food meat which is not fit therefor.(*g*) Butchers and victuallers committing such an offence have long been punishable by statute.(*h*)

The main enactments now in force for preventing the sale of unsound food are to be found in the Public Health Act, 1875,(*i*) which applies to all places except the metropolis,(*j*) the Public Health (London) Act, 1891,(*k*) which applies to the county of London,(*l*) and the Towns

(*a*) I.e. 36 trusses ; s. 3.   (*b*) s. 13.   (*c*) *Ibid.*
(*d*) s. 21.   (*e*) s. 1.   (*f*) s. 3.
(*g*) Shillito *v.* Thompson (1875) 1 Q.B.D. 12 ; R. *v.* Stevenson (1862) 3 F. & F. 106 ; R. *v.* Jarvis, Id. 108 ; R. *v.* Crawley, Id. 109.
(*h*) See Judicium Pillorie, 51 Hen. III. St. 6. (Ruff), repealed by 7 & 8 Vict. c. 24, s. 2.
(*i*) 38 & 39 Vict. c. 55, ss. 116–119 ; as extended by 53 & 54 Vict. c. 59, s. 28.
(*j*) ss. 2, 4.   (*k*) 54 & 55 Vict. c. 76, s. 47.   (*l*) ss. 132, 141.

Sale of Unwholesome Meat and Provisions 105

Improvement Clauses Act, 1847,(a) which applies only where it has been made applicable by some special Act.(b) The provisions of these Acts, and also of the Sale of Food and Drugs Acts, 1875 and 1879,(c) which are aimed against the sale of adulterated food, are general, and are not confined to sales in markets and fairs. On the other hand, the Markets and Fairs Clauses Act, 1847,(d) contains, in s. 15, like provisions against the sale of unsound food, which concern only such markets and fairs as are governed by that Act.(e)

The Sale of Food and Drugs Act, 1875, empowers (amongst other persons specified) any inspector of a market, under the direction and at the cost of the local authority appointing him, or charged with the execution of the Act, to procure samples of food, and, if he suspect the same to have been sold contrary to any provision of the Act, to submit them to be analysed, with a view to taking proceedings against the offender.(f) The Sale of Food and Drugs Act, 1879, gives similar powers in respect of milk in course of delivery to a purchaser or consignee in pursuance of a contract for the sale to him thereof.(g) A person exposing an article of food for sale is liable to a penalty if he refuse to sell it to the inspector or other persons specified.(h) It is not altogether clear who is an 'inspector of a market' within the meaning of the Acts; but the expression probably includes such an official as an 'inspector of provisions' appointed by the undertakers of a market to which the Markets and Fairs Clauses Act, 1847, applies.(i) The Acts contemplate that the inspector shall act 'under the direction and at the cost of the local authority appointing' him, 'or charged with the execution of' the Acts.(j) Probably an urban district council, owning a market to which the Markets and Fairs Clauses Act applies, and appointing an inspector of provisions, would be a 'local authority' within the meaning of the Acts, but it may be doubted whether a market com-

---

(a) 10 & 11 Vict. c. 34, s. 131.   (b) ss. 1, 2.
(c) 38 & 39 Vict. c. 63; 42 & 43 Vict. c. 30. See also the Margarine Act, 50 & 51 Vict. c. 29, and the Acts relating to the adulteration of seeds and of fertilisers and feeding stuffs.
(d) 10 & 11 Vict. c. 14.   (e) See *post*, p. 154.
(f) s. 13.   (g) s. 3.
(h) Act of 1875, s. 17; Act of 1879, s. 4.
(i) See 10 & 11 Vict. c. 14, s. 15.
(j) 38 & 39 Vict. c. 63, s. 13; 42 & 43 Vict. c. 30, s. 3.

pany would be such. The local authorities 'charged with the execution' of the Acts are probably those referred to in s. 10 of the Act of 1875, as amended by the Local Government Act, 1888.(a) The inspector must act under the direction and at the cost of such local authority, or of the local authority (if any) by which he is appointed.

§ 4. *Diseases of animals.*

By the Diseases of Animals Act, 1894,(b) the Board of Agriculture have extensive powers of control over the holding of markets and fairs, for the purpose of preventing or checking pleuro-pneumonia, foot-and-mouth disease, and other diseases of animals.

The Board are empowered to make orders, from time to time, for prohibiting or regulating the holding of markets and fairs for the sale of animals, or for allowing them to be held only on such terms and conditions as the Board prescribe ;(c) for prohibiting or regulating the exposure of diseased or suspected animals in markets or fairs, or the placing of them in lairs or other places adjacent to, or connected with, markets or fairs ;(d) for dealing with animals found to be affected whilst exposed for sale in a market or fair, or in transit ;(e) for prescribing or regulating the cleansing or disinfection of places used for holding markets or fairs or for lairage,(f) and generally for the purpose of the prevention of the spread of disease.(g)

The orders have effect as if they were parts of the Act,(h) and severe penalties are imposed for disobedience.(i)

The orders which have been made in accordance with the provisions of this Act are far too numerous to be set out in this work, and many of them are of only local and temporary operation.

(a) 51 & 52 Vict. c. 41, ss. 3 (x.), 38, and 39 : in the City of London, the common council ; elsewhere in the metropolis, the vestries and district boards ; in counties (including the smaller boroughs), the county councils ; in boroughs which according to the census of 1881 had a population of not less than 10,000, the borough councils.
(b) 57 & 58 Vict. c. 57 (as amended by 59 & 60 Vict. c. 15).
(c) 57 & 58 Vict. c. 57, ss 9 and 22 (xix.).
(d) *Ibid.* s. 22 (ix.).   (e) *Ibid.* s. 21.
(f) *Ibid.* s. 22 (xx.).   (g) *Ibid.* s. 22 (xxxvii.).
(h) *Ibid.* s. 49.   (i) *Ibid.* ss. 51 to 57.

§ 5. Licences for sale of intoxicating drinks.

The Licensing Acts contain special provisions for meeting the requirements of persons who attend at markets and fairs. These provisions are of two kinds—(1) for granting occasional licences for selling at fairs, and (2) for granting exemptions from the provisions of the Acts as to closing, in respect of licensed premises near markets.

Occasional licences for selling intoxicating liquors at fairs are granted (*a a*) according to the following rules :— Occasional licences for fairs

1. A licence may be granted to any of the following persons :—

(i.) Any person authorised to keep a common inn, or alehouse, or victualling-house, who holds excise licences to sell therein beer, spirits, wine, or tobacco.(*a*)

(The occasional licence will empower him to sell at the specified place the like articles for which he holds licences).(*b*)

(ii.) Any person holding an excise licence, either (A) to keep a refreshment house (under 23 & 24 Vict. c. 27), or (B) to sell by retail in a refreshment house foreign wine to be consumed therein (under 23 & 24 Vict. c. 107), or (C) to retail beer to be consumed on the premises where sold (under 4 & 5 Will. IV. c. 85).(*b*)

(The occasional licence will authorise him to carry on at the specified place the same trade as he is authorised to carry on by his licence).(*b*)

2. The written consent must first be obtained of a justice of the peace usually acting at the petty sessions for the petty sessional division within which the proposed place of sale is situate.(*c*)

But the licence will not be void because of a mere irregularity (without fraud) in obtaining the consent of a wrong justice.(*d*) The excise authorities provide forms for the justice to sign in giving his consent.

3. Upon such consent being obtained, the licence may be granted by an officer of excise authorised by the Commissioners of Inland Revenue. It may be granted in cases within

---

(*a a*) As to a licence being necessary, see 37 & 38 Vict. c. 49, s. 18.
(*a*) 25 & 26 Vict. c. 22, s. 13.   (*b*) 27 & 28 Vict. c. 18, s. 5.
(*c*) 25 & 26 Vict. c. 22, s. 13, as amended by, and 27 & 28 Vict. c. 18, s. 5, as subject to, 26 & 27 Vict. c. 33, s. 20.
(*d*) Stevens *v.* Emson (1876) 1 Ex. D. 100.

Rule 1 (i.) whenever the commissioners consider it conducive to public convenience, comfort and order :(*a*) in cases within Rule 1 (ii.) whenever they consider it necessary for the accommodation of the public.(*b*)

4. The licence holds good for the specified period of time, not exceeding six (*c*) consecutive days in cases within Rule 1 (i.), or three (*b*) in cases within Rule 1 (ii.) ; after which a new licence must be taken out, if required, upon a new consent by a justice.

5. The licence may authorise sales from such hour, not earlier than sun-rise, until such hour, not later than ten o'clock at night, as may be specified in the consent given by the justice.(*d*)

6. The licence will be no protection to the licensee unless he produce it whenever requested so to do by an officer of excise or constable or police-officer.(*e*)

7. No licence may be granted for any Sunday, Christmas Day, Good Friday, or day appointed for a public fast or thanksgiving.(*a*)

8. The duty payable in cases within Rule 1 (i.) is half-a-crown a day, provided that if consecutive licences are taken out, and the first is for six days, the duty is not to exceed ten shillings for any licence after the first :(*f*) in cases within Rule 1 (ii.) (B) or (C), one shilling a day :(*g*) in cases within Rule 1 (ii.) (A) nil.(*g*)

Exemptions from closing licensed premises near markets

Orders exempting licensed premises near markets from the provisions of the Licensing Acts with respect to closing are granted according to the following rules(*h*) :—

1. The order may be made by the local authority of the licensing district, upon the production of such evidence as the authority may deem sufficient to show that the order is necessary or desirable for the accommodation of any considerable number of persons attending a public market.

(*a*) 25 & 26 Vict. c. 22, s. 13. (*b*) 27 & 28 Vict. c. 18, s. 5.
(*c*) 25 & 26 Vict. c. 22, s. 13, as amended by 26 & 27 Vict. c. 33, s. 19.
(*d*) 26 & 27 Vict. c. 33, s. 20, as amended by 37 & 38 Vict. c. 49, s. 19.
(*e*) 25 & 26 Vict. c. 22, s. 13; 27 & 28 Vict. c. 18, s. 5.
(*f*) 26 & 27 Vict. c. 33, s. 19.
(*g*) 27 & 28 Vict. c. 18, Sched. B.
(*h*) 35 & 36 Vict. c. 94, s. 26, as amended by 37 & 38 Vict. c. 49, s. 5.

Licences for Sale of Intoxicating Drinks 109

2. The order may be granted, if the local authority think fit, to any licensed victualler, or any licensed keeper of a refreshment house, or person licensed to sell beer or cider by retail to be consumed upon the premises, in respect of premises in the immediate neighbourhood of the market.

3. The order entitles the holder of the order to keep the premises open on such days, and during such time except between 1 A.M. and 2 A.M., as may be specified in the order ; and protects him from any penalty for keeping the premises open on such days and during such time, but does not exempt him from any other penalty under the Licensing Acts, or otherwise.

4. The holder of the order must affix in a conspicuous place outside the premises a notice, in the form prescribed by the local authority, stating the days and hours during which the premises are permitted by the order to be kept open. He is liable to a penalty not exceeding £5 if he makes default in affixing the notice or in keeping it affixed during any part of the time for which his exemption is granted.

5. Any person who keeps affixed to his premises any such notice when he does not hold an order is liable to a penalty not exceeding £5.

6. The local authority may at any time, if it seem fit to them, withdraw the order, or alter it by way of extension or restriction, as they may deem necessary or expedient, so, however, as not to render any person liable to any penalty for anything done under the order before the holder was informed of the withdrawal or alteration.

7. The local authority in the metropolitan police district is the commissioner of police for the metropolis, subject to the approbation of a principal Secretary of State : in the city of London and its liberties, so far as they are not included in the metropolitan police district, the commissioner of city police, subject to the approbation of the Lord Mayor of London : in any other place, two justices of the peace in sessions assembled.

§ 6. *Licences for theatrical performances at fairs.*

The Theatres Act, 1843,(*a*) provides by section 23 that nothing contained in that Act 'shall be construed to apply to

(*a*) 6 & 7 Vict. c. 68.

any theatrical representation in any booth or show which,(a) by the justices of the peace or other persons having authority in that behalf, shall be allowed in any lawful fair, feast, or customary meeting of the like kind.' This section does not exempt from the operation of the Act a theatrical representation in a booth, unless the booth has been duly 'allowed.'

Section 2 of the Act imposes penalties on any person who keeps 'any house or other place of public resort in Great Britain for the public performance of stage plays' without authority under letters-patent from the crown, or without a licence from the Lord Chamberlain, or the justices, as provided by the Act. But it has been held, apparently, that this section does not affect the owner of a temporary booth for theatrical representations.(b)

Section 11, however, imposes penalties on any person who for hire (c) acts, or presents, or causes, permits, or suffers, to be acted, or presented, any part in any stage play 'in any place not being a patent theatre or duly licensed as a theatre;' and it has been held that this section applies to a stage play in a temporary booth, if the booth be neither patented nor licensed, nor within the protection of s. 23.(d)

To come within the protection of s. 23, a booth at a fair must have been allowed 'by the justices of the peace, or other persons, having authority in that behalf.' If the fair is held anywhere outside the limits of the Lord Chamberlain's authority,(e) the allowance may be obtained from the authority which now conducts the licensing business formerly entrusted by the Theatres Act, 1843, to justices at special sessions: namely, in county boroughs, the council of the borough, and, elsewhere, the county council.(f) The council of the county or county borough, however, have power to delegate the business to a committee of the council, or to the justices of the county or county borough sitting in petty sessions.(g)

(a) 'Which' appears to refer to 'booth or show,' not to 'theatrical representation.'
(b) Davys v. Douglas (1859) 4 H. & N. 180. The judges gave no reasons for their decision in this case.
(c) See s. 16 of the Act.
(d) Fredericks v. Payne (1862) 1 H. & C. 584; Tarling v. Fredericks (1872) 28 L.T. 814.
(e) As to which see 6 & 7 Vict. c. 68, s. 3. As to letters patent from the crown, see Id. s. 2.
(f) 51 & 52 Vict. c. 41, ss. 7, 34 and 36.
(g) Or in the case of a county council to a district council; Id. ss. 28 and 34.

Councils which retain the business in their own hands, may, by standing orders for the regulation of their proceedings, prescribe the procedure whereby licences may be obtained ; but in the absence of such standing orders they must follow, as nearly as circumstances admit, the procedure prescribed by the Theatres Act, 1843.(a)   If the business be delegated to justices at petty sessions, it would seem that the justices must follow the procedure prescribed by the Theatres Act, 1843.(b)

With regard to other forms of amusement frequently offered to the public at fairs, it may be observed that under the Public Health Acts Amendment Act, 1890,(c) s. 38, an urban authority (d) which has adopted the Act may make by-laws for the prevention of danger from whirligigs and swings when such whirligigs and swings are driven by steam power, and from the use of firearms in shooting ranges and galleries. A person living in the neighbourhood of a fair can obtain an injunction to restrain a nuisance to him arising from the noise of steam organs played in the fair.(e) By-laws for whirligigs

Nuisances

§ 7. *Accounts.*

At common law the owner of a market or fair, as such, is under no obligation to keep accounts or publish returns of his receipts or expenditure in connection with his franchise ; and at the present day, apart from the law relating to rates and taxes, no such obligation lies upon private persons who own common law markets or fairs and take tolls under charters or by prescription for their private benefit. Various statutes, however, with reference to accounts and returns affect, as a rule, municipal corporations and district councils owning markets or fairs, undertakers of statutory markets, and public trustees or commissioners or local authorities levying tolls in markets under the authority of Parliament. These statutes may be shortly referred to by grouping markets and fairs under the following heads :—

1. *Markets and fairs owned by a municipal corporation subject to the Municipal Corporations Act,* 1882.—The municipal

(a) See 51 & 52 Vict. c. 41, s. 78. As to the proceedings of a committee of a council, see Id. s. 82.
(b) 51 & 52 Vict. c. 41 apparently gives no directions on the point.
(c) 53 & 54 Vict. c. 59.
(d) Or a rural authority with the necessary urban powers ; see ss. 5, 50.
(e) See Lambton v. Mellish [1894] 3 Ch. 163.

corporation, and their officers, must comply, with regard to accounts and returns, with the provisions contained in ss. 25-28 of the above Act.(*a*) These provisions contain nothing which relates peculiarly to markets and fairs. They concern rather the general administration of municipal corporations, and therefore no further mention need be made of them.

2. *Markets established or regulated under the Public Health Act*, 1875.—The district council owning the market, and their officers, must comply, with regard to accounts and returns, with the provisions of the Public Health Act, 1875,(*b*) the District Auditors Act, 1879,(*c*) and the Local Government Act, 1894.(*d*) These provisions contain nothing which relates peculiarly to markets.

3. *Markets and fairs constructed or regulated under a special Act which incorporates s. 50 of the Markets and Fairs Clauses Act*, 1847.—Under this section, the undertakers of the market or fair must, at the end of each financial year, cause an account in abstract to be prepared, showing the whole receipt and expenditure of all rents and other moneys levied by virtue of their statutory powers during that year, under the several distinct heads of receipt and expenditure, with a statement of the balance of such account, duly audited or certified by the chairman of the undertakers, and by the auditors, if any; and, on or before the expiration of one calendar month from the day on which such accounts end, they must send a copy of the account, free of charge, to the clerk of the peace of the county in which the market or fair is situate. The section is set out in full *post*, p. 170. This section is not incorporated with the Public Health Act, 1875, and therefore its provisions do not apply to a market established or regulated under s. 167 of that Act. But they apply to a market or fair constructed or regulated by a municipal corporation under a special Act which incorporates the section.

4. *Markets provided by a local authority under the Diseases of Animals Act*, 1894, *s.* 32, *or under the earlier Contagious Diseases (Animals) Acts.*—Section 50 of the Markets and Fairs

(*a*) 45 & 46 Vict. c. 50. As to the desirability of keeping market accounts separate from other accounts, for purposes of assessment to the income tax, see A.-G. *v.* Scott (1873) 28 L.T. 302, and *post*, p. 116.
(*b*) 38 & 39 Vict. c. 55, ss. 245-250.
(*c*) 42 Vict. c. 6; see 50 & 51 Vict. c. 72.
(*d*) 56 & 57 Vict. c. 73, ss. 21 and 58.

Clauses Act, 1847, mentioned above, applies to the market, and the local authority must comply with the provisions of that section. The local authority must also comply with the provisions of s. 32 of the Diseases of Animals Act, 1894, and must therefore carry the tolls received by them to a separate account, and apply them as directed by the section, and make such periodical returns to the Board of Agriculture of their expenditure and receipts in respect of the market as the Board require. The section is set out in full *post*, p. 191.

5. *Markets in respect of which tolls or dues are levied by authority of parliament.*—Under the Local Taxation Returns Acts, 1860 and 1877,(*a*) the clerk or treasurer of a market authority which levies, or orders to be levied, under the authority of parliament, any tolls or dues in respect of the market, is required to make an annual return to the Local Government Board of the sums levied or received by or in respect of such tolls and dues and of the expenditure thereof. As a rule, the accounts must be made up to Lady Day in each year, and the return sent in within one month after being audited. The material provisions of these Acts are set out *post*, p. 202.

These Acts do not extend to 'any tolls or dues taken by any joint stock company as profits of their undertaking, or to any tolls or dues taken by prescription or otherwise as private property.'(*b*) And the following classes of markets are exempt from the operation of the Acts :—

(1) Markets which belong to municipal corporations to which the Municipal Corporations Act, 1882, applies.(*c*)

(2) Markets provided under the Diseases of Animals Act, 1894, by a county council (*d*) or borough council.(*e*)

(3) Markets belonging to a district council the accounts of which are audited by a district auditor: *unless* the Local Government Board require the return to be made.(*f*)

The Acts, however, apply to markets with statutory tolls, if vested in public bodies other than those above mentioned ; unless the officers of such bodies are exempted from the operation of the Acts by any other Act of Parliament.

(*a*) 23 & 24 Vict. c. 51 ; 40 & 41 Vict. c. 66.
(*b*) 23 & 24 Vict. c. 51, s. 8.
(*c*) 45 & 46 Vict. c. 50, s. 5, and Sched. I. part 2.
(*d*) *Ibid.* and 51 & 52 Vict. c. 41, s. 71.
(*e*) *Ibid.* (*f*) 42 Vict. c. 6, s. 3.

CHAPTER VIII

RATES AND TAXES

§ 1. *Land tax.*

UNDER the Land Tax Acts, 1797 and 1798,(*a*) all lands and tenements, tolls, yearly profits, and all hereditaments of what nature or kind soever they be, and all persons having or holding the same, stand charged with the land tax. Market-places are lands and tenements, and franchises of markets and fairs are hereditaments. They are therefore liable to the tax.

'Tolls' here include tolls leviable by authority of a statute in respect of a franchise created by statute or otherwise, or in respect of the user of land,(*b*) and the latter tolls form a separate tenement and hereditament distinct from the land.(*c*) Stallages seem to be included in the word 'tolls'; at any rate, they are included in the word 'tenements.'(*d*)

Land tax is generally payable by four quarterly payments in every year ;(*e*) but as fairs are usually held only for some short time in the year, this method of payment is unsuitable to fairs. Accordingly, the entire sum assessed for the whole year on a fair, and the booths, stalls, and standings in the fair, is to be demanded by the collector, at any time within seven days after the first proclaiming of the fair, from the persons who set to sale any goods or merchandises in the fair, booths, stalls, or standings, or otherwise occupy the same, or, if they cannot be found, upon the premises charged with the assessment.(*f*) And in default of payment, the sum assessed is to be levied by distress and sale of all the goods and chattels to

(*a*) 38 Geo. III. c. 5, s. 4; 38 Geo. III. c. 60.
(*b*) Charing Cross Bridge Co. *v.* Mitchell (1855) 4 E. & B. 549; Vauxhall Bridge Co. *v.* Sawyer (1851) 6 Exch. 504.
(*c*) *Ibid.*
(*d*) *Ibid.*
(*e*) 38 Geo. III. c. 5, s. 4.
(*f*) *Ibid.* s. 125. As to the town of Cambridge, see s. 124.

Land Tax

be found in the booths, stalls or standings.(*a*) But the tenants of the booths, stalls, and standings which are rated are required and authorised to pay the sum or sums rated thereon, and to deduct the same out of the rent payable for such booths to their landlords.(*b*)

In case of non-payment, within six days after demand, of the tax charged on any tolls or profits of a market or fair, which are not distrainable, the collector, constable, or other officer thereunto appointed by warrant under the hands and seals of any two of the commissioners, may seize and sell so much of the tolls or profits as may be sufficient for levying the tax and all the charges occasioned by non-payment, rendering any overplus to the owner.(*c*)

Under the Taxes Management Act, 1880,(*d*) if a person charged with the tax refuses to pay it on demand made by the collector, the collector may distrain him by his goods and chattels, and may sell the distress by public auction at the expiration of five days ; and if there be no sufficient distress the defaulter is liable to be committed to prison.

§ 2. *Income tax.*

Under Schedule (A) of the Income Tax Act, 1853,(*e*) income tax is payable yearly in respect of the property in rights of markets and fairs, and in tolls, upon the annual value of the property.

The general rules for estimating such property are contained in Schedule (A), No. iii., of the Income Tax Act, 1842.(*f*)

Under these rules, the annual value of the property is understood to be the full amount of profits received from the property within the preceding year. The tax may be charged either on the persons or corporation carrying on the concern or on their agents having the management thereof or being in receipt of the profits thereof.(*g*) It is to be charged on the amount of the profits before they are paid or distributed to or between the persons who claim the profits ; and such persons

---

(*a*) 38 Geo. III. c. 5, ss. 125, 126. As to distress, see s. 17.
(*b*) *Ibid.* s. 126. As to deducting from rent, see ss. 17, 18. The deduction must be made from the current rent ; Andrew *v.* Hancock (1819) 1 Bro. & Bing. 37 ; Stubbs *v.* Parsons (1820) 3 B. & Ald. 516.
(*c*) *Ibid.* s. 42.   (*d*) 43 & 44 Vict. c. 19, ss. 86 *et seq.*
(*e*) 16 & 17 Vict. c. 34, s. 2.
(*f*) 5 & 6 Vict. c. 35, s. 60, Schedule (A), No. iii., third case.
(*g*) *Ibid.*

must allow the tax to be deducted out of the profits. The charge is to be made on the profits of the concern, exclusive of profits from land used in the concern.(*a*)

Under the Revenue Act, 1866,(*b*) the concern is made chargeable and assessable to the tax in the manner mentioned in the Income Tax Act, 1842, Schedule (A), No. iii., according to the rules prescribed by Schedule (D) of that Act, so far as such rules are consistent with Schedule (A), No. iii.

But, though the rules prescribed by Schedule (D) apply to the concern, the concern still remains chargeable under Schedule (A) ; and therefore, notwithstanding s. 101 of the Act of 1842, the tax must be assessed on the profits of a market or fair as a separate concern, and the accounts of the market or fair may not be combined with the accounts of any other concern for the purpose of setting off profits from the former against losses in the latter.(*c*)

The Act of 1842 requires the persons or corporation carrying on the concern, or their agents liable to be charged with the tax, to make an annual return of the amount of the profits received from the concern in the preceding year.(*d*) And the Act renders every owner or occupier of a market or fair, or receiver of the profits thereof, answerable for the tax charged thereon : and entitles every such receiver to retain and deduct the tax out of such profits : and authorises the collector to recover the tax by distress upon any person answerable therefor.(*e*)

Proceedings for the recovery of the tax by distress upon the goods and chattels of a defaulter are regulated by the Taxes Management Act, 1880,(*f*) which renders the defaulter liable to be committed to prison in the absence of such distress.(*g*)

(*a*) 5 & 6 Vict. c. 35, s. 60, Schedule (A), No. iii., third case.
(*b*) 29 & 30 Vict. c. 36, s. 8. For Schedule (D), see the Act of 1842, s. 100. The concern falls within the first case mentioned in the rules.
(*c*) A.-G. *v.* Scott (1873) 28 L.T. 302 ; Re Corporation of Birmingham (1875) 1 Tax Cas. 26. In these cases the question arose with regard to corporations owning markets; but it seems that the principle applies equally to individuals. See also Coltness Iron Co. *v.* Black (1881) 6 App. Cas. 315.
(*d*) 5 & 6 Vict. c. 35, s. 190, Schedule (G), iii. See also ss. 47 *et seq.*
(*e*) s. 72. As to the right of receivers to deduct the tax out of all moneys coming to their hands as such receivers, see also s. 44.
(*f*) 43 & 44 Vict. c. 19, ss. 86–88, 90. See *ante*, p. 115.
(*g*) ss. 89–91.

§ 3. Rates.

A market-place, or market-house, is rateable property under 43 Eliz. c. 2. In estimating the yearly value of a market-place profits from stallage and piccage must be taken into account, as enhancing the value of the occupation.(a) A person using a stall has, for the time being, the use and occupation of that portion of the soil on which the stall stands, and whatever profit is made by the occupation of the soil is properly rated.(a)

But franchise tolls, which are payable merely as market tolls for the use of a market, must not be taken into account in estimating the yearly value of the occupation of the market-place ; nor are such tolls rateable property.(b)

Such tolls are incorporeal hereditaments, not incident to or arising out of the occupation of the soil. They are usually payable in respect of goods sold in the market-place, and are quite different in their nature from a compensation paid to the owner of the soil or his lessee for the use of the soil. They are payable irrespective of the ownership or occupation of the soil.(c)

Tolls payable by statute, not upon the sale of goods in a market, but upon the mere entry of goods into the market, have been held to be franchise tolls for the use of the market, and not stallage tolls for the occupation of the soil. Such tolls, therefore, must not be considered in rating the market-place.(d)

But charges made by the occupier of a market for admission thereto are necessarily incidental to the use of the soil, if they cannot be supported as due to a franchise, whether by charter, prescription, statute, or otherwise ; and such charges must be taken into consideration in estimating the value of the occupation.(e) This rule, it seems, must apply equally

---

(a) Roberts v. Overseers of Aylesbury (1853) 1 E. & B. 423 ; and see Worcester v. St. Clement's (1858) 22 J.P. 319 ; Reg. v. Derby J.J. (1856) 28 L.T.O.S. 89 ; Reg. v. Barnard Castle (1863) 27 J.P. 534 ; and as to deductions see Brecon Markets Co. v. St. Mary's, Brecon (1877) 36 L.T.N.S. 109.

(b) R. v. Casswell (1872) L.R. 7 Q.B. 328 ; R. v. Bell (1816) 5 M. & S. 221.

(c) See Roberts v. Overseers of Aylesbury (1853) 1 E. & B. 423.

(d) R. v. Casswell (1872) L.R. 7 Q.B. 328 ; Mayor of London v. Overseers of St. Sepulchre (1871) Id. 333 n.

(e) Percy v. Ashford Union (1876) 34 L.T.N.S. 579.

whether the market itself can be supported as a franchise or not.

The onus of showing that a charge is due to a franchise lies upon the person who asserts that it is.(a)

All payments made for any occupation of the soil of a market-place beyond that to which the general public is entitled are payments in the nature of stallage, and therefore to be taken into account in making the rate. It is not necessary that the payments should be made in respect of a single separate stall for each holder, so long as a distinct portion of the soil is allotted. A payment is stallage equally whether there be a single stall for each holder or a comparatively small portion of the market be assigned to a certain number of holders by a sort of tenancy in common. It is enough if the payment be made for some standing room in the market, as distinct from the mere entrance into it. Such a payment is made in respect of the soil, and enhances the value of the occupation.(b)

Accordingly, payments taken at Deptford Foreign Cattle Market on the landing of cattle there, for 'wharfage, lairage, market dues and charges,' under which the cattle might be kept in the market for ten days, were held to be payments for the use and occupation of the soil, and therefore rateable.(c) In this case the consignees had no right to have the cattle kept in any particular pens, but only in such pens as the clerk of the market authority might direct, and the clerk was entitled to have the cattle shifted from one pen to another.

Stall-holders

Holders of stalls in markets are not generally rateable in respect of their occupation of such stalls. It is submitted that a stall-holder might have such an occupation as would make him liable to be rated ; and as a matter of fact the holders of stalls in the central avenue of Covent Garden Market pay rates in respect of their stalls. But usually a stall-holder's occupation is too fleeting to render him properly liable.(d)

In 1880 an attempt was made to rate a stall-holder in

(a) Percy v. Ashford Union (1876) 34 L.T.N.S. 579, per Field, J.
(b) Duke of Bedford v. Overseers of St. Paul, Covent Garden (1881) 51 L.J.M.C. 41.
(c) Mayor of London v. Assessment Committee of Greenwich Union (1883) 48 L.T.N.S. 437.
(d) Per Coleridge, J., in Roberts v. Overseers of Aylesbury (1853) 1 E. & B. 423 ; see also R. v. Mosley (1823) 2 B. & C. 226.

Bodmin Market.(a) It appeared that his stalls were capable of being removed, and were liable to be removed from one spot to another, provided that they continued in the same position relatively to other stalls. He therefore had no exclusive right to any definite portion of the soil, and for this reason it was held that he had no rateable occupation.

But this reason would not apply to fixed stalls, occupied exclusively for a year or a longer period, such as are found in some markets ; and there seems to be no reason why the holders of such stalls should not be rated.

Stall-holders who occupy fixed spaces at a fixed rent of not less than ten pounds a year may be qualified to be on the Parliamentary and Local Government Registers as occupation voters.(b)

(a) Spear v. Guardians of Bodmin Union (1880) 49 L.J.M.C. 69.
(b) Hall v. Metcalfe [1892] 1 Q.B. 208 ; 48 Vict. c. 3, s. 5 ; 51 & 52 Vict. c. 10, s. 3.

CHAPTER IX

SALES IN MARKETS AND FAIRS

§ 1. *The law as to sale of goods in market overt.*

The rule   As a general rule, where goods are sold by a person who is not the owner, and who does not sell them under the authority or with the consent of the owner, the buyer acquires no better title than the seller had. But where goods are sold in market overt, according to the usage of the market, the buyer acquires a good title to the goods, provided he buys them in good faith and without notice of any defect or want of title on the part of the seller.(*a*)

Origin of the rule   The law as to sales in market overt arose at a time when there was much greater simplicity in transactions between buyer and seller. The practice then was to sell and buy in markets and fairs. Shops were very few, and persons whose goods were taken feloniously knew where to resort in order to prevent their being sold. We can therefore well understand how the law was established for the protection of buyers. If a man did not pursue his goods to market, where such goods were openly sold, he ought not to interfere with the right of the honest and *bona fide* purchaser. But still, the law gives him this protection, that the goods must be exposed for sale and the whole transaction begun, continued, and completed in open market, so as to give full opportunity to the owner to pursue them and prevent their sale.(*b*)

(*a*) See the Sale of Goods Act, 1893 (56 & 57 Vict. c. 71) ss. 21, 22. The sections contain certain qualifications to the general rule, not expressed in the text. As to horses, see *post*, p. 126. For a clear statement of the common law, see per Lord Cairns (1878) Cundy *v.* Lindsay, 3 App. Cas. 459, 463.

(*b*) See per Cockburn, C.J., in Crane *v.* London Dock Co. (1864) 5 B. & S. 313, 318; 33 L.J.Q.B. 224, 228. The law on this subject was well established by the time of Henry VI.; see Y.B. 9 Hen. VI. f. 45 b: 35 Hen. VI. f. 29: 11 Ed. IV. f. 6: 12 Ed. IV. ff. 8, 12 b: Jenk. Rep. 83. It probably originated in the merchant law administered in courts of pie

The Law as to Sale of Goods in Market Overt

It seems to be clear that at common law a sale in an open fair gives the same protection as a sale in an open market,(a) and that in the Sale of Goods Act, 1893, which now contains the law on this subject, the word 'market' includes 'fair.'(b) *In what markets*

The market must be an open, public and legally constituted market.(c) Therefore a sale by public auction at a horse repository is generally not within the rule.(d) Whether a sale in a modern statutory market is within the rule is perhaps doubtful. In one English case counsel seem to have admitted that such a sale was not a sale in market overt ;(e) but in the Irish Courts (f) the contrary has been decided. It is difficult to see upon what principle a sale in a statutory market should not have the same effect as a sale in a market granted by charter, as the doctrine of market overt depends not on the origin of the market, but on the publicity of the sale. Moreover, we have seen that there is some ground for the opinion that modern statutory markets have all the incidents of franchise markets, except in so far as such incidents are expressly or impliedly modified or taken away by the Acts under which the markets are established.(g)

A sale in market overt does not protect the buyer unless the whole transaction of contract and sale is begun and concluded in the market.(h) A bargain outside the market that the buyer shall have the option of purchasing in the market at a particular price, followed by such purchase, is not a sale in *What is a sale in market overt*

---

powder. The custom seems to have been known on the continent as early as the ninth century A.D. Notker, who was living about 850 A.D., says that 'merchants contend that the purchase which is made at an annual fair should be valid, whether it be just or unjust, because it is their custom ;' see *Report of Royal Commission*, vol. i. p. 4. The Anglo-Saxon law required that all goods above a certain value should be sold in market-towns (ports), and that the sale should be witnessed by the port-reeve or other persons. A sale so conducted did not give the buyer an absolute title available against the true owner of goods which had been stolen, but it protected him from the consequences of being found in possession of stolen property ; see the *Laws of Ina, Athelstan, Cnut, and William the Conqueror*, edit. of 1840, pp. 51, 87, 88, 167, 209, 212.

(a) See, e.g., Comyns *v.* Boyer (1596) Cro. Eliz. 485; and see 2 Black. Comm. 449 ; 2 Inst. 713.
(b) s. 22 (1). 'Every fair is a market'; 2 Inst. 406 ; cf. *ante*, p. 100.
(c) Lee *v.* Bayes (1856) 18 C.B. 599.   (d) *Ibid.*
(e) Moyce *v.* Newington (1878) 4 Q.B.D. 32. The case was overruled, but not on this point, in Bentley *v.* Vilmont (1887) 12 App. Cas. 471.
(f) Ganly *v.* Ledwidge (1876) 10 Ir. Rep. C.L. 33.
(g) See *ante*, pp. 26, 87, 121.   (h) 2 Inst. 713 (9th point).

market overt.(a) Nor is a sale by sample, for a sale in market overt requires that the commodity should be openly sold and delivered in the market.(b). The sale must take place in the usual market-place, upon the lawful day for holding the market, during the usual market hours, and not at night.(c). In markets in which tolls are payable the buyer is not protected unless payment be made of the toll which is due upon the sale; but in markets which are toll-free the sale changes the property, though no toll be paid.(d) It has been held that the burden of showing that toll was due, and was not paid, lies upon the party impeaching the sale.(e) The protection only extends to things which are vendible in the market.(f)

City of London

By the custom of the city of London, every shop in the city which is open to the public is market overt between sunrise and sun-set, on all days except Sundays and holidays; but it is market overt only for such goods as the shop-keeper professes to trade in; and it seems that the custom does not apply where the shop-keeper is the buyer, and not the seller, of the goods.(g)

Limitations of rule

The principal limitation upon the doctrine of sale in market overt is that the buyer is not protected unless he buy 'in good faith and without any notice of any defect or want of title on the part of the seller.' The common law limitation to this effect (h) is expressly retained by the Act of 1893.(i) The Act also provides that the sale must be 'according to the

(a) Roll. Abr. 'Market,' E; Dyer, p. 99 b, pl. 66.
(b) Hill v. Smith (1812) 4 Taunt. 520, 532; Crane v. London Dock Co. (1864) 5 B. & S. 313.
(c) 2 Black. Comm. 449; 2 Inst. 713 (2nd, 3rd, 11th points); Clifton v. Chancellor (1600) Moore, 624; Harvey v. Facy (1594) 2 And. 115; Godb. 131.
(d) Comyns v. Boyer (1596) Cro. Eliz. 485; 2 Inst. 713 (10th point); Y.B. 12 Ed. IV. ff. 8, 9; 35 Hen. VI. f. 29; Jenk. Rep. 83.
(e) Comyns v. Boyer, supra; but see Moran v. Pitt (1873) 42 L.J.Q.B. 47.
(f) Case of Market Overt (1896) 5 Co. Rep. 83 b; 2 Inst. 713.
(g) 2 Blac. Com. 449; case of Market Overt (1596) 5 Rep. 83 b, Cro. Eliz. 454; S.C. sub. nom. L'Evesque de Worcester's case, Moore 360, Popham 84; Taylor v. Chambers (1604) Cro. Jac. 68; Anon. (1701) 12 Mod. 521; Wilkinson v. King (1810) 2 Camp. 335; Lyons v. De Pass (1840) 11 A. & E. 326; Hargreave v. Spink [1892] 1 Q.B. 25. In Clifton v. Chancellor (1600) Moore, 624, a similar custom was alleged to exist in Bristol.
(h) See 2 Inst. 713 (5th, 6th, and 7th points).
(i) 56 & 57 Vict. c. 71, s. 22 (1) and s. 62 (2).

The Law as to Sale of Goods in Market Overt 123

usage of the market'; (*a*) and that there is to be no change in the law relating to the sale of horses.(*b*) Buyers of horses, therefore, are not protected unless the sale take place with the formalities prescribed by 2 Ph. & M. c. 7, and 31 Eliz. c. 12.(*c*)

Before the passing of the Sale of Goods Act, the crown was not affected by an unauthorised sale in market overt of goods belonging to the crown ;(*d*) and the Act, though silent upon the point, has not altered the law in this respect, as it does not purport to bind the crown. Before the Act, the rule was that the property in goods was not affected by a transaction in market overt if one of the parties to the transaction had no capacity to buy or sell ;(*e*) and the Act appears to have preserved this rule.(*f*)

The doctrine does not protect the seller, against whom an action of trover may lie, though he act innocently,(*g*) and even though he be a public sales-master selling by auction in a market in the ordinary course of his duty.(*h*)

It remains to be stated that in the case of stolen goods (*i*) the title acquired by a buyer in market overt is liable to be defeated. 'Where goods have been stolen and the offender is prosecuted to conviction, the property in the goods so stolen revests in the person who was the owner of the goods, or his personal representative, notwithstanding any intermediate dealing with them, whether by sale in market overt or otherwise.'(*j*)

If the conviction be upon an indictment by or on behalf of the owner or his personal representative, the court before whom the offender is tried (*k*) has power to award a writ of restitution for the stolen goods, or to order their restitution in summary manner.(*l*)

Revesting and restitution.

(*a*) s. 22 (1).
(*b*) s. 22 (2), which prevents s. 22 (1) from applying to the sale of horses. But s. 24 (see *post*) applies. (*c*) See *post*, p. 126.
(*d*) 2 Blac. Comm. 449 ; 2 Inst. 713 (1st point).
(*e*) 2 Inst. 713 (8th point). (*f*) See s. 2.
(*g*) Peer *v.* Humphrey (1835) 2 A. & E. 495 ; Delaney *v.* Wallis (1883) 14 L.R. Ir. 31.
(*h*) Ganly *v.* Ledwidge (1876) 10 Ir. Rep. C.L. 33. See further, as to the liability of auctioneers, Consolidated Co. *v.* Curtis [1892] 1 Q.B. 495.
(*i*) Including horses. As to horses, see also *post*, p. 127.
(*j*) Sale of Goods Act, 1893 (56 & 57 Vict. c. 71) s. 24 (1).
(*k*) See Reg. *v.* Mayor of London (1869) L.R. 4 Q.B. 371.
(*l*) The Larceny Act, 1861 (24 & 25 Vict. c. 96) s. 100.

124   *Sales in Markets and Fairs*

The same court (a) has similar power where the prosecution is by the Director of Public Prosecutions, provided that the owner has given to the Director all reasonable information and assistance.(b) If he fail or neglect to obtain such writ or order, and though he have taken no part in the prosecution, the owner can still recover his goods by action.(c)

The rule that the goods are to be restored upon an indictment and conviction for stealing is as old as 21 Henry VIII. c. 11.(d) The provisions in the Larceny Act, 1861, s. 100, widened the rule by providing for the restoration of the goods upon a conviction for any offence mentioned in that Act, and consisting in 'stealing, taking, obtaining, extorting, embezzling, converting, or disposing of, or in knowingly receiving' the goods.(e) In Bentley *v.* Vilmont (f) the House of Lords decided, with some reluctance, that the effect of this section was to revest the goods, even as against an innocent buyer in market overt, upon a conviction for obtaining the goods by false pretences, notwithstanding that the owner had been induced to pass to the offender the property in the goods, as well as their possession.

It is probably in consequence of this decision that the Sale of Goods Act, 1893, provides that 'notwithstanding any enactment to the contrary, where goods have been obtained by fraud or other wrongful means not amounting to larceny, the property in such goods shall not revest in the person who

(a) See Reg. *v.* Mayor of London (1869) L.R. 4 Q.B. 371.
(b) 42 & 43 Vict. c. 22, s. 7. As to orders for restitution upon a summary conviction, see the Summary Jurisdiction Act, 1879 (42 & 43 Vict. c. 49) s. 27 (3).
(c) Scattergood *v.* Sylvester (1850) 15 Q.B. 506. The Sale of Goods Act, 1893, does not make prosecution by the *owner* a condition of the goods revesting.
(d) Repealed by 7 & 8 Geo. IV. c. 27. The substituted enactment in 7 & 8 Geo. IV. c. 29, s. 57, was repealed by 24 & 25 Vict. c. 95. The Act of Hen. VIII. does not seem to have altered the earlier law, except by putting an indictment on the same footing as a writ of appeal; see Golightly *v.* Reynolds (1772) Lofft. 88, 90, per Lord Mansfield; 2 Inst. 714; Bracton, lib. 3, cap. 32, fol. 151.
(e) 24 & 25 Vict. c. 96, s. 100. Under this section the goods do not revest unless the indictment be by or on behalf of the owner or his personal representative. The section contains a proviso that nothing in the section shall apply to the case of any prosecution of any trustee, banker, merchant, attorney, factor, broker, or other agent entrusted with the possession of goods or documents of title to goods, for any *misdemeanour* against the Act. As to this proviso, see Payne *v.* Wilson [1895] 1 Q.B. 653, 659; 2 Q.B. 537.
(f) (1887) 12 App. Cas. 471.

was the owner of the goods, or his personal representative, by reason only of the conviction of the offender.'(a) The effect of this provision appears to be that the decision in Bentley v. Vilmont (b) is no longer law, and that, notwithstanding the Larceny Act, 1861, s. 100, goods do not now revest upon a conviction unless they were obtained by wrongful means amounting to larceny.

None but *stolen* goods revest under s. 24 (1) of the Sale of Goods Act, 1893. It seems that if goods are embezzled by a clerk or servant, they are 'stolen' within the meaning of that sub-section, and do not fall within the provision in s. 24 (2), which relates to goods obtained by fraud or other wrongful means not amounting to larceny.(c)

Before the Sale of Goods Act, 1893, stolen goods revested upon the conviction of a receiver for knowingly receiving them, and it was not essential to obtain the conviction of the actual thief.(d) It is submitted that this is still the law, although the Act of 1893 is not explicit upon the point. There seems to be nothing in s. 24 (2) to alter the law in this respect.

Notwithstanding the prosecution of the thief to conviction, the title acquired by a buyer in market overt will not be defeated if the buyer can avail himself of the provisions of the Factors Acts or any enactment enabling the apparent owner of goods to dispose of them as if he were the true owner.(e)

Although the conviction revests the property, yet until the conviction the title acquired by buying in market overt remains good. Accordingly, the owner has no right of action against the buyer if the buyer parts with or consumes the goods before the conviction, even though he does so with notice of the theft.(f) Nor has the buyer any claim against the owner for the expenses he incurred in keeping the goods before they revested.(g)

(a) 56 & 57 Vict. c. 71, s. 24 (2).   (b) *Supra*.
(c) See 24 & 25 Vict. c. 96, ss. 67-73. The misdemeanours dealt with in ss. 75-87 of that Act seem not to 'amount to larceny.'
(d) See 24 & 25 Vict. c. 96, s. 100.
(e) Sale of Goods Act, 1893 (56 & 57 Vict. c. 71) s. 21 (2) (a); see Payne v. Wilson [1895] 1 Q.B. 653, 661; 2 Q.B. 537.
(f) Horwood v. Smith (1788) 2 T.R. 750. Only persons in possession of the goods at or after the date of the conviction are liable to the owner; *Ibid.*; see Lindsay v. Cundy (1878) 3 Q.B.D. 348, 3 App. Cas. 459.
(g) Walker v. Matthews (1881) 8 Q.B.D. 109.

§ 2. *Sale of horses.*

Sales of horses, mares, geldings, colts, and fillies in markets and fairs ought to be conducted with the formalities prescribed by the statutes passed in 1555 and 1589 to prevent horse-stealing.(*a*) These statutes modify in the case of such sales the general doctrine as to the title acquired by buying in market overt.(*b*) But subject to those modifications the doctrine applies to such sales, by the common law.(*c*)

It is the duty of the owner, bailiff, or steward of every market or fair at which horses are sold to appoint and limit out yearly a certain and special open place for such sales, and to put in and appoint a sufficient person to take toll (if any) and keep the open place from 10 A.M. until sunset on every market or fair day.(*c*) The duties of the toll-gatherer are to take the toll payable on any sale at the open place, and between 10 A.M. and sunset on the day of the sale, and not at any other place or time : to have before him at the taking of the toll the parties to the sale and also the horse sold : and then and there to make the necessary entries relating to the sale in the book to be kept for that purpose.(*e*) The toll-gatherer or book-keeper must, within one day after the market or fair, deliver the book to the owner, bailiff, or steward, who must then make and sign a note of the true number of sales at the market or fair.(*f*) Penalties are imposed for breaches of these duties.(*g*)

Every horse which is sold in the market or fair must be openly exposed in the open place appointed for the sales, in the time of the market or fair at which it is sold, by the space of one hour together at least, between 10 A.M. and sunset.(*h*) And the parties to the sale must, before sunset on the day of the sale,(*i*) come together, bringing the horse with them, into

---

(*a*) 2 & 3 Ph. & M. c. 7 ; 31 Eliz. c. 12. As to the extent to which horses were stolen, and stolen horses sold in markets and fairs, in the sixteenth century, see the 'Description of England' in Holinshed's *Chronicles* (edit. 1587), Bk. 2, ch. 11

(*b*) See *ante*, pp. 120 *et. seq.* For a form of proclamation, in connection with these statutes, used at the opening of the horse-fairs held at York, see Drake's *History of York* (1736), p. 218.

(*c*) 56 & 57 Vict. c. 71, s. 22 (1) does not apply to the sale of horses ; see s. 22 (2) ; but s. 24 applies.

(*d*) 2 & 3 Ph. & M. c. 7, s. 1. (*e*) *Ibid.* (*f*) *Ibid.*
(*g*) *Ibid.* : see ss. 2 *ad fin.*, 3. (*h*) *Ibid.* s. 2.
(*i*) 2 & 3 Ph. & M. c. 7, s. 1.

Sale of Horses

the open place to the toll-gatherer or book-keeper there, and cause him to make the necessary entries in the book, at the same time paying to him the toll, if there be any, or, if there be no toll, then one penny for making the entries.(*a*)

The entries prescribed by the earlier statute are the colour or colours and at least one special mark of the horse, and the full names and dwelling-places of the buyer and seller.(*b*) The later statute requires entries also to be made of the true price or value given for the horse, and (besides the full name, dwelling-place and occupation of the seller) either an entry that the book-keeper knows the seller, and his name, dwelling-place and occupation, or, if that be not the case, then an entry of the name, dwelling-place, and occupation of some creditable person known to the book-keeper, then and there declaring that he has the necessary knowledge of the seller.(*c*) This statute imposes penalties in respect of false declarations and entries ;(*d*) and gives the buyer a right to receive a copy of the entries upon payment of twopence.(*e*)

If the requirements of the statutes are not strictly complied with, and the horse has been stolen or wrongfully taken from its owner, the sale does not take the property out of the owner, who may retake the horse wherever he happens to find it, or may recover it by action.(*f*) This appears to be the case, notwithstanding the *bona fides* of the buyer, if the seller or his voucher be entered in the book by a false name.(*g*) The onus of proving that the requirements of the statutes were complied with lies upon the buyer or other person relying upon that fact.(*h*)

Moreover, although all the requirements of the statutes be complied with, yet if the sale be of a horse stolen within six months before the sale, the property is not taken away from the owner, provided that he take the prescribed steps to recover

Recovery of stolen horse

(*a*) 2 & 3 Ph. & M. c. 7, s. 2; cf. ss. 1, 4.
(*b*) 2 Ph. & M. c. 7, ss. 1, 2.   (*c*) 31 Eliz. c. 12, s. 1.
(*d*) *Ibid.*   (*e*) *Ibid.*
(*f*) 2 & 3 Ph. & M. c. 7, s. 2; 31 Eliz. c. 12, s. 1 ; see 2 Inst. 717 ; Com. Dig. Market, E ; 2 Black. Com. 451; Moran *v*. Pitt (1873) 42 L.J.Q.B. 47.
(*g*) Gibb's case (1588) Owen 27, 1 Leon. 158 ; Barker *v*. Reading (1627) W. Jones, 163 ; Palm. 485 ; 2 Inst. 717. The decision in Wikes *v*. Morefoots (1588) Cro. Eliz. 86, was probably wrong.
(*h*) Moran *v*. Pitt (1873) 42 L.J.Q.B. 47 ; see North *v*. Jackson (1859) 2 F. & F. 198.

the horse.(a) For this purpose he must, within six months after the theft, make a claim to the horse before some justice of the peace at the place where the horse happens to be found, and then within the next forty days prove by two sufficient witnesses his title to the horse and its theft from him within six months before his claim. If he establish his case he is entitled to recover the horse upon paying or tendering to the person in possession of it the sum which that person deposes that he paid for the horse *bona fide* and without fraud or collusion.(b)

Until the theft has been proved, a justice ought not to order a seizure of the horse if in the hands of an innocent buyer.(c)

§ 3. *Sale of hay and straw in markets in and near the metropolis.*

Markets for the sale of hay or straw which are held in or within thirty miles of the cities of London and Westminster are subject to the provisions of the Hay and Straw Acts, 1796, 1834, 1856.(d) Reference has already been made to the provisions of these Acts with regard to market hours,(e) and the weighing of hay and straw.(f) But there still remain some other provisions to which it is necessary to refer, and particularly the provision of the Act of 1796 which requires a public book or register of sales to be kept in each of these markets.(g)

Register of sales

In the city of London this book or register must be kept by the clerk or toll-gatherer appointed by the corporation; and elsewhere by 'the clerk or toll-gatherer appointed within their several jurisdictions.'(h)

Upon any sale of hay or straw exceeding four trusses in one quantity being made within the limits within which the Act applies,(i) it is the duty of the seller to make and subscribe the prescribed entries in the register of the market in which the sale was made, or, if it was made out of the market, then in the register of the market nearest to the place of sale. The

(a) 31 Eliz. c. 12, s. 3.　　　　(b) *Ibid.*
(c) Joseph *v.* Adkins (1817) 2 Stark. 76.
(d) 36 Geo. III. c. 88 ; 4 & 5 Will. IV. c. 21 ; 19 & 20 Vict. c. 114.
(e) See *ante*, p. 53.
(f) See *ante*, p. 103.　　(g) 36 Geo III. c. 88, s. 10.　　(h) *Ibid.*
(i) I.e. in, or within 30 miles of, the cities of London and Westminster.

Sale of Hay and Straw in and near the Metropolis 129

prescribed entries are the names and places of abode of the buyer and seller, and their principals (if any), the place of sale, and the price paid or agreed. These entries must be made and subscribed before 6 P.M. on the day of the sale if it was made in any market, or within seven days after the sale if it was made out of market ; and the book-keeper is entitled to a fee of 1*d.* for each sale entered.(*a*)

The book must be kept at some convenient place in the market, and must be open to every person applying to inspect it and paying 1*d.* for the inspection, at all times between 9 A.M. and 6 P.M. on every day except Sundays.(*a*)

Penalties are imposed upon sellers who omit to make the required entries in the register and upon keepers of registers who knowingly suffer untrue entries to be made or refuse inspection of the book to a person tendering the inspection fee.(*a*)

The Act expressly provides that no entries need be made in the register with regard to hay or straw delivered within the above-mentioned limits under a special contract, but that entries must be made of all hay and straw which is sent to a market or place within those limits to be there sold, and which is accordingly sold there.(*b*)

The Act of 1796 imposes penalties for buying hay or straw on its way to the market (forestalling), and for buying in the market for the purpose of selling again in the market (regrating) ;(*c*) and also for not bringing to the market on the ensuing market-day hay or straw exposed for sale, and not sold, on any market-day.(*d*) Forestalling and regrating

With regard to other provisions of the Acts, it may be mentioned that the Act of 1796 prohibits the clerk or toll-gatherer of any market to which the Act applies from buying or selling, or being concerned in the buying or selling of, any hay or straw within the limits of the Act.(*e*) It also prohibits common salesmen from dealing in hay, straw or grass on their own account.(*f*) The Act of 1856 requires salesmen selling in any market or place within the limits of the Act to deliver, with the delivery of any hay or straw sold by them, a ticket stating the number of trusses sold and the name and address of the owner.(*g*)

(*a*) 36 Geo. III. c. 88, s. 10.   (*b*) *Ibid.* s. 11.
(*c*) *Ibid.* s. 18.   (*d*) *Ibid.* s. 23.   (*e*) *Ibid.* s. 12.
(*f*) s. 8.   (*g*) 19 & 20 Vict. c. 114, s. 2.

CHAPTER X

PROCEDURE AND EVIDENCE

§ 1. *Scire facias.*

The appropriate process for obtaining the repeal of a charter or letters patent for holding a market or fair is that of *scire facias*. The action of *scire facias* to repeal a grant by charter or letters patent is a proceeding taken by or on behalf of the crown upon information that the grant is void because unadvisedly made or improperly obtained, or that it has become forfeited through misuse or abuse, or through non-fulfilment of conditions attached to the grant.(*a*) These grounds for instituting proceedings by *scire facias* have been already referred to in earlier pages of this work.(*b*)

The writ of *scire facias* was formerly issued from the Petty Bag Office in Chancery. It now issues, since the abolition of that office, from the Crown Office.(*c*) It can only issue upon a fiat of the Attorney-General, who has the right and duty of controlling the action, and of determining upon what and whose information, and on what terms and security as to costs, he will permit the action to be prosecuted. The writ issues as of right for every subject aggrieved, but not as of course for every subject applying for it.(*d*) Formerly the practice was for the Attorney-General not to grant his fiat until he had received a warrant under the sign manual directing him to cause the writ to be issued; and the warrant had to be obtained by a memorial to the crown, and was only issued upon

---

(*a*) See Eastern Archipelago Co. *v.* The Queen (1853) 2 E. & B. 856; G. E. R. Co. *v.* Goldsmid (1884) 9 App. Cas. 927, 965; Peter *v.* Kendal (1827) 6 B. & C. 703, 710; 3 Blac. Comm. 261; 4 Inst. 88.
(*b*) See *ante*, pp. 21, 90–93.
(*c*) Short & Mellor, Crown Office Pr. 444.
(*d*) R. *v.* Prosser (1848) 11 Beav. 316; Eastern Archipelago Co. *v.* The Queen (1853) 2 E. & B. 856.

Scire Facias

the Attorney-General's advice ;(a) but the modern practice seems to be for the Attorney-General to act on his own initiative.(b) He endorses his fiat upon a draft of the proposed writ, which must be submitted to him.(c)

The writ may now be issued to the sheriff of any county,(d) and it directs the sheriff to make known (e) to the defendant that he must appear and show why the charter or letters patent should not be cancelled. The sheriff, by a summons to the defendant, warns him to appear to the writ. If he fail to appear, judgment that the grant be cancelled will go against him by default. As it is unlikely that proceedings by *scire facias* will now be taken in connection with a market or fair, no further description of the practice will be given here. It is considered sufficient to refer the reader to the authorities mentioned below.(f)

§ 2. *Quo Warranto*.

A person who holds a market or levies toll without charter or other lawful authority may be proceeded against by information in the nature of a *Quo Warranto* to compel him to show by what authority the market is held or the toll levied.

Formerly the process was by Writ of *Quo Warranto*, and in the printed volume of the " Placita de Quo Warranto " (g)

(a) See Richardson's C.P. Practice, 391-398 ; Tidd's Practice, 9th ed. 1094 ; Chitty, Prerog. of Crown, 331.
(b) See 1 Webster's Patent Cases, 669 n (f) ; Foster *on Scire Facias*, 247.
(c) 1 Webster, 64 n (a) ; Foster, 249.
(d) 12 & 13 Vict. c. 109, s. 29.
(e) Hence the title 'scire facias.'
(f) See Foster *on Scire Facias* ; Godson *on Patents*, 2nd. ed. p. 269 ; 2 Tidd's Pr., 9th ed., pp. 1093 *et seq* ; Chitty, Prerog., 330, 331 ; 2 Saund. Rep. 72 a ; 1 Webster's Patent Cases, 64 n (a), 669 n (f) ; Grady & Scotland's Pr., 290 ; 2 Richardson's C.P. Pr., 391 *et seq.* ; Eastern Archipelago Co. *v.* The Queen (1853) 2 E. & B. 856, 1 Id. 310 ; R. *v.* Aires (1717) 10 Mod. 258, 354 ; R. *v.* Buller (1685) 3 Lev. 220, 2 Vent. 344 ; Basset's case (1568) Dyer, 276 b ; also Dyer, 197, 198 ; 4 Inst. 72, 88 ; R. *v.* Eyre (1717) 1 Str. 43 ; R. *v.* Miles (1797) 7 T.R. 367 ; 11 & 12 Vict. c. 94 ; Rules in Chancery of December 29, 1848, and August 3, 1849 ; 12 & 13 Vict. c. 109 ; 37 & 38 Vict. c. 81, ss. 5, 12 ; 42 & 43 Vict. c. 78, s. 4 ; R.S.C. January 30, 1889.

(g) The volume entitled *Placita de Quo Warranto* was printed under the superintendence of the Record Commission in 1818. The volume contains records of most of the *quo warranto* proceedings in the reigns of Edw. I., II., and III. As to the nature and purpose of these proceedings, see Introduction to the volume, and Stuart Moore *on Foreshore*, pp. 42-46 & 69-72.

Procedure and Evidence

many cases occur in which the titles of market-owners were enquired into and the markets seized for want of title. This writ was a writ of right for the crown against subjects who claimed or usurped any office, franchise, liberty, or privilege belonging to the crown, to enquire by what authority they maintained their claim, in order to have the right determined. It also lay in case of non-user or long neglect of a franchise, or misuser or abuse thereof; being a writ commanding the defendant to show by what warrant he exercised such a franchise, having never had any grant of it, or having forfeited it by neglect or abuse.(*a*)

Informations

This writ having fallen into disuse on account of the delay with which it was attended,(*b*) a more expeditious mode of proceeding has been adopted, viz., an information in the nature of a *quo warranto*.(*c*) This was formerly a proceeding of a criminal nature, but is now a civil proceeding for all purposes.(*d*) The proceeding supposes the defendant to be in actual, though not in legal, possession of the franchise, and judgment of ouster is necessary to dispossess him.(*e*) It is the proper process where it is desired to oust the defendant on the ground that he never had a charter,(*f*) or has lost it by misuse :(*g*) *scire facias*, where it is sought to repeal the charter under which he holds.(*h*)

To found an information in the nature of a *quo warranto* there must be both a claim of the franchise and actual user,(*i*) as by taking tolls (*j*) or holding a court of pie powder.(*k*) It is insufficient to show that the defendant holds an informal market without demanding toll,(*l*) or that he has promoted or encouraged a market : for mere promotion or encouragement is

---

(*a*) 3 Blac. Comm. 262; Com. Dig. 'Quo Warranto.'
(*b*) A very different objection to it was that judgment thereon against the crown was final; see R. *v.* Trinity House (1666) 1 Sid. 86; Anon. 12 Mod. 225.
(*c*) See 3 Blac. Comm. 262; R. *v.* Ponsonby (1755) Sayer, 245.
(*d*) 47 & 48 Vict. c. 61, s. 15.
(*e*) Peter *v.* Kendal (1827) 6 B. & C. 703, 710.
(*f*) Per Holt, C.J., R. *v.* London (1691) 1 Show 240, 4 Mod. 53.
(*g*) R. *v.* Staverton (1611) Yelv. 190.
(*h*) See *ante*, p. 130.
(*i*) Com. Dig., ' Quo Warranto,' C. (5).
(*j*) Plac. Quo Warr. (Crossthweyt) p. 115, (Emmeseye) p. 212.
(*k*) *Ante*, p. 3.
(*l*) R. *v.* ——— (1682) 2 Show. 201 ; S. C. sub. nom. R. *v.* Bradley, Tremaine, P.C. 449; Plac. Quo. Warr. (Ramesbury) p. 801.

not usurpation of the franchise.(a) So holding an annual gathering or wake is not an encroachment of a franchise, although the people buy and sell there, if no toll be taken or other franchise exercised.(b)

An information in the nature of a *quo warranto* for levying a market or fair without lawful warrant may be filed by the Attorney-General *ex officio*, in his own name, without any relator, without leave of the court, and without any recognisance. Such an information may also be exhibited and filed, by express leave of the court, in the name of the Queen's Coroner and Attorney, at the instance of a private prosecutor. Leave must be obtained in open court, by moving for a rule nisi, and the prosecutor will be required to enter into a recognisance in £50 effectually to prosecute.(c) No order for filing any information will be granted unless, at the time of moving, an affidavit be produced by which some person deposes on oath that such motion is made at his instance as relator (d)

If, upon the trial, judgment be given for the defendant, he has an allowance of his franchise.(e) If it appear that he has levied the market by wrong and without title, the judgment is that he be ousted of the market, for it has no legal existence. But if the crown granted the market to the defendant or his predecessors in title, and he has either misused or not used the market, then the judgment should be that the market be seized by the crown to be granted out again to whomsoever the crown please,(f) for the franchise is not thereby extinguished.(g) So also if the defendant does not appear, the judgment should be for seizure by the crown.(h)

(a) R. v. Marsden (1766) 1 W. Bl. 579; 3 Burr. 1812.
(b) Plac. Quo Warr., pp. 115, 212, 801; Abb. Plac. (Salingeford) p. 85.
(c) See C.O.R. 1886, r. 46; Corner, C. Pr. 180 *et seq.*; Shortt, Informations, part ii.; Short & Mellor, C.O. Pr. 279. For a precedent of an information by the A.-G., see Tremaine, P.C. 449.
(d) C.O.R. 1886, r. 54.
(e) 3 Blac. Comm. 263.
(f) Y.B. 15 Ed. IV. f. 7 b, per Billing, J., and agreed; 3 Blac. Comm. 263.
(g) Peter v. Kendal, 6 B. & C. 703, 710.
(h) Y.B. 15 Edw. IV. f. 7; R. v. Trinity House (1666) 1 Sid. 86. The only forms of judgment given by the C.O.R. 1886 are for ouster; see forms No. 36 (judgment after disclaimer), and No. 123 (after trial by jury); but rule 308 contemplates that cases may arise to which the forms given are inapplicable. As to disclaimer, see rule 59.

Procedure and Evidence

§ 3. *Summary proceedings for declaring fairs in the metropolis unlawful.*

The Metropolitan Fairs Act, 1868,(*a*) supplies a simple process to prevent the holding of unlawful fairs within the limits of the metropolitan police district. If a fair be held, or notice be given of any fair proposed to be held, on any ground within the district other than that on which a fair has been held during each of the seven years immediately preceding, the Commissioner of Police can, under this Act, have the question whether the fair is legal summarily raised before a magistrate, and, if the fair be declared to be unlawful, he can take summary steps to suppress it.

§ 4. *Evidence.*

It is proposed here to treat shortly of the evidence which may be available to establish market and fair rights.

Grants — From the close of the twelfth century to the year 1516, the king's grants of franchises were made by charter, and thenceforward by letters patent. All these grants are recorded respectively in the Charter Rolls and Patent Rolls deposited at the Record Office. The grants recorded in the charter rolls may be either grants of liberties which had not been previously granted, or confirmation charters, i.e. charters confirming previous grants with or without the addition of further privileges. When the original grant is recited in the confirmation charter, the latter is called an inspeximus charter.(*b*) The origin of a fair or market may be proved by a charter of one of the above kinds, or by letters patent.

Both charters and letters patent may be proved by the production of the original under the great seal, of which the court takes judicial notice.(*c*) Primary evidence of charters or letters patent may also, it seems, be given (without accounting for the original) by an exemplification or enrolment.(*d*) An

---

(*a*) 31 & 32 Vict. c. 106. See also 2 & 3 Vict. c. 47, ss. 39, 40 (as amended by 30 & 31 Vict. c. 134, s. 21), *post*, p. 204.

(*b*) See Introduction to printed volume of the Rotuli Chartarum, by Sir T. Duffus Hardy, 1837. Palmer's Index, No. 93, in the Record Office, contains a list of grants of markets and fairs from 1 John to 22 Edw. IV.

(*c*) Lawe's case (1596) 2 Rep. 17 b.

(*d*) See the Introduction to the Rotuli Chartarum by Sir T. Duffus Hardy (1837) pp. xviii. and ix.

exemplification is an exact copy sealed with the great seal.(*a*) An enrolment is the roll of charters and letters patent now preserved in the Public Record Office ;(*b*) and the enrolment is itself a public document, which need not be produced in court, but may be proved by an exemplification, or by an examined copy,(*c*) or by a copy examined and certified by the deputy keeper of the records or one of the assistant record keepers, and sealed or stamped with the seal of the Record Office.(*d*)

Most local and personal Acts passed before 1851 contain a section declaring them public, and every Act passed after the year 1850 is a public Act, unless the contrary is expressly provided.(*e*) The courts take judicial notice of public Acts.(*f*) If, however, an Act is not public, it must be proved. This is most conveniently done by producing a copy purporting to be printed by the Queen's printer, or under the authority or superintendence of Her Majesty's Stationery Office.(*g*)

Acts of Parliament

To establish a market or fair by prescription, or presumption of lost grant,(*h*) or to prove customary rights therein,(*i*) user within the time of living memory will usually be proved by the evidence of living witnesses. Though not absolutely necessary,(*j*) it is always advisable to carry the evidence further back than the date to which the memory of the oldest living witnesses can carry it. For this purpose, evidence of reputation and documentary evidence of various kinds may be used, and a careful search should therefore be made in the Record Office, and in the muniment room of the supposed owner of the franchise.

Evidence of ancient user

Some documents are admissible in evidence as acts of ownership. Among these are old leases and conveyances of the market or fair, or of the tolls,(*k*) tables of tolls which have

Acts of ownership

(*a*) See the Introduction to the Rotuli Chartarum by Sir T. Duffus Hardy (1837) p. vii.
(*b*) *Ibid.* pp. i. and vii. ; and see 1 & 2 Vict. c. 94.
(*c*) I.e. a copy which a witness swears he has examined with the original and found to be correct.
(*d*) 1 & 2 Vict. c. 94, ss. 12 and 13; 8 & 9 Vict. c. 113, s. 1 ; 14 & 15 Vict. c. 99, s. 14.
(*e*) 52 & 53 Vict. c. 63, s. 9.
(*f*) R. *v.* Sutton (1816) 4 M. & S. 532, 542.
(*g*) 8 & 9 Vict. c. 113, s. 3 ; 45 Vict. c. 9, s. 2
(*h*) See *ante*, p. 22. (*i*) See *ante*, pp. 64, 86. (*j*) See *ante*, p. 23.
(*k*) Mayor of Penryn *v.* Best (1878) 3 Ex. D. 292, 296 ; Bristow *v.* Cormican (1878) 3 App. Cas. 641, 653 ; Malcolmson *v.* O'Dea (1863) 10

136   *Procedure and Evidence*

been exhibited in the market or used by collectors of toll,(a) appointments of stewards, bailiffs, or other officers,(b) writs, pleadings, and other proceedings in actions brought by the owner for toll or disturbance, proceedings in the court of pie powder, and proceedings relating to the market or fair in the court leet or borough court.(c)

Declarations against interest
Accounts made out by deceased bailiffs or stewards, wherein they debit themselves with tolls which they profess to have collected personally, are admissible in evidence, as declarations by deceased persons against their interest, to prove that tolls were in fact paid.(d) And payments of rent for a market may be proved in the same way.

Evidence of reputation
The public have a right to enter and buy and sell,(e) and it seems that the public interest in market-rights is sufficient to let in evidence of reputation when the question is as to the existence of a market or the right to take toll.(f) If so, the mere statements of deceased persons, whether oral or written, which embody a common report, and were made before any controversy had arisen, are admissible, and may be proved by a living witness.(g) Of greater value are formal written statements in the nature of reputation. Among writings of this kind are depositions,(h) rates and assessments,(i) recitals or descriptions in leases and conveyances,(j) or in Acts

H.L.C. 593, 672, 614; De Rutzen v. Farr (1835) 4 A. & E. 53; Mosley v. Walker (1827) 7 B. & C. 40, 43; Duke of Beaufort v. Smith (1849) 4 Exch. 450, 471.
(a) Brett v. Beales (1816) M. & M. 416, 419; Lawrence v. Hitch (1868) L.R. 3 Q.B. 521.
(b) Mayor of Penryn v. Best, *supra*; Malcolmson v. O'Dea, *supra*; Earl of Carnarvon v. Villebois (1844) 13 M. & W. 313, 329.
(c) Mosley v. Walker, *supra*.
(d) De Rutzen v. Farr (1835) 4 A. & E. 53; Mayor of Exeter v. Warren (1844) 5 Q.B. 773; Doe v. Thynne (1808) 10 East, 206; Doe v. Michael (1851) 17 Q.B. 276; Duke of Beaufort v. Smith (1849) 4 Exch. 450, 471; and see notes to Higham v. Ridgway (1808) 2 Smith, L.C. (10th ed.), 317.
(e) See *ante*, pp. 31, 38, 56.
(f) Cf. Earl of Carnarvon v. Villebois (1844) 13 M. & W. 313, 332; Brett v. Beales (1829) M. & M. 416; Drinkwater v. Porter (1835) 7 C. & P. 181; Pim v. Currell (1840) 6 M. & W. 234.
(g) See Crease v. Barrett (1835) 1 C. M. & R. 919, 929; Barraclough v. Johnson (1838) 8 A. & E. 99; Thomas v. Jenkins (1837) 6 A. & E. 525; R. v. Cotton (1813) 3 Camp. 444; R. v. Bliss (1837) 7 A. & E. 550.
(h) Freeman v. Phillips (1816) 4 M. & S. 486.
(i) See R. v. Cotton (1813) 3 Camp. 444.
(j) Plaxton v. Dare (1829) 10 B. & C. 17; Brett v. Beales (1829) M. & M. 416.

of Parliament.(a) And some evidence may be found in presentments of manorial and other customary courts.(b) Extracts from Domesday Book are probably admissible as evidence of this kind. That book contains many references to markets existing at the time of its compilation.(c)

Upon the same principle verdicts and judgments in previous actions in which the existence of a market or fair, or the right to take toll, was in issue are receivable in evidence in subsequent actions where the same matter is in issue, although the parties be different, provided they have the same relative interests.(d) So the proceedings, and the judgment and finding of the jury, in *quo warranto* proceedings,(e) allowances before Justices in Eyre,(f) inquisitions to ascertain the extent of crown lands,(g) the returns to inquisitions *post mortem*(h) and extents of manors,(i) may be given in evidence. The 'Placita de Quo Warranto,' 'Abbrevatio Placitorum,' and 'Rotuli Hundredorum' all contain many records relating to markets and fairs.

Verdicts and judgments

(a) Earl of Carnarvon v. Villebois (1844) 13 M. & W. 313, 332; R. v. Sutton (1816) 4 M. & S. 532.
(b) See Duke of Beaufort v. Smith (1849) 4 Exch. 450; Roe v. Parker (1792) 5 T.R. 26; Talbot v. Lewis (1834) 1 C.M. & R. 495.
(c) Extracts from Domesday may be proved by an examined or certified copy in accordance with 1 & 2 Vict. c. 94, ss. 12 and 13.
(d) Pim v. Currell (1840) 6 M. & W. 234; Briscoe v. Lomax (1833) 8 A. & E. 198, 214; Earl of Carnarvon v. Villebois (1844) 13 M. & W. 313, 331; Reed v. Jackson (1801) 1 East, 355. Cf. Duke of Beaufort v. Smith (1849) 4 Exch. 450.
(e) Earl of Carnarvon v. Villebois (1844) 13 M. & W. 313, 331; Earl of Egremont v. Saul (1837) 6 A. & E. 924.
(f) Per Parke, B., in Earl of Carnarvon v. Villebois (1844) 13 M. & W. 313, 331; Doe d. William IV. v. Roberts (1844) 13 M. & W. 520.
(g) Rowe v. Brenton (1828) 8 B. & C. 737, 747.
(h) Mosley v. Walker (1827) 7 B. & C. 40, 42, and see the *Calendarium Inquisitionum post mortem*, vol. i., introductory note (1806).
(i) See the statute Extenta Manerii, 4 Ed. I. Stat. 1 (Ruff.); Incert. Temp. (Stat. Realm); repealed by S. L. R. Act, 1863.

PART II

PUBLIC STATUTES RELATING TO
THE ESTABLISHMENT OF MARKETS AND FAIRS

141

THE MARKETS AND FAIRS CLAUSES ACT, 1847.

(10 & 11 VICT. c. 14.)

An Act for consolidating in one Act certain provisions usually contained in Acts for constructing or regulating markets and fairs. [23 April 1847.]

[[1] WHEREAS it is expedient to comprise in one Act sundry provisions usually contained in Acts of Parliament authorising the construction or regulation of markets and fairs, and that as well for avoiding the necessity of repeating such provisions in each of the several Acts relating to such undertakings as for ensuring greater uniformity in the provisions themselves: Be it enacted by the Queen's most Excellent Majesty, by and with the advice and consent of the Lords Spiritual and Temporal, and Commons, in this present Parliament assembled, and by the authority of the same, That [1]]this Act shall extend only to such markets or fairs as shall be authorised by any Act of Parliament hereafter to be passed which shall declare that this Act shall be incorporated therewith; and all the clauses of this Act, save so far as they shall be expressly varied or excepted by any such Act, shall apply to the undertaking authorised thereby, so far as the same shall be applicable to such undertaking,[2] and shall, with the clauses of every other Act which shall be incorporated therewith, form part of such Act, and be construed therewith as forming one Act.

Extent of Act

[1] The preamble and other words in the brackets may now be omitted from any revised edition of the statutes published by authority; S. L. R. Act, 1891 (54 & 55 Vict. c. 67), s. 1, and schedule. Provisions relating only to Scotland or Ireland are omitted, but the omission is indicated by asterisks.

[2] It is important to notice this qualification; for, notwithstanding the incorporation of the whole of this Act, the undertaking will not be affected by any provisions of this Act which are not applicable thereto. For instance, if the undertaking be merely a market, it will not be affected by provisions of this Act which relate exclusively to a fair or a slaughterhouse, unless the incorporating Act, by apt words, renders such provisions applicable. See also as to the application of the provisions of such an Act as this, Dartford Rural Council v. Bexley Heath R. Co [1898] A. C. 210.

And with respect to the construction of this Act, and any Act incorporated therewith,[1] be it enacted as follows:

The headings to the various portions of this Act are to be referred to, to determine the sense of any doubtful expression in a section occurring nder a particular heading.(a)

Clauses 2 and 3 are not incorporated with the Public Health Act, 1875, but they are incorporated with the Diseases of Animals Act, 1894, by s. 32 thereof.

[1] The only Act which, by this Act, is incorporated therewith is the Railways Clauses Consolidation Act, 1845, ss. 140-161; see s. 52 of this Act.

Interpretations in this Act

S. 2. The expression *the special Act* used in this Act shall be construed to mean any Act which shall be hereafter passed authorising the construction or regulation of a market or fair, and with which this Act shall be incorporated; and the word *prescribed* used in this Act in reference to any matter herein stated shall be construed to refer to such matter as the same shall be prescribed or provided for in the special Act, and the sentence in which such word occurs shall be construed as if instead of the word 'prescribed' the expression 'prescribed for that purpose in the special Act' had been used; and the expression *the lands* shall mean the lands which shall by the special Act be authorised to be taken or used for the purposes thereof; and the expression *the undertaking* shall mean the market or fair, and the works connected therewith, by the special Act authorised to be constructed or regulated; and the expression *the undertakers* shall mean the persons authorised by the special Act to construct or regulate the market or fair.

Interpretations in this and the special Act

S. 3. The following words and expressions in both this and the special Act, and any Act incorporated therewith, shall have the meanings hereby assigned to them,[1] unless there be something in the subject or context repugnant to such construction; (that is to say,)

> Words importing the singular number shall include the plural number, and words importing the plural number shall include also the singular number:[2]
> Words importing the masculine gender shall include females:
> The word *person* shall include a corporation, whether aggregate or sole:
> The word *lands* shall include messuages, lands, tenements, and hereditaments ... of any tenure:[3]
> The word *lease* shall include ... an agreement for a lease:
> The expression *the market or fair* shall mean the market

(a) See Hammersmith Rly. Co. v. Brand (1869) L.R. 4 H.L. 171.

or fair, and the works connected therewith, by the special Act authorised to be constructed or regulated : ²
The word *cart* shall include waggon, and also any carriage used wholly or chiefly for the conveyance of goods :
The word *driver* shall include the carter or other person having the care of any cart :
The word *cattle* shall include horse, ass, mule, ram, ewe, wether, lamb, goat, kid, or swine : ⁴
The expression *the collector* shall mean the person appointed by the undertakers to collect the stallages, rents, or tolls authorised by the special Act, and shall include the assistants of the collector :
The word *month* shall mean calendar month :
The expression *superior courts* when the matter submitted to the cognisance of the court arises in England . . . shall mean her Majesty's [⁵ superior courts of record at Westminster⁵] . . . [⁶and shall include the court of common pleas of the county palatine of Lancaster, and the court of pleas of the county of Durham.⁶]. . .
The word *oath* shall include affirmation in the case of quakers, and any declaration lawfully substituted for an oath in the case of any other persons allowed by law to make a declaration instead of taking an oath : ⁷
The word *county* shall include riding or other division of a county having a separate commission of the peace ; . . . and it shall also include county of a city or county of a town :
The word *justice* shall mean justice of the peace acting for the place where the matter requiring the cognisance of any such justice arises ; and if such matter arise in respect of lands situated not wholly in any one jurisdiction shall mean a justice acting for the place where any part of such lands shall be situated; and where any matter is authorised or required to be done by two justices, the expression *two justices* shall be understood to mean two or more justices assembled and acting together : ⁸
The expression *quarter sessions* shall mean quarter sessions as defined in the special Act : and if such expression be not there defined it shall mean the general or quarter sessions of the peace which shall be held at the place nearest to the market or fair, or the principal office thereof for the county or place in which the market or fair is situate, or for some division of such county having a separate commission of the peace.'

¹ The effect of not incorporating this section with the special Act seems to be that it is not decisive upon the meaning of words in the special Act,

but is nevertheless decisive upon the meaning of words in the sections of this Act which are incorporated with the special Act.
² A special Act authorising the erection of 'a market-house' may be construed as authorising the erection of two market-houses.(*a*)
³ I.e. 'of any tenure, if any,' for 'hereditaments' here include incorporeal hereditaments.(*b*)
⁴ The expression 'animals,' in s. 32 of the Diseases of Animals Act, 1894, is defined by s. 59 of that Act, and includes 'cattle,' as defined by the same section; but neither 'animals' nor 'cattle,' as thereby defined, include horse, ass, or mule. It is submitted that the definition of 'cattle' in this Act does not override that in the Act of 1894, as regards markets provided under s. 32 of that Act.
⁵ For the words in brackets read now 'High Court of Justice.' See the Supreme Court of Judicature Act, 1873 (36 & 37 Vict. c. 66), ss. 16, 76).
⁶ The words in brackets were repealed by the S. L. R. Act, 1891. The jurisdiction of the Courts referred to was transferred to the High Court of Justice by the Judicature Act, 1873, s. 16.
⁷ See the Oaths Act, 1888 (51 & 52 Vict. c. 46).
⁸ See s. 55, *infra*.

And with respect to citing this Act or any part thereof, be it enacted as follows:

Short title of this Act
S. 4. In citing this Act in other Acts of Parliament, and in legal instruments, it shall be sufficient to use the expression 'The Markets and Fairs Clauses Act, 1847.'

Form in which portions of this Act may be incorporated in other Acts
S. 5. For the purpose of incorporating part only of this Act with any Act hereafter to be passed it shall be enough to describe the clauses of this Act with respect to any matter in the words introductory to the enactment with respect to such matter, and to enact that the clauses so described, or that this Act, with the exception of the clauses so described, shall be incorporated with such Act, and thereupon all the clauses of this Act so incorporated shall, save so far as they shall be expressly varied or excepted by such Act, form part of such Act, and such Act shall be construed as if such clauses were set forth therein with reference to the matter to which such Act relates.¹

¹ If the special Act incorporates or excepts any part of this Act merely by a description in the words of an introductory heading, all the clauses of this Act which occur between that heading and the next are incorporated or excepted, as the case may be.(*c*) But if the special Act excepts clauses occurring under one heading, the exception does not extend to clauses referring to the same subject matter, but falling under another heading.(*d*)

(*a*) Richards *v.* Scarborough Public Market Co. (1853) 23 L.J. Ch. 110.
(*b*) See G. W. R. Co. *v.* Swindon and Cheltenham Rly. Co. (1884) 9 App. Cas. 787.
(*c*) Ferrar *v.* Commissioners of Sewers (1869) L.R. 4 Ex. 227; Dungey *v.* Mayor of London (1869) 38 L.J.C.P. 298.
(*d*) R. *v.* Mayor of London (1867) L.R. 2 Q.B. 292.

S. 6   Construction of Market or Fair   145

And with respect to the construction of the market or fair, and the works connected therewith, be it enacted as follows :

Clauses 6-11 are not incorporated with the Public Health Act, 1875. Clauses 6-9 are not incorporated with the Diseases of Animals Act, 1894, s. 32, but clauses 10 and 11 are.
As to the acquisition of lands for markets to be established under the Public Health Act, 1875, see ss. 166, 175-178 of that Act, and as to the acquisition of lands for markets to be provided under the Diseases of Animals Act, 1894, see s. 33 of that Act.
For a case in which a special Act provided that this Act should be read as if the words 'enlarging the market' had been inserted, instead of 'constructing the market,' see A.-G. v. Mayor of Cambridge.(a)

S. 6. Where [1] by the special Act the undertakers shall be empowered, for the purpose of constructing the market or fair, to take or use any lands [2] otherwise than with the consent of the owners and occupiers thereof, they shall, in exercising the power so given to them, be subject to the provisions and restrictions contained in this Act and in the Lands Clauses Consolidation Act, 1845,[3] when the special Act relates to England ; . . . and the undertakers shall make to the owners and occupiers of and all other parties interested in any lands taken or used for the purposes of the special Act, or injuriously affected by the construction of the works thereby authorised, full compensation for the value of the lands so taken or used, and for all damage sustained by such owners, occupiers, and other persons by reason of the exercise, as to such lands, of the powers vested in the undertakers by this or the special Act, or any Act incorporated therewith ; and, except where otherwise provided by this or the special Act, the amount of such compensation shall be determined in the manner provided by the said Lands Clauses Consolidation Act . . . for determining questions of compensation with regard to lands purchased or taken under the provisions thereof ; and all the provisions of the said last-mentioned Act . . . shall be applicable to determine the amount of any such compensation, and to enforce payment or other satisfaction thereof.

Construction of markets or fairs to be subject to the provisions of this Act, and the Lands Clauses Consolidation Act, 1845

[1] Compare with the provisions in ss. 6 and 11 of this Act the like provisions in ss. 6 and 16 (proviso *ad fin.*) of the Railways Clauses Act, 1845 (8 & 9 Vict. c. 20), and in ss. 6 and 12 (proviso *ad fin.*) of the Waterworks Clauses Act, 1847 (10 & 11 Vict. c. 17).
It is not intended to insert here a review of all the provisions of the Lands Clauses Acts or the numerous decisions thereon. For that the reader is referred to some standard work on the law of compensation. It has been thought, however, that it might be useful to mention certain established propositions, which appear to be applicable to ss. 6 and 11 of this Act :—

(a) (1873) L.R. 6 H.L. 303.

1. There is no remedy, unless a remedy is given by statute, for damage arising from the lawful exercise, without negligence, of statutory powers.(*a*)

2. The compensation provided by ss. 6 and 11 is compensation for damage done in the lawful exercise, in a lawful manner, of the statutory powers therein referred to ; and not compensation for injury done by the undertakers while exceeding their powers or while exercising them in an unlawful or negligent manner; but for such injury the ordinary remedy by action for damages or an injunction remains unimpaired.(*b*)

3. S. 11 does not curtail the right of the undertakers to exercise their statutory powers therein referred to, but controls the manner in which such powers may be lawfully exercised. Undertakers who, in exercising such powers, do unnecessary damage, are liable to an action.(*c*)

4. If the undertakers, in pursuance of their powers, take lands compulsorily from a person who holds other lands besides the lands so taken, such person is entitled to compensation for any diminution in the value of such other lands, whether arising from the construction on the lands so taken of the works authorised to be constructed thereon, or arising, after the construction of such works, from the authorised use of such works and lands.(*d*)

5. A person who neither owns nor has any interest in the lands which the undertakers take compulsorily is only entitled to compensation for damage arising from the exercise by the undertakers of their statutory powers if it arises under the following circumstances :

(i.) The damage must arise from an act done in the lawful exercise by the undertakers of their statutory powers ; see propositions 2 and 3, *supra*.

(ii.) The damage must be such damage as would have rendered the undertakers liable to an action therefor if they had not obtained their statutory powers.(*e*)

(iii.) The damage must be an injury to lands, or to a right incident thereto ; and not merely a personal injury or injury to trade.(*f*)

(iv.) The damage must arise from the construction of the authorised works, and not from their user after construction. But construction may include works made after the market is opened. The scope of s. 11 of this Act is limited by the words introductory to the group of sections to which it belongs.(*g*)

Consequently the owner of a common law market or fair has no

(*a*) R. *v.* Pease (1832) 4 B. & Ad. 30; Vaughan *v.* Taff Vale Rly Co. (1860) 5 H. & N. 679 ; Hammersmith Rly. Co. *v.* Brand (1868) L.R. 4 H.L. 171 ; L. B. & S. C. Rly. Co. *v.* Truman (1885) 11 App. Cas. 45.
(*b*) Broadbent *v.* Imperial Gaslight Co. (1857) 7 De G. M. & G. 436, 7 H.L.C. 600 ; Lawrence *v.* G. N. R. Co. (1851) 16 Q.B. 643 ; Clowes *v.* Staffordshire Potteries Waterworks Co. (1872) L.R. 8 Ch. 125 ; Biscoe *v.* G. E. R. Co. (1873) L.R. 16 Eq. 636.
(*c*) Per Lord Campbell, R. *v.* E. & W. India Docks Co. (1853) 2 E. & B. 466, 474 ; Fenwick *v.* East London Rly. Co. (1875) L.R. 20 Eq. 544 ; A.-G. *v.* Metr. Rly. Co. [1894] 1 Q.B. 384, 391.
(*d*) Re Stockport, Timperley and Altrincham Rly. Co. (1869) 33 L.J.Q.B. 251 ; Cowper Essex *v.* Local Board for Acton (1889) 14 App. Cas. 153.
(*e*) Re Penny (1857) 7 E. & B. 660 ; Ricket *v.* Metr. Rly. Co. (1867) L.R. 2 H.L. 175 ; Hammersmith Rly. Co. *v.* Brand (1868) L.R. 4 H.L. 171 ; Caledonian Rly. Co. *v.* Walker's Trustees (1882) 7 App. Cas. 259.
(*f*) Ricket *v.* Metr. Rly. Co. (1867) L.R. 2 H.L. 175 ; Beckett *v.* Midland Rly. Co. (1868) L.R. 3 C.P. 82 ; Metr. B. of W. *v.* McCarthy (1874) L.R. 7 H.L. 243 ; Caledonian Rly. Co. *v.* Walker's Trustees (1882) 7 App. Cas. 259.
(*g*) Hammersmith Rly. Co. *v.* Brand (1869) L.R. 4 H.L. 171 ; Caledonian Rly. Co. *v.* Walker's Trustees (1882) 7 App. Cas. 259 ; A.-G. *v.* Metr. Rly. Co. [1894] 1 Q.B. 384.

S. 6 Construction of Market or Fair

right, under s. 11, to compensation for any damage to his franchise caused by the undertakers holding their statutory market.(a)
² See s. 3. The definition of lands there given is the same as that in the Lands Clauses Act, 1845, s. 3, and includes incorporeal hereditaments ;(b) but in the absence of a special provision in the special Act, the undertakers will have no power to compel landowners to grant easements in their favour.(c)
³ 8 & 9 Vict. c. 18, amended by 23 & 24 Vict. c. 106, 32 & 33 Vict. c. 18, and 46 & 47 Vict. c. 15.

S. 7. If[1] any omission, mis-statement, or wrong description shall have been made of any lands, or of the owners, lessees, or occupiers of any lands, described or purporting to be described in the special Act, or in the schedule thereto, the undertakers, after giving ten days' notice to the owners, lessees, and occupiers of the lands affected by such proposed correction, may apply in England ... to two justices[2] ... for the correction thereof; and if it appear to such justices ... that such omission, mis-statement, or wrong description arose from mistake, they ... shall certify the same accordingly, and shall in such certificate state the particulars of any such omission, mis-statement, or wrong description ; and such certificate shall be deposited in England ... with the clerk of the peace ... of the county[3] in which the lands affected thereby shall be situated ; ... and such certificate shall be kept by such clerk of the peace ... with the other documents to which they relate,[4] and thereupon the special Act or schedule shall be deemed to be corrected according to such certificate ; and the undertakers may make the works in accordance with such certificate as if such omission, mis-statement, or wrong description had not been made.

<small>Errors and omissions in special Act, or schedules thereto, may be corrected by justices, who shall certify the same</small>

<small>Certificate to be deposited</small>

[1] Cf. the corresponding provisions in s. 7 of the Railways Clauses Act, 1845, and s. 7 of the Waterworks Clauses Act, 1847. The object of the section is to provide for cases in which it may be difficult to identify the lands described in the special Act or the schedule thereto, owing to some omission or mis-statement by mistake in the description there given of the lands or the persons having interests therein.(d)
[2] See ss. 3, 55.   [3] See s. 3.
[4] The documents referred to include the copy of the special Act, which must be deposited with the clerk of the peace, under s. 58.

S. 8. Copies of any such alteration or correction thereof, or extracts therefrom, certified by any such clerk of the peace, ...

<small>Copies of alterations</small>

(a) See Hopkins v. G. N. Rly. Co. (1877) 2 Q.B.D. 224.
(b) See G. W. R. Co. v. Swindon and Cheltenham Rly. Co. (1884) 9 App. Cas. 787.
(c) Pinchin v. L. & Blackwall Rly. Co. (1855) 5 De G. M. & G. 851 ; Hill v. Mid. Rly. Co. (1882) 21 Ch.D. 143 ; G. W. R. Co. v. Swindon, etc., Co. supra.
(d) Kemp v. W. End of London Rly. Co. (1855) 1 K. & J. 681.

148 Markets and Fairs Clauses Act, 1847   S. 8

to be evidence

in whose custody the same may be, which certificate [1] such clerk shall give to all parties interested when required, shall be received in all courts of justice and elsewhere as evidence of the contents thereof.[2]

[1] I.e. the clerk's certificate that the copy is a true copy of the justices' certificate. It is not expressly provided that interested parties may inspect the justices' certificate, and make extracts or copies therefrom, but the clerk is bound to give them his certificate when required, and is not expressly empowered to charge any fee. It might perhaps be held that an inspection or copy of the justices' certificate may only be had on the same terms as an inspection or copy of the special Act under s. 58 (q.v.).

[2] A copy of the justices' certificate, purporting to be certified as a true copy, and to be signed as such, by a clerk of the peace having the custody of the original, is admissible in evidence without proof of the signature or official character of the clerk; see the Evidence Act, 1845.(a)

Additional land may be taken for extraordinary purposes

S. 9. The undertakers, in addition to the lands authorised to be taken compulsorily, or to be appropriated by them for the purposes of the market or fair under the powers of this and the special Act, may appropriate any lands vested in them, or may contract with any person willing to sell the same, for the purchase of any land within the limits of the special Act,[1] not exceeding in the whole the prescribed[2] number of acres, for extraordinary purposes; (that is to say,)

[1] For providing slaughter-houses, (if the undertakers shall be authorised by the special Act to provide slaughter-houses,) and houses and places for weighing carts:

[2] For making convenient roads and approaches to the market or fair:

[3] For any other purpose which may be necessary[3] for the formation or convenient use of the market or fair.

[1] See s. 12, and note (2) thereon, *infra*. [2] See s. 2.
[3] A purpose does not become 'necessary' within the meaning of this clause because it is convenient to the undertakers on the score of economy.(b)

Undertakers, subject to provisions of this and the special Act, may execute the works herein named

S. 10. Subject to the provisions in this and the special Act, and any Act incorporated therewith, the undertakers, for the purpose of constructing a place for holding the market or fair, may execute any of the following works; (that is to say,)

[1] They may enter [1] upon any lands described in the special Act, or the schedule thereto, and other lands purchased by them or belonging to them, and set out such parts as they think necessary for the purposes of the market or fair, and thereupon from time to time build and maintain such market-places or places for fairs, and such stalls,

(a) 8 & 9 Vict. c. 113, s. 1.
(b) See Fenwick v. E. London Rly. Co. (1875) 20 Eq. 544.

sheds, pens, and other buildings or conveniences for the use of the persons frequenting the market or fair, and for weighing and measuring goods sold in the market or fair, and for weighing carts, as they may think necessary.[2]

[2] They may from time to time on such lands as aforesaid make and maintain all such roads and approaches as they may think necessary for the convenient use of the persons resorting to the market or fair.

[1] With regard to lands to be taken or used compulsorily, the undertakers' right of entry is subject to the Lands Clauses Act, 1845, ss. 84-92; see also ss. 124-126.

[2] Unless the special Act otherwise provides, the words 'lands purchased by them,' as used in this section, will, it seems, include all lands from time to time purchased by the undertakers, whether purchased before or after the passing of the special Act, provided that they have power to purchase such lands and devote them to the purposes mentioned in the section. But the special Act usually limits the scope of this section either to specified lands or to lands within a specified district.

This Act does not expressly confer upon the undertakers any right to remove a market from one place to another. The provisions of s. 14, *infra*, seem to be imperative, and if they be so, then, subject to the provisions of the special Act, the undertakers, when once they have opened a market-place for public use, must continue to hold markets therein. Under s. 9, however, it seems that they may have power from time to time to extend the market-place.

If powers of removal are desired, it seems advisable to make express provision for them in the special Act.

S. 11. Provided[1] always, that in the exercise of the powers by this or the special Act granted the undertakers shall do as little damage as can be, and shall make full satisfaction in manner herein[2] and by the special Act and any Act incorporated therewith provided to all parties interested for all damages sustained by them by reason of the exercise of such powers.

Undertakers to make satisfaction for damage done

[1] See s. 6, *supra*, and note (1) thereon.
[2] The reference seems to be to s. 6, and not to s. 52, of this Act; even in cases where compensation for lands injuriously affected is claimed by persons having no interest in lands taken.(a)

And with respect to the holding of the market or fair, and the protection thereof, be it enacted as follows :

Clauses 12-16 are incorporated with the Public Health Act, 1875, see s. 167, *post*, p. 184; and also with the Diseases of Animals Act, 1894, see s. 32, *post*, p. 190.

S. 12. Before the market or fair shall be opened for public use the undertakers shall give not less than ten days' notice of

Before the market or

(a) See R. v. Edwards (1884) 13 Q.B.D. 586.

fair shall be opened, notice to be given by undertakers	the time when the same will be opened,[1] and such notice shall be given by the publication thereof in some newspaper circulating within the limits of the special Act,[2] and by printed handbills posted on some conspicuous place within those limits.[3]

[1] I.e. 'the time when it will *for the first time* be opened for public use'; but it is advisable to state in the notice the days and hours on and during which the market or fair will be held.

[2] The phrase 'within the limits of the special Act' occurs also in ss. 9, 17, 19, and 42. It is not defined by this Act, and its meaning must be sought for in the special Act. It is therefore advisable, in drafting a special Act, to insert therein a definition of the phrase as used in the incorporated sections. For markets under the Public Health Act, 1875, the phrase is defined by s. 316 of that Act; see *post*, p. 188.

[3] No penalty is imposed by this Act upon undertakers who open their market or fair without giving the notice prescribed by this section; but (assuming that s. 12 is incorporated by the special Act) it is doubtful whether the undertakers of a market can take the benefit of s. 13 of this Act if they have not complied with s. 12, or whether a market or fair is a legal market or fair for any purpose until s. 12 has been complied with. In a prosecution under s. 13 it is advisable to prove that s. 12 has been complied with, as was apparently done in Hooper *v.* Kenshole.(*a*)

Sales elsewhere than in markets prohibited under a penalty not exceeding 40*s*.	**S. 13.** After[1] the market-place is opened for public use[2] every person other than a licensed hawker[3] who shall sell or expose for sale in any place within the prescribed limits,[4] except[5] in his own dwelling-place or shop,[6] any articles[7] in respect of which tolls are by the special Act authorised to be taken in the market, shall for every such offence be liable to a penalty[9] not exceeding forty shillings.[10]

[1] The effect of this section on the undertakers' right of action for disturbance of their market is discussed *ante*, p. 87.

[2] See s 12 and note (3) thereon, *supra*. This section (unlike ss. 12 and 14-16) applies only to a market, and not to a fair. It seems that it would not apply to a fair regulated by a special Act merely because such Act incorporated this Act.

This section comes into force as soon as the market-place has been opened for public use; and its operation appears not to be confined to the days on which, or the hours during which, the market is held.

[3] A licensed hawker here means a hawker trading as such, who holds a licence under the Hawkers Act, 1888,(*b*) or a pedlar trading as such, who holds a certificate under the Pedlars Acts, 1871 and 1881.(*c*)

For the purposes of the Hawkers Act, 1888, a 'hawker' means 'any person who travels *with a horse or other beast bearing or drawing burden*, and goes from place to place or to other men's houses carrying to sell or exposing for sale any goods, wares, or merchandise, or exposing samples or patterns of any goods, wares, or merchandise to be afterwards delivered, and includes any person who travels by any means of locomotion to any place in which he does not usually reside or carry on business, and there sells or exposes for sale any goods, wares, or merchandise, in or at any house, shop, room, booth, stall, or other place whatever hired or used by him for that purpose' (s. 2). The Act requires every hawker annually

---

(*a*) (1877) 2 Q.B.D. 127.   (*b*) 51 & 52 Vict. c. 33.
(*c*) 34 & 35 Vict. c. 96; 44 & 45 Vict. c. 45.

S. 13   Holding of Market, etc.   151

to take out a licence (s. 3 (1)), which, whenever issued, expires on the 31st March in each year (s. 3 (2)); but exempts from this requirement certain persons, including persons who sell fish, fruit, victuals, or coal. But a person so exempted, who does not take out a licence, is not 'a licensed hawker' within the meaning of the above section 13.(*a*)   S. 5 of the Act of 1888 requires a hawker to keep his name and the words 'licensed hawker' on every box, package, and vehicle used for the carriage of his goods.   If a local Act which incorporates the above section 13 prohibits the sale of tollable articles in the street unless sold by a licensed hawker in the 'lawful exercise of his calling,' the prohibition extends to a licensed hawker who does not comply with s. 5 of the Act of 1888.(*b*)

For the purposes of the Pedlars Acts, a 'pedlar' means 'any hawker, pedlar, petty chapman, tinker, caster of metals, mender of chairs, or other person who, *without any horse or other beast bearing or drawing burden*, travels and trades on foot and goes from town to town or to other men's houses, carrying to sell or exposing for sale any goods, wares, or merchandise, or procuring orders for goods, wares, or merchandise immediately to be delivered, or selling or offering for sale his skill in handicraft' (Act of 1871, s. 3).   The Acts prohibit any person from acting as a pedlar without the prescribed certificate, which lasts for one year from the date of its issue, but provide that it shall not be necessary for a certificate to be obtained by certain persons, including commercial travellers and sellers of vegetables, fish, fruit, or victuals.(*c*)   The Act of 1871, s. 6, provides that a certificate under that Act shall, for the purpose of the Markets and Fairs Clauses Act, 1847, and any Act incorporating the same, have the same effect as a hawker's licence, and that the term 'licensed hawker' in the Markets and Fairs Clauses Act shall be construed to include a pedlar holding such a certificate.   A person, however, who holds only a pedlar's certificate is exempted from the provisions of the above s. 13 only while trading as a pedlar; and he is not exempted therefrom if he trade as a hawker with a horse and cart without a hawker's licence ;(*d*) nor is a person without a pedlar's certificate exempted therefrom by reason that the Act of 1871, s. 23, renders it unnecessary for him to take out a pedlar's certificate.(*a*)   Where a special Act prohibited persons from selling tollable articles in the streets without a licence from the *undertakers*, and made no exception in favour of licensed hawkers or certificated pedlars, it was held that such hawkers and pedlars were subject to the prohibition|;(*a*) but such prohibition does not prevent them from selling non-tollable articles.(*e*)

' 'The prescribed limits' mean 'the limits prescribed for that purpose in the special Act'; see s. 2, *supra*.   If the special Act provides that such Act shall for all purposes be in force within a specified district, the boundaries of that district are the prescribed limits.(*f*)   In the case of a market under the Public Health Act, 1875, the limits of the district of the urban authority are the prescribed limits.(*g*)   In the case of a market under the Diseases of Animals Act, 1894, the limits of the land acquired or appropriated for the purposes of the market are the prescribed limits.(*h*)

There have been several decisions upon the question what constitutes

---

(*a*) Openshaw *v.* Oakeley (1889) 60 L.T. 929.
(*b*) Hooper *v.* Kenshole (1877) 2 Q.B.D. 127.
(*c*) Act of 1871, ss. 4, 5, 23; Act of 1881, s. 2.
(*d*) Woolwich L.B. of Health *v.* Gardiner [1895] 2 Q.B. 497.
(*e*) Loftos *v.* Gleave (1890) 55 J.P. 149; Loftos *v.* Kiggins (1890) Id. 151.
(*f*) Caswell *v.* Cook (1862) 11 C.B.N.S. 637; and see Kilminster *v.* Fitton (1886) 53 L.T. 959; Collier *v.* North (1876) 35 L.T. 345.
(*g*) Spurling *v.* Bantoft [1891] 2 Q.B. 384.
(*h*) 57 & 58 Vict. c. 57, s. 32 (3).

a *sale within* the prescribed limits. The effect of these decisions, with regard to contracts for the sale and delivery of tollable articles, seems to be as follows :—

1. The section does not affect a delivery within the limits under a contract made outside the limits, provided that the goods were outside the limits at the time when the contract was made, and were appropriated to the contract before they were brought within the limits.(*a*) According to the Irish case of Newtownards Town Commissioners *v.* Woods,(*b*) the section does not affect a delivery within the limits, under a contract of sale made by sample within the limits, if the bulk of the goods was outside the limits at the time when the contract was made; but this case seems to be at variance with the cases next to be mentioned.

2. The section applies to cases in which the goods are delivered within the limits without having been appropriated to the contract before being brought within the limits; and it seems to be immaterial in these cases whether the contract was made within the limits or outside them.(*c*) *A fortiori*, the section applies where the contract was made within the limits and the goods appropriated to the contract were within the limits at the time when the contract was made.(*d*) It applies notwithstanding that the seller previously bought the goods in the market.(*e*)

A baker does not 'expose for sale' bread which he brings to a customer's house merely for the purpose of making a delivery under a previous contract.(*f*)

³ The only place expressly excepted is the seller's own dwelling-place or shop, but the section can scarcely be construed as prohibiting sales in the market-place while the market is in progress.

⁴ It is a question of fact whether a place is a man's own dwelling-place or shop; but in determining that question regard must be had to the object of the section, which is, on the one hand, that the market should be protected from the establishment, within the district, of a rival market, but, on the other hand, that the established traders of the district who carry on their business in their own dwelling-places or shops should not be interfered with.(*g*)

'Dwelling-*place*' has been said by Earle, C.J., to be a wider expression than 'dwelling-house,' which occurs in some local Acts, and to be capable of including a yard attached to a dwelling-house ;(*h*) but in Fearon *v.* Mitchell,(*i*) Cockburn, C.J., thought that no distinction was to be drawn between the two expressions; and in that case, and in McHole *v.* Davies,(*j*) it was held that a large yard adjoining a man's dwelling-house,

---

(*a*) Bourne *v.* Lowndes (1858) 22 J.P. 354; Stretch *v.* White (1861) 25 Id. 485; see Pletts *v.* Campbell [1895] 2 Q.B. 229; Pletts *v.* Beattie [1896] 1 Q.B. 519.
(*b*) (1877) 11 Ir.Rep.C.L. 506.
(*c*) Mayor of Exeter *v.* Heaman (1877) 37 L.T. 534; Torquay Market Co. *v.* Burridge (1884) 48 J.P. 71; see Pletts *v.* Campbell, Pletts *v.* Beattie, *supra*.
(*d*) Mayor of Londonderry *v.* M'Elhinney (1875) 9 Ir.Rep.C.L. 61.
(*e*) Black v. Sackett (1869) 10 B. & S. 639.
(*f*) White *v.* Mayor of Yeovil (1892) 61 L.J.M.C. 213. Cf. Luke *v.* Charles (1861) 25 J.P. 148.
(*g*) Llandaff Market Co. *v.* Lyndon (1860) 8 C.B.N.S. 515, 524; Pope *v.* Whalley (1865) 6 B. & S. 303; Ashworth *v.* Heyworth (1869) L.R. 4 Q.B. 316; Fearon *v.* Mitchell (1872) L.R. 7 Q.B. 690; McHole *v.* Davies (1875) 1 Q.B.D. 59.
(*h*) Llandaff Market Co. *v.* Lyndon, *supra*; and per Cockburn, C.J., in McHole *v.* Davies, *supra*.
(*i*) *Supra*.   (*j*) *Supra*.

S. 13 Holding of Markets, etc. 153

and used by him for extensive sales of cattle and sheep, was neither his dwelling-place nor his shop.

In considering whether a place is a shop, 'it is necessary to have regard to the nature, character, and extent of the trade' which is carried on therein.(a) In Fearon v. Mitchell it was held that a large hall, used for sales of cattle by public auction, was not a shop, but a rival market. An auction-room may be a shop, and if a place be a shop 'the mode of selling therein cannot deprive it of the ordinary privilege attached to a shop';(b) but *prima facie* auctioneers' premises are not shops.(c)

A distinction is drawn not only between 'shop' and 'rival market,' but also between 'shop' and 'stall.' 'Shop' imports something more than a mere place for sale : it imports a place for storing also, so far as the nature of the commodities admit of storing ;(d) and it means a man's 'real permanent private shop,' as distinguished from a mere temporary stall.(e) In determining whether a particular structure is a shop or a stall, it is proper to consider whether the building is of a substantial character, or a mere alteration of what was formerly a stall: whether it admits of the entrance of buyers: whether it protects the goods from the weather, and admits of their being left therein at night with reasonable safety : and also what is the nature and duration of the tenant's holding thereof; but no one of these considerations is conclusive of itself.(e) Thus it was held in Ashworth v. Heyworth (f) that a wooden shed which was affixed to a house and stood upon premises held therewith, and which had for many years been used for exposing goods for sale, was a shop; and in Hooper v. Kenshole,(g) that a covered and enclosed skittle-alley was not the shop of a hawker who hired it for two days to sell his goods therein. A ship moored to a wharf in a canal is not a shop.(h)

In Spurling v. Bantoft (i) a cattle market was established in a borough by the corporation, acting as sanitary authority. Prior to the establishment of such market, they had granted to a cattle salesman a lease of a yard, with a covenant for quiet enjoyment. It was held that the lease and covenant did not exempt the tenant from the operation of this section.

⁷ 'Article' is the word usually employed to cover all marketable commodities, and a horse may be an article within the meaning of the section.(j)

⁸ 'Toll' here means a market toll payable in respect of articles sold or exposed for sale in the market, and does not include a toll in the nature of stallage or rent payable for the occupation of a stall in the market-place.(k)

⁹ For the recovery of penalties, see s. 52. The offence cannot be condoned by payment of toll, nor toll claimed in lieu of penalty.(l)

¹⁰ The effect of this section may be considerably altered by the provisions of the special Act, with which it must be read.(m)

(a) Per Mellor, J., Fearon v. Mitchell (1872) L.R. 7 Q.B. 690.
(b) Per Byles, J., Wiltshire v. Willett (1861) 11 C.B.N.S. 240.
(c) Per Blackburn, J., and Cockburn, C.J., in Fearon v. Mitchell, *supra*.
(d) Per Mellor, J., Pope v. Whalley (1865) 6 B. & S. 303.
(e) Per Blackburn, J., *Id.* (f) (1869) L.R. 4 Q.B. 316.
(g) (1877) 2 Q.B.D. 127. See also Perkins v. Arber (1873) 37 J.P. 406.
(h) Wiltshire v. Baker (1861) 11 C.B.N.S. 237.
(i) [1891] 2 Q.B. 384.
(j) Llandaff Market Co. v. Lyndon (1860) 8 C.B.N.S. 515. See also Shepherd v. Folland (1884) 49 J.P. 165; Morgan v. Kingdon (1875) 39 Id. 471.
(k) Caswell v. Cook (1862) 11 C.B.N.S. 637.
(l) Carter v. Parkhouse (1870) 22 L.T.N.S. 788; Quilligan v. Limerick (1883) 14 L.R. Ir. 265.
(m) See Rutherford v. Straker (1887) 42 Ch.D. 85 n.

Market days	**S. 14.** After the market-place or place for fairs is opened for public use¹ the undertakers shall² hold markets and fairs therein on the prescribed³ days (if any), and on such other days as the undertakers shall² appoint from time to time by any by-law⁴ to be made in pursuance of this or the special Act.

¹ See s. 12, and note (3) thereon, *supra*.
² The section provides no remedy for non-compliance with its provisions, which seem to be imperative; and if they are imperative, then (subject to the provisions of the special Act) mandamus is the proper legal remedy.
³ I.e. prescribed for that purpose in the special Act; see s. 2.
⁴ See ss. 42-49, *infra*.

Penalty for selling or exposing for sale unwholesome meat, etc.	**S. 15.** Every person who shall sell or expose for sale any unwholesome meat or provisions¹ in the market or fair shall be liable to a penalty² not exceeding five pounds for every such offence; and any inspector of provisions appointed by the undertakers may seize such unwholesome meat or provisions, and carry the same before a justice, and thereupon such proceedings shall be had as are herein-after³ directed to be had in the case of any cattle or carcase seized in any slaughter-house and carried before a justice.
Penalty on obstructing inspector	And every person who shall obstruct or hinder the inspector of provisions from seizing or carrying away such unwholesome meat or provisions shall be liable to a penalty² not exceeding five pounds for every such offence.

¹ As to selling unwholesome meat and provisions, see further, *ante*, p. 104. As to making by-laws for preventing the sale or exposure for sale of unwholesome provisions in the market or fair, see s. 42, *infra*; and see also, *post*, p. 208.
² As to the recovery of penalties, see s. 52, *infra*.
³ See s. 20, *infra*.

Penalty for obstructing market or fair keeper	**S. 16.** Every person who shall assault or obstruct any person appointed by the undertakers to superintend the market or fair, or to keep order therein, whilst in the execution of his duty, shall for every such offence be liable to a penalty¹ not exceeding forty shillings.

¹ As to the recovery of penalties, see s. 52, *infra*.

And with respect to slaughter-houses, be it enacted as follows:

Clauses 17-20 relate to slaughter-houses, a subject which does not fall within the scope of this book. It seems sufficient, therefore, to point out that Clauses 17-20 are incorporated with the Diseases of Animals Act, 1894, but are not incorporated with the Public Health Act, 1875. Cl. 15, however, of this Act, which is incorporated with the Public Health Act, 1875, refers to cl. 20 of this Act for the proceedings to be taken upon the seizure of unwholesome meat or provisions exposed for sale.

S. 17. Where by the special Act the undertakers shall be empowered to provide slaughter-houses they may from time to time erect, on any land purchased by them under the provisions of this or the special Act, or any Act incorporated therewith, any buildings, or set apart and improve any buildings belonging to them, for the slaughtering of cattle,[1] and so soon as the same shall be ready for public use the undertakers shall give notice to that effect by the publication thereof in some newspaper circulating within the limits of the special Act,[2] and by printed handbills posted on some conspicuous place within the said limits. *[marginal: Power to erect slaughter-houses if authorised by the special Act]*

[1] See s. 3.   [2] See s. 12 and note (2) thereon, *supra*.

S. 18. Provided that nothing in this or the special Act, or any Act incorporated therewith, shall protect the undertakers from an indictment for nuisance,[1] or from any other legal proceeding, in respect of any such slaughter-house as aforesaid. *[marginal: Nothing to protect undertakers from an indictment for nuisance]*

[1] The keeper of a slaughter-house which is a public nuisance is liable to be indicted,(a) and is also liable to an action for damages or an injunction at the suit of a person who sustains particular damage therefrom beyond that suffered by the general public.(b)

S. 19. After the expiration of ten days from the publication and posting of such notice [1] no person shall slaughter any cattle or dress any carcase, for sale as human food or food of man, in any place within the limits of the special Act other than a slaughter-house which was in use as such before and at the time of the passing of the special Act, and has so continued ever since, or the slaughter-houses made in pursuance of this and the special Act; and every person who shall, after such notice as aforesaid, slaughter any such cattle [2] or dress for sale any such carcase within the limits of the special Act in any place other than one of such slaughter-houses, shall be liable to a penalty [3] not exceeding five pounds for every such offence. *[marginal: Penalty on slaughtering cattle, etc., elsewhere than in an authorised slaughterhouse]*

[1] See s. 17.
[2] It is not an offence under this section to slaughter cattle on private premises for any purpose other than that of their being sold as human food or food of man.(c)
[3] As to the recovery of penalties, see s. 52, *infra*.

S. 20. The inspector of provisions, or any officer appointed by the undertakers for that purpose, may at all times of the day, with or without assistants, enter into and inspect all buildings erected or set apart by the undertakers for slaughtering cattle, and examine whether any cattle or the carcase of any cattle *[marginal: Inspector may enter and inspect slaughterhouses]*

(a) R. v. Cross (1826) 2 C. & P. 483; R. v. Watts, Id. 486.
(b) 3 Blac. Comm. 220; Benjamin v. Storr (1874) L.R. 9 C.P. 400; Crump v. Lambert (1867) L.R. 3 Eq. 409; see 1 Sm. L.C. (10th ed.), pp. 274, 828.
(c) Elias v. Nightingale (1858) 8 E. & B. 698.

is deposited there; and in case such officer shall find any cattle, or the carcase or part of the carcase of any such cattle, which shall appear unfit for the food of man, he may seize and carry the same before a justice, and such justice shall forthwith order the same to be further inspected and examined by competent persons; and in case upon such inspection and examination such cattle, carcase, or part of a carcase, shall be found unfit for the food of man, such justice shall order the same to be immediately destroyed or otherwise disposed of in such way as to prevent the same being exposed for sale or used for the food of man; and every person who shall obstruct or hinder such inspector or other officer in the discharge of any of the duties aforesaid shall be liable to a penalty [1] not exceeding five pounds for every such offence.

[1] As to the recovery of penalties, see s. 52, *infra*.

And with respect to weighing goods and carts, be it enacted as follows:

Clauses 21-30 are incorporated with the Public Health Act, 1875, see s. 167, *post*, p. 184; and also with the Diseases of Animals Act, 1894, see s. 32 (2), *post*, p. 190.

In these clauses, the legislature speaks sometimes of 'commodities' (see s. 21, and cf. s. 34), sometimes of 'articles' (see ss. 22, 23, and cf. ss. 13, 38, 42), and sometimes of 'goods,' as above (see ss. 24, 25, 28, and cf. s. 34). The words 'articles' and 'commodities' appear to be synonymous, and to be capable of including all things for the buying and selling of which the market or fair is held.(*a*) 'Articles' may sometimes include horses,(*a*) and also, it seems, cattle; see s. 38, *infra*, where the legislature speaks of 'cattle or *other* articles.' Apart from the above heading, the legislature uses the word 'goods' in this group of clauses only when referring to goods brought in carts; and the word 'goods' as here used seems not to be applicable to cattle; see the preamble and provisions of 50 & 51 Vict. c. 27, *post*, p. 196. If that is so, it may perhaps be contended that the meaning of the words 'commodities' and 'articles,' whenever they occur in *this* group of clauses, is cut down by the word 'goods,' as used in the heading, so as not to include cattle; and there seems to be nothing in this group of clauses which is inconsistent with such contention.

As to weighing and measuring, see further, *ante*, pp. 98-104.

Undertakers to provide proper weights and measures for weighing commodities sold at markets and fairs

S. 21. The undertakers shall [1] provide sufficient and proper weighing houses or places for weighing or measuring the commodities sold in the market or fair, and shall keep therein proper weights, scales, and measures, according to the standard weights and measures for the time being, for weighing such commodities as aforesaid, and shall appoint proper persons to attend to the weighing or measuring such commodities at all times during which the market or fair is holden.

[1] See s. 14, *supra*, and note (2) thereon.

(*a*) See per Byles, J., Llandaff Market Co. *v.* Lyndon (1860) 8 C.B.N.S. 515, 521.

S. 22. Every person selling or offering for sale any articles in the market or fair shall, if required so to do by the buyer,[1] cause [2] the same to be weighed or measured by the weights and scales or measures provided by the undertakers; and any such person who shall refuse, on demand, to cause such articles to be weighed or measured in manner aforesaid, shall be liable to a penalty [3] not exceeding forty shillings. *Articles to be weighed if requested by the buyer*

Penalty for refusal

[1] Including, perhaps, any person to whom the articles are offered for sale. The request, it is submitted, must be made before the articles are delivered to, and accepted by, the buyer.

[2] The section is silent upon the question whether the buyer or seller is to bear the expense of weighing or measuring; but as the section imposes upon the seller the duty of *causing* the articles to be weighed or measured, it seems that generally he must pay the necessary tolls; see s. 34, *infra*.

[3] As to the recovery of penalties, see s. 52, *infra*.

S. 23. Every person appointed by the undertakers to weigh or measure any articles sold [1] in the market or fair who shall refuse or neglect to weigh or measure the same when required shall be liable to a penalty [2] not exceeding forty shillings. *Penalty on persons appointed refusing to weigh*

[1] Including, possibly, 'articles offered for sale'; see s. 22, *supra*. Perhaps 'any articles sold in the market' means 'any articles of a kind which may be sold in the market,' and not merely the particular articles which are actually sold therein.

[2] As to the recovery of penalties, see s. 52, *infra*.

S. 24. The undertakers shall provide sufficient and proper buildings or places for weighing carts in which goods are brought for sale within the market or fair or the prescribed limits,[1] and shall keep therein machines and weights proper for that purpose, and shall from time to time appoint a person in every such building or place to afford the use of such machines to the public by weighing such carts, with or without their loading, as may be required. *Undertakers to keep proper machines for weighing carts laden with goods*

[1] See s. 13, and note (4) thereon, *supra*.

S. 25. The driver [1] of every such cart [1] shall, at the request of the buyer or seller of such goods, or his agent, take such cart, with or without the loading thereof, to the nearest of the said weighing machines, and shall permit [2] the same to be weighed; and if such cart be weighed with its load thereupon the driver shall, if required, take such cart after its load has been discharged to the weighing machine nearest to such place of discharge, and permit [2] it to be re-weighed without such load; and if any such driver shall for the purposes aforesaid be required to take such cart a greater distance than half a mile, including the going to and returning from such machines respectively, the owner of the cart shall be paid for every horse which shall be used in drawing such cart twopence for the first half mile, and a like sum for *Carts to be weighed at one of the machines erected by the undertakers* every additional half mile; and such payment shall be made[3] by the person requiring such cart to be weighed as aforesaid before the driver thereof shall be obliged to take it as aforesaid for the purpose of having it weighed.

[1] See s. 3.
[2] The driver's duty under this section is to 'permit,' not to 'cause,' the weighing. As between the driver and the person who requires him to permit the weighing, the toll for weighing must be paid, it is submitted, by the latter, as he seems to be the person who 'brings' the cart to be weighed, within the meaning of s. 34, *infra*. Under s. 26 it is the driver's duty to assist in weighing the cart if requested.
[3] Or tendered; see s. 26, *infra*. The section says that the *owner* of the cart is to be paid for the cartage; but it is submitted that, in the absence of the owner, the driver has an irrebuttable authority to accept payment; otherwise the provisions of the section could be readily defeated.

Penalty on drivers for refusing to take carts to be weighed, etc.

S. 26. The driver of any such cart who shall not, upon being so requested as aforesaid, and having such payment[1] made or tendered as aforesaid, take the same to such weighing machine as herein-before directed, or who shall refuse to assist in the weighing of the same, shall forfeit to the person requiring such cart to be weighed a sum not exceeding twenty shillings.[2]

[1] I.e. the payment for cartage mentioned in s. 25.
[2] Recoverable in the manner provided by s. 52, *infra*.

Penalties on drivers of carts, etc., committing frauds in weighing

S. 27. Every driver of any such cart weighed at any weighing machine to be provided in pursuance of this or the special Act who shall commit any of the following offences shall be liable to a penalty[1] not exceeding five pounds for each offence; (that is to say,)

[1] If he at the time of weighing any such cart knowingly[2] have anything in or about the same other than the proper loading thereof:

[2] If he alter any ticket denoting the weight of any such cart or the loading of the same:

[3] If he make or use, or be privy to making or using, any ticket falsely stating the weight of any such cart or the loading thereof:

[4] If he, after the weighing of any such cart with the loading thereof, remove any part of such loading, and afterwards dispose of or attempt to dispose of or represent the residue of such loading as being the full loading denoted by such ticket:

[5] If he, between the time when the cart and the loading thereof have been so weighed and the time when such cart is weighed without such loading, change the wheels of such cart, or make any other change upon it after being

required to allow such cart to be weighed without the loading thereof:

[6] If he be guilty of any other fraudulent contrivance to misrepresent the weight of any such cart or of the loading thereof.

¹ As to recovery of penalties, see s. 52, *infra*.
² The word 'knowingly' is not used in the description of the other offences described by the section, but from the use of the word 'other' in the description of the last offence thereby described, it seems that a driver does not commit any offence against the section unless he be guilty of some *fraudulent* contrivance to misrepresent the weight of a cart or its loading.

S. 28. If the buyer or seller of any goods brought in any cart for sale within the market or fair,¹ and which shall be required to be weighed as aforesaid,² shall do³ anything to such cart or its loading whereby the true weight thereof respectively shall be altered before⁴ such weighing, he shall for every such offence be liable to a penalty⁵ not exceeding five pounds. *Penalty on buyers or sellers for committing frauds in weighing*

¹ The words 'or the prescribed limits,' which occur in s. 24, are here omitted.
² I.e. it seems, as provided by either s. 22 or s. 25; for the expression 'articles,' as used in s. 22, includes 'goods brought in any cart for sale.'
³ Notwithstanding the marginal note to this section, it seems doubtful whether the word 'knowingly' or 'fraudulently' can be read into the section before the word 'do'; for if the scope of the section be limited by reading such word into it, the section seems unnecessary, having regard to s. 30, *infra*.
⁴ I.e. it seems, 'after the cart or its loading has been required to be weighed and before the weighing thereof.'
⁵ As to the recovery of penalties, see s. 52, *infra*.

S. 29. The person for the time being appointed to keep any weighing machine provided in pursuance of this or the special Act shall be liable to a penalty¹ not exceeding five pounds in any of the following cases; (that is to say,) *Penalties for frauds committed by the machine keeper*

[1] If he wilfully neglect, on application, duly to weigh any cart, with or without its loading, as the case may be, that is brought to the machine kept by him to be weighed:²

[2] If he do not fairly weigh every such cart, with or without loading, as the case may be:²

[3] If he do not deliver to the buyer or seller of any such loading, or to any person interested therein, on application, a ticket or account specifying the true weight of such cart, with or without such loading, as may be required:²

[4] If he give to the driver of any such cart a false ticket or account of the weight of such cart, with or without the loading thereof:²

[5] If he weigh any cart, with or without its loading, knowing

160   *Markets and Fairs Clauses Act*, 1847   S. 29

that anything had been done to such cart or to the loading thereof to alter the true weight thereof respectively :²

[6] If he knowingly assist in or connive at any fraud concerning the weighing of any cart or the loading thereof, or make or connive at making any false representation of the weight of the same respectively.

¹ As to the recovery of penalties, see s. 52, *infra*.
² Notwithstanding the marginal note to the section, the machine-keeper is probably liable for a breach of this clause, whether committed with fraudulent intent or not. The Act seems to cast certain duties on him, and to render him liable to a penalty if he fails to perform these duties.

Penalty on other parties committing frauds as to weighing.

S. 30. Every person¹ who shall knowingly act or assist in committing any fraud respecting the weighing or weight of any cart, or the loading thereof,² in pursuance of this or the special Act, shall for every such offence be liable to a penalty³ not exceeding five pounds.

¹ Notwithstanding the marginal note, the words 'every person' probably includes buyers, sellers, drivers, and machine-keepers.
² It seems strange that no provision is here made for the punishment of frauds in respect of the weighing or measuring of articles under s. 22. Ss. 27-30 are limited to the weighing of carts and their loads.
³ As to recovery of penalties, see s. 52, *infra*.

And with respect to the stallages, rents, and tolls to be taken by the undertakers, be it enacted as follows :

Clauses 31-41 are incorporated with the Public Health Act, 1875 ;(*a*) but with regard to tolls, as distinct from stallages and rents, s. 167 of that Act prohibits an urban authority from levying in a market established by them under that Act any toll which has not been approved by the Local Government Board.

Clauses 31-41 were incorporated with the repealed Local Government Act, 1858 ;(*b*) but with regard to tolls, as distinct from stallages and rents, s. 50 (2) prohibited the local board from levying any toll which had not been approved by a Secretary of State. Upon the establishment of the Local Government Board the approval of that Board was substituted for that of a Secretary of State, by the Local Government Board Act, 1871.(*c*)

Clauses 31-41 are incorporated with the Diseases of Animals Act, 1894, but the tolls require the approval of the Board of Agriculture.(*d*)

Clauses 36-41 apply to tolls in respect of the weighing of cattle levied by a market authority under the Market and Fairs (Weighing of Cattle) Act, 1887, s. 8 ; see *post*, p. 198.

For the distinction between tolls and stallages or rents, see *ante*, pp. 55 and 63.

Tolls, etc., not to be

S. 31. Unless it be otherwise provided by the special Act, the undertakers shall not demand or receive any stallage, rent, or

---

(*a*) S. 167, *post*, p. 184.   (*b*) 21 & 22 Vict. c. 98.   (*c*) 34 & 35 Vict. c. 70.
(*d*) 57 & 58 Vict. c. 57, s. 32, *post*, p. 190.

S. 31   *Stallages, Rents and Tolls*

toll until the market-place or place for a fair or slaughter-house **demanded** in respect of the use of which the same shall be demanded shall **until market** be completed and fit for the use of the persons resorting there- **ket or fair** unto. **completed**

S. 32. A certificate under the hand of any two justices[1] shall **Certificate** be conclusive evidence that the same is completed and fit for **of two justices to be** public use as aforesaid; and any such justices shall sign such **evidence** certificate on proof being adduced to them that the market-place **that market** or place for a fair or slaughter-house is so completed and fit for **ket or fair** public use. **is completed**

[1] See ss. 3, 55. The certificate may be proved by producing the original document, purporting to be signed by two justices, without proof of their signature or official character;(a) or by producing a copy, provided (1) that it be proved to be an examined copy, or (2) that it purport to be signed and certified as a true copy by the officer to whose custody the original is entrusted.(b) The certificate is made conclusive evidence, but it is not the only admissible evidence of the completion and fitness of the place.

S. 33. The several stallages, rents, or tolls payable in respect **Stallages,** of the market or fair or slaughter-house shall be paid from time **etc., when** to time, on demand, to the undertakers or the collector,[1] or other **to be paid** person authorised by the undertakers to receive the same.

[1] See s. 3.

S. 34. The tolls payable in respect of weighing or measuring **Tolls for** marketable commodities, or carts with or without goods, shall be **weighing,** paid to the person authorised by the undertakers to weigh or **etc., to be** measure the same by the persons bringing [1] such marketable com- **paid before** modities or carts to be weighed or measured before the same are **goods are** weighed or measured. **weighed, etc.**

[1] See s. 22, *supra*, and note (2) thereon; and s. 25, *supra*, and note (2) thereon.

S. 35. The tolls[1] in respect of cattle[2] brought to the market[3] **Tolls in** for sale shall become due as soon as the cattle in respect whereof **respect of** they are demandable are brought into the market-place, and **cattle** before the cattle are put into any pen, or tied up in such market- **market,** place; and if the cattle be not removed within one hour after the **when due** close of the market, another toll[4] shall become due in respect of the cattle so omitted to be removed.[5]

[1] This section applies, it seems, only to tolls, and not to stallages or rents; and it depends upon the terms of the special Act whether any tolls are payable 'in respect of cattle brought to the market for sale.'
[2] See s. 3.

(a) 8 & 9 Vict. c. 113, s. 1.   (b) 14 & 15 Vict. c. 99, s. 14.

² The words 'or fair' are omitted, and consequently it seems that the section cannot apply to a fair, unless the special Act by apt words renders it applicable thereto.
⁴ I.e., it seems, a second toll of the same amount, unless the authorised scale of tolls provides otherwise.
⁵ This clause, it is submitted, does not *entitle* persons to keep their cattle in the market-place after the close of the market, but merely fixes, in a somewhat unsatisfactory manner, the compensation to be paid for non-removal.

Stallages, tolls, etc., may be varied from time to time

S. 36. The undertakers may from time to time change the stallages, rents, and tolls to be taken in respect of the market or fair, or for the slaughter-houses, or for weighing and measuring, provided that the stallages, rents, and tolls in no case exceed the amounts authorised by the special Act.¹

¹ Tolls taken in respect of a market established under the Public Health Act, 1875, must be authorised by the Local Government Board.(*a*) Tolls taken in respect of a market provided under the Diseases of Animals Act, 1894, must be approved by the Board of Agriculture.(*b*)

Penalty on taking a greater toll than authorised by this or the special Act

S. 37. Every person who shall demand or receive a greater toll¹ than that authorised to be taken under the provisions of this or the special Act² shall for every such offence be liable to a penalty³ not exceeding forty shillings.

¹ 'Toll,' probably, does not here include stallage or rent.
² See s. 36, *supra*, and note (1) thereon.
³ As to the recovery of penalties, see s. 52, *infra*.

Recovery of tolls by distress, etc.

S. 38. If any person liable to the payment of any stallage, rent, or toll authorised by this or the special Act to be taken do not pay the same when demanded, the undertakers or their lessee,¹ or any person authorised by the undertakers or their lessee to collect the same, may levy the same in England . . . by distress ² . . . of all or any of the cattle or other articles in respect of which such stallage, rent, or toll is payable, or of any other cattle or other articles in the market,³ belonging to the person liable to pay such stallage, rent, or toll, or under his charge, or⁴ such tolls⁵ may be recovered in any court having competent jurisdiction.⁶

¹ See s. 41, *infra*, and note (1) thereon.
² This section, in giving a right of distress, gives no right to sell the articles distrained, sale not being incident to distress at common law; but if cattle be distrained under this section, it seems that the undertakers are bound to provide them, while detained, with sufficient food, and have the remedies for recovering the cost of so doing conferred by 17 & 18 Vict. c. 60, s. 1. S. 52 of this Act incorporates s. 148 of the Railways Clauses Consolidation Act, 1845,(*c*) but, having regard to the difference between the last-mentioned section and this section with respect to the goods made

(*a*) See 38 & 39 Vict. c. 55, s. 167, *post*, p. 184.
(*b*) See 57 & 58 Vict. c. 57, s. 32, *post*, p. 191.
(*c*) See *post*, pp. 171 and 177.

S. 38   Stallages, Rents and Tolls

distrainable, and having regard also to the words introductory to the group of sections to which s. 148 belongs, it seems doubtful whether a distress under s. 38 of this Act is in any case affected by s. 148 of the Railways Clauses Act. In the case of markets established or regulated under the Public Health Act, 1875, s. 148 of the Railways Clauses Act has no application, inasmuch as s. 52 of this Act is not incorporated with the Public Health Act.

In the case, however, of a distress for any 'rent' in respect whereof the relation of landlord and tenant subsists between the undertakers and their debtor, the undertakers are probably not prevented by the remedy expressly given by this section from distraining as landlords and exercising a landlord's statutory powers of sale; but it seems that they cannot first distrain under this section, and then sell the distress as if they had distrained as landlords. Under this section they can distrain the debtor's articles wherever found in the market; as landlords they can only distrain upon the demised premises.

³ See s. 35, *supra*, and note (3) thereon. The section appears to be so framed as to authorise a distress only in the market-place. It is submitted that toll payable in respect of cattle not removed within one hour after the close of the market (see s. 35) may be levied by distress.

¹ The remedies seem to be alternative, not concurrent.

⁵ 'Such tolls,' perhaps, here include stallage and rent.

⁶ The effect of merely incorporating both s. 38 and s. 39 appears to be that in case a dispute arises concerning any stallage, rent or toll, the only tribunal competent to determine such dispute is that of a justice, as provided by s. 39; but a mere refusal to pay appears not to be a dispute within the meaning of s. 39, and in cases merely of non-payment without any dispute the proper course seems to be to sue the defaulter either in the County Court or the High Court. (*a*) It is doubtful whether a justice has any jurisdiction if there be no 'dispute.'

S. 39. If any dispute ¹ arise concerning any such stallage, rent, or toll, such dispute shall be determined in England ... by a justice,² ... and such justice ... shall, on application made to him, determine the same, and make such order therein, and award such costs to either party as to him shall seem proper; and in default of payment, on demand, of the money which shall be so awarded, and of the costs, the same shall be forthwith levied in England ... by distress, ... and the justice ... shall issue his warrant accordingly.

Disputes respecting tolls, how to be settled

¹ See s. 38, *supra*, and note (6) thereon. The justice, probably, has no jurisdiction where the dispute concerns, not the stallage, rent, or toll, but the validity of a distress levied to recover the same under s. 38.

² See s. 3. If the special Act incorporates s. 52 of this Act, the method of procedure under this section, so far as it is not thereby specially provided for, is regulated by s. 52, *infra*, and the clauses of the Railways Clauses Consolidation Act, 1845, thereby incorporated.

S. 40. Every person who shall assault or obstruct any person authorised to collect any stallage, rent, or toll authorised by this or the special Act shall for every such offence be liable to a penalty ¹ not exceeding forty shillings.

Penalty for obstructing collector of rates, etc.

¹ As to the recovery of penalties, see s. 52, *infra*.

(*a*) See the County Courts Act, 1888, 51 & 52 Vict. c. 43, s. 56.

164   Markets and Fairs Clauses Act, 1847   S. 41

List of tolls, etc., to be set up and placed in conspicuous places

S. 41. The undertakers or their lessee[1] shall from time to time cause to be painted on boards, or to be printed and attached to boards, in large and legible characters, a list of the several stallages, rents, and tolls from time to time payable under this and the special Act,[2] and shall cause a board containing such list to be conspicuously set up and continued in the market or fair, and in each weighing-house and slaughter-house provided by the undertakers, to which each such list shall relate, and no stallage, rent, or toll shall be payable during the time such list is not so set up, or for anything not specified therein: Provided always, that if such list shall be destroyed, injured, or obliterated, the stallages, rents, and tolls shall continue to be payble during such time as shall be reasonably required for the restoration of such list, in the same manner as if such list had continued in the state required by this Act.

[1] The only references in this Act to the undertakers' lessee are those in this section and s. 38, *supra*. The undertakers' right (if any) to lease their undertaking must be sought for outside this Act.

[2] The actual sums for the time being payable must be stated in the list, and not merely the maximum sums which the undertakers have power to charge.(a)

And with respect to the by-laws to be made by the undertakers, be it enacted as follows:

Clauses 42-49 were incorporated with the Local Government Act, 1858, s. 50, now repealed. But they are not incorporated with the Public Health Act, 1875. S. 167 of the latter Act, however, provides that the urban authority may with respect to any market belonging to them make by-laws for any of the purposes mentioned in s. 42 of this Act. With regard to the making, confirmation, publication, and proof of such by-laws, see the Public Health Act, 1875, ss. 182, *et seq*. And as to by-laws made before that Act was passed, see ss. 315, 326, and 4; see also, *post*, p. 201.

Clauses 42-49 are incorporated with the Diseases of Animals Act, 1894; see s. 32 (2), *post*, p. 190; but s. 32 (3) of that Act enacts that, as regards markets provided under the Diseases of Animals Act, 1894, or under the earlier Contagious Diseases (Animals) Acts, the by-laws shall be approved by the Board of Agriculture, and that such approval 'shall be sufficient without any other approval or allowance, notice of application for approval being given, and proposed by-laws being published before application, as required by' ss. 45 and 46 of this Act.

Expressions used in any by-laws made since 1889 have, unless the contrary intention appears, the same respective meanings as in the Act conferring the power to make them (52 & 53 Vict. c. 63, s. 31).

Model by-laws, applicable to markets under the Public Health Act, are printed *post*, p. 208; and these may be adapted for use in other statutory markets.

(a) Gregson *v.* Potter (1879) 4 Ex. D. 142.

S. 42. The undertakers may from time to time make such by-laws as they think fit for all or any of the following purposes ; (that is to say),

[1] For regulating the use of the market-place and fair,[1] and the buildings, stalls, pens, and standings therein, and for preventing nuisances or obstructions therein, or in the immediate approaches thereto :

[2] For fixing the days, and the hours during each day, on which the market or fair shall be held :[2]

[3] For inspection of the slaughter-houses, and for keeping the same in a cleanly and proper state, and for removing filth and refuse at least once in every twenty-four hours, and for requiring that they be provided with a sufficient supply of water, and preventing the exercise of cruelty therein :[3]

[4] For regulating the carriers resorting to the market or fair, and fixing the rates for carrying articles carried therefrom within the limits of the special Act :[4]

[5] For regulating the use of the weighing machines provided by the undertakers, and for preventing the use of false or defective weights, scales, or measures :

[6] For preventing the sale or exposure for sale of unwholesome provisions in the market or fair :

And the undertakers may from time to time, as they shall think fit, repeal or alter any such by-laws ; Provided always, that such by-laws shall not be repugnant to the laws of that part of the United Kingdom where the same are to have effect, or to the provisions of this or the special Act, or of any Act incorporated therewith ; and such by-laws shall be reduced to writing under the common seal of the undertakers if they be a body corporate, or the hands and seals of two of the undertakers if they be not a body corporate, and, if affecting other persons than the officers and servants of the undertakers, shall be printed and published as herein[5] provided.

By-laws may be made for all or any of the purposes herein-named

By-laws may be repealed or altered from time to time

[1] A by-law providing that no auctioneer shall sell cattle by auction in the market-place before noon on the market-day is valid.(*a*) So is a by-law which reserves a part of the market-place for the sale only of particular commodities, or for sale only by wholesale, and imposes a penalty for selling other commodities, or for selling by retail, in that part.(*b*) But a by-law is void if its effect is to prohibit a marketable commodity from being brought into the market at all without leave of the market officials.(*c*)

(*a*) Collins *v.* Corporation of Wells (1885) 1 T.L.R. 328.
(*b*) Savage *v.* Brook (1863) 15 C.B.N.S. 264 ; Strike *v.* Collins (1888) 55 L.T.N.S. 182.
(*c*) Wortley *v.* Nottingham L. B. (1870) 21 L.T.N.S. 582.

² As to the days on which markets and fairs may be lawfully held, see *ante*, p. 50.
³ An urban authority appears to have no power under s. 167 of the Public Health Act, 1875, to make by-laws for the purposes mentioned in this clause.
⁴ As to the words 'within the limits of the special Act,' see s. 12, and note (2) thereon, *supra*.
⁵ See s. 47, *infra*.

By-laws may be enforced by imposition of penalties

S. 43. The undertakers, by the by-laws so to be made by them,¹ may impose such reasonable penalties as they shall think fit, not exceeding five pounds for each breach of such by-laws;² provided that every such by-law shall be so framed as to allow the justices . . . before whom any penalty imposed thereby shall be sought to be recovered to order the whole or part only of such penalty to be paid.³

¹ Including, it seems, by-laws which relate solely to the officers and servants of the undertakers, although such by-laws are not required by the Act to be either confirmed (see s. 44) or published (see s. 42, *ad fin.*).
² The undertakers are given some discretion (which they ought to exercise) with respect to the amount of the penalty to be imposed by a by-law for a breach thereof; but if the penalty imposed for a breach exceed £5 the by-law is void; and since the penalty is required to be reasonable, it seems that a by-law which imposes an unreasonable penalty is void, although the penalty does not exceed £5. Subject to these observations, it seems to be sufficient, in making a set of by-laws, to provide by one of them that 'every person who is guilty of any breach of any of these by-laws shall be liable for each such breach to a penalty of £5.'
³ Any by-law not so framed is void; but in making a set of by-laws it seems to be sufficient to provide by one of them that 'the justices before whom any penalty imposed by any of these by-laws shall be sought to be recovered may order the whole or part only of such penalty to be paid.'

No bylaws to come into operation until allowed in the manner prescribed

S. 44. No by-laws made under the authority of this or the special Act (except such as may relate solely to the officers or servants of the undertakers) shall come into operation until the same shall be allowed in the manner prescribed by the special Act, or, if no manner be prescribed, until the same shall be [¹ allowed by the justices at quarter sessions if the market or fair be in England, . . . and . . . approved under the hand of one of her Majesty's principal secretaries of state; and it shall be incumbent on the justices at quarter sessions, . . . on the request of the undertakers, to examine into the by-laws which may be tendered to them for that purpose, and to allow of or disallow the same as to them may seem meet.¹]

¹ 'Confirmed by the Local Government Board' may now be read for the words in brackets, as regards by-laws made on or after August 10, 1872. The Public Health Act, 1872,(*a*) substituted the consent, sanction,

---

(*a*) 35 & 36 Vict. c. 79, s. 34.

S. 44 By-laws 167

or confirmation of the Local Government Board for that of a secretary of state where required in any *local Act* to give effect to any by-law ; and this enactment was preserved by the Public Health Act, 1875.(*a*) Questions having arisen as to the effect of the enactment,(*b*) the Public Health (Confirmation of By-laws) Act, 1884,(*c*) was passed. The effect of that Act is that a by-law made under s. 42 of the Markets and Fairs Clauses Act, by reason of the incorporation thereof with any local Act, and confirmed before August 10, 1872, by a secretary of state, or on or after that date by the Local Government Board, is valid without any other confirmation, allowance or approval ; unless by the express provisions of the local Act, and without reference to ss. 44-46 of the Markets and Fairs Clauses Act, some other confirmation, allowance, or approval is required.

A by-law relating solely to the officers or servants of the undertakers is not affected by the Public Health (Confirmation of By-laws) Act, 1884 (see s. 4), and comes into force without any confirmation, approval, or allowance.

S. 45. Provided always, That no such by-law shall be allowed in manner herein mentioned [1] unless notice of the intention to apply for an allowance of the same shall have been given in one or more newspapers of the county [2] in which the market or fair shall be situated, or, if there be no newspaper in such county, in one or more newspapers of the adjoining county, one month [2] at least before the hearing of such application ; and any party aggrieved by any such by-law, on giving notice of the nature of his objection to the undertakers ten days before the hearing of the application for the allowance thereof, may, by himself or his counsel, attorney, or agent, be heard thereon, but not so as to allow more than one party to be heard upon the same matter of objection.

Notice of allowance of by-laws to be given in one or more newspapers, etc.

[1] 'Allowed in the manner herein mentioned' seems to refer to an allowance in the manner prescribed by the special Act, or if none be prescribed thereby, to an allowance by justices (see s. 44). An allowance by justices is no longer necessary, unless expressly required by the special Act (see s. 44, *supra*, and note (1) thereon). If s. 45 be now incorporated by a special Act which does not expressly require some 'allowance' of by-laws, there will be nothing upon which the section can operate, unless it be construable as referring to a confirmation by the Local Government Board ; but there will be difficulties in the way of such construction. The Local Government Board, however, before confirming by-laws, can probably require steps to be taken similar to those mentioned in the section.

[2] See s. 3.

S. 46. For one month [1] at least before any such application for allowance [2] of any by-laws a copy of such proposed by-laws shall be kept at the principal office of the undertakers, and shall be put up in some conspicuous place in the market-place or fair, and all persons at all reasonable times may inspect such copy

A copy of proposed by-laws to be open for inspection

(*a*) 38 & 39 Vict. c. 55, s. 343, and Sch. V. pt. 3 ; see 54 & 55 Vict. c. 76, s. 142 (5).
(*b*) See Wallasey Tramway Co. *v.* Wallasey L. B. (1883) 47 J.P. 821.
(*c*) 47 Vict. c. 12, ss. 3 and 4 ; see *post*, p. 200.

without fee or reward, and the undertakers shall furnish every person who shall apply for the same with a copy thereof or of any part thereof on payment of sixpence for every one hundred words so to be copied.

¹ See s. 3.   ² See s. 45, *supra*, and note (1) thereon.

Publication of by-laws

S. 47. The said by-laws¹ shall be published in the prescribed² manner, and when no manner of publication is prescribed they shall be printed, and the clerk of the undertakers shall give a printed copy thereof to every person applying for the same without charge, and a copy thereof shall be painted or placed on boards, and put up in some conspicuous part of the principal office of the undertakers, and also in some conspicuous place in the market-place or fair, and such boards, with the by-laws thereon, shall be renewed from time to time as occasion shall require, and shall be open to inspection without fee or reward; and in case the said clerk shall not permit the same to be inspected at all reasonable times he shall for every such offence be liable to a penalty³ not exceeding five pounds.

¹ These words, 'the *said* by-laws,' do not, it seems, include by-laws which relate solely to the officers or servants of the undertakers (see s. 42, *ad fin.*).
² See s. 2, *supra*.
³ As to recovery of penalties, see s. 52, *infra*.

By-laws to be binding on all parties

S. 48. All by-laws made¹ and confirmed² according to the provisions of this and the special Act, when so published and put up,³ shall be binding upon and be observed by all parties, and shall be a sufficient warrant for all persons acting under the same.⁴

¹ By-laws are not made 'according to the provisions of this Act' if they be repugnant to the laws of England, or to the provisions of this or the special Act or any Act incorporated therewith (see s. 42, *supra*); and they are repugnant to the laws of England if they be unreasonable. Such repugnant by-laws are not rendered valid by the confirmation of any confirming authority.(*a*)
² As to confirmation, see s. 44, *supra*, and note (1) thereon.
³ See s. 47, *supra*.
⁴ Apparently, by-laws affecting only the officers and servants of the undertakers do not require to be published in order to become operative; see s. 42, *ad fin.*, *supra*.

Proof of publication of by-laws

S. 49. The production of a written or printed copy of the by-laws requiring confirmation by the court of quarter session ... authenticated by the signature of the judge or of the chairman of the court ... who shall have approved of the same, and requiring

---

(*a*) See Ellwood *v.* Bullock (1844) 6 Q.B. 383; R. *v.* Wood (1855) 5 E. & B. 49; Saunders *v.* S. E. R. Co. (1880) 5 Q.B.D. 456; Dyson *v.* L. & N. W. R. Co. (1881) 7 Q.B.D. 32; Kruse *v.* Johnson [1898] 2 Q.B. 91.

approval under the hand of one of her Majesty's principal secretaries of state, and a written or printed copy of the by-laws not requiring such confirmation or approval, authenticated by the common seal of the undertakers if they be a body corporate, or under the hands of the undertakers if not incorporated, or any two of them, shall be evidence [1] of the existence and making of such by-laws in all cases of prosecution under the same, without proof of the signature of such judge, chairman . . . or such secretary of state, or the common seal or signature of the undertakers ; [2]

And with respect to the proof of the publication of any such by-laws,[3] it shall be sufficient to prove that a painted board containing a copy thereof was put up and continued in manner by this Act directed, and in case of its afterwards being displaced or damaged, that such board was replaced or restored as soon as conveniently might be, unless proof be adduced by the party complained against that such painted board did not contain a copy of such by-laws, or was not duly put up or continued as directed by this Act.

[1] I.e. *prima facie*, not conclusive, evidence.
[2] The effect of the Public Health (Confirmation of By-laws) Act, 1884, is that, unless the special Act expressly requires by-laws to be confirmed by justices, such confirmation is now, and is deemed to have always been, unnecessary; and the only confirmation which need be proved is either that of a secretary of state before August 10, 1872, or that of the Local Government Board on or after that date ; see s. 44, and note (1) thereon.

S. 49 is somewhat obscurely worded, so far as it relates to by-laws confirmed by a secretary of state ; but the meaning seems to be that such by-laws may be proved by the production of a written or printed copy, purporting to be authenticated by the signature of the judge or chairman of the quarter sessions which approved them. Whether the copy must also purport to be signed by a secretary of state is not clear. These by-laws are now deemed not to have required approval by quarter sessions; but it is not clear that a copy purporting only to be signed by a secretary of state would comply with this section. The safest course, if feasible, is to produce a copy purporting to be signed by the chairman or judge of quarter sessions and by the secretary of state. Such a copy would seem to be sufficient evidence of the by-laws. The copy so signed seems to be 'a document of such a public nature as to be admissible in evidence on its mere production from the proper custody,' within the meaning of the Evidence Act, 1851,(a) and therefore by reason of that Act, (unless the special Act renders the document provable by a copy, in which case its provisions must be followed), the by-laws may be proved by producing a copy of such document, *proved* to be an examined copy, or *purporting* to he signed and certified as a true copy by the officer of the undertakers to whose custody the original is entrusted.

With regard to by-laws confirmed since August 9, 1872, by the Local Government Board, s. 49 does not provide any means of giving secondary

---

(a) 14 & 15 Vict. c. 99, s. 14 ; see Motteram *v.* Eastern Counties Rly. Co. (1859) 7 C.B.N.S. 58.

evidence thereof. It seems not unlikely, however, that such by-laws might be proved by the production of the original copy, showing on its face the confirmation by the Local Government Board. The courts would perhaps take judicial notice of the seal of the Board and of the signatures of the president or members of the Board or of the secretary or assistant-secretary,(a) and presume therefrom that the by-laws had been made by the undertakers and duly confirmed. If the production of the original, purporting to show the confirmation by the Local Government Board, would be evidence of the by-laws on its mere production from the proper custody, so also would an examined copy thereof, or a copy or extract purporting to be signed and certified as a true copy by the clerk or other officer of the undertakers to whose custody the original is entrusted.(b)

Publication of these by-laws must be proved; and may be proved in accordance with the latter part of the above section, as this provision does not seem to be affected by the Public Health (Confirmation of By-laws) Act, 1884.

² I.e. if they require publication (see s. 42, *ad fin.*).

S. 50. And with respect to the receipts and expenditure of the undertakers, be it enacted : [1]

Annual account to be made up by the undertakers, and transmitted to the clerk of the peace, and to be open to inspection

That the undertakers shall in every year cause an annual account in abstract to be prepared, showing the whole receipt and expenditure of all rents and other moneys levied by virtue of this or the special Act for the year ending the thirty-first day of December, or some other convenient day in each year, under the several distinct heads of receipt and expenditure, with a statement of the balance of such account, duly audited or certified by the chairman of the undertakers, and by the auditors, if any, and shall send a copy of the said account, free of charge, to the clerk of the peace in England ... of the county ² in which the market or fair is situate, on or before the expiration of one month ³ from the day on which such accounts shall end, which account shall be open to the inspection of the public at all seasonable hours, on payment of the sum of one shilling for every such inspection ; and if the undertakers omit to prepare or send such account as aforesaid they shall forfeit for every such omission the sum of twenty pounds.[3]

[1] Clause 50 is not incorporated with the Public Health Act, 1875. As to the accounts with regard to a market established or regulated under that Act, see *ante*, p. 112.
Clause 50 is incorporated with the Diseases of Animals Act, 1894.(c) S. 32 (6) of that Act requires a local authority, which has provided a market under that Act, or the earlier Contagious Diseases (Animals) Acts, to make such returns to the Board of Agriculture of their expenditure and receipts in respect of the market as the Board require.
² See s. 3, *supra*.
³ Recoverable in the manner provided by s. 52, *infra*.

(a) See 34 & 35 Vict. c. 70, s. 5.
(b) 14 & 15 Vict. c. 99, s. 14 ; Motteram *v.* Eastern Counties Rly. Co. (1859) 7 C.B.N.S. 58.
(c) 57 & 58 Vict. c. 57, s. 32 (2) *post*, p. 190.

S. 51. With respect to the tender of amends.

Repealed by the S.L.R. Act, 1894.(a) The Public Authorities Protection Act, 1893,(b) now regulates actions against any person for any act done 'in pursuance, or execution, or intended execution, of any Act of Parliament,' or 'in respec tof any alleged neglect or default in the execution of any such Act,' and enables the defendant, if the action be for damages, to plead tender of amends before action brought.

And with respect to the recovery of damages not specially provided for, and of penalties, and to the determination of any other matters referred to justices in England, . . . be it enacted as follows :

Clauses 52–57 are not incorporated with the Public Health Act, 1875. With regard to markets established or regulated under s. 167 of that Act, penalties under the incorporated provisions of this Act, or under by-laws made with respect to such markets, are recoverable in the manner directed by the Summary Jurisdiction Acts before a court of summary jurisdiction.(c)

Clauses 52–57 are not incorporated with the Diseases of Animals Act, 1894. S. 54 of that Act provides for the summary prosecution of offences against that Act, but the Act contains no provision for the summary prosecution of offences against the incorporated clauses of this Act, or against by-laws made thereunder, unless s. 54 can be construed as such.

One of the results of incorporating clause 52 is that no penalty imposed by this Act, or the special Act, or by s. 144 of the Railways Clauses Consolidation Act, 1845, can be recovered unless such penalty has been published and kept published, as required by s. 143 of the last-mentioned Act.

S. 52. If the market or fair be in England . . . the clauses of the Railways Clauses Consolidation Act, 1845,[1] with respect to the recovery of damages not specially provided for, and penalties, and to the determination of any other matter referred to justices, shall be incorporated with this and the special Act ; . . . and such clauses shall apply to the market or fair and the undertakers respectively, and shall be construed as if the word 'undertakers' had been inserted therein instead of the word 'company.' *Railways Clauses Consolidation Act, 1845, as to damages, etc., to be incorporated with this and the special Act*

[1] 8 & 9 Vict. c. 20, ss. 140-161 ; see *post*, pp. 175 *et seq.*

S. 53. Applied only to Ireland ; and was repealed by S.L.R. Act, 1875.

S. 54. And be it enacted, that nothing in this or the special Act shall be deemed to extend to or affect any Act of Parliament relating to her Majesty's duties of customs or excise, or any other revenue of the crown, or to extend to or affect any claim of her Majesty in right of her crown, or otherwise howsoever, or any proceedings at law or in equity by or on behalf of her *Nothing in this or the special Act to affect the rights of the crown*

(a) 57 & 58 Vict. c. 56, s. 1, and first schedule.
(b) 56 & 57 Vict. c. 61.,
(c) See the Public Health Act, 1875, ss. 316, 251, 183.

172 *Markets and Fairs Clauses Act*, 1847 S. 54

Majesty, in any part of the United Kingdom of Great Britain and Ireland.

All things required to be done by two justices may in certain cases be done by one

S. 55. All things herein or in the special Act, or any Act incorporated therewith, authorised or required to be done by two justices, may and shall be done in England . . . by any one magistrate having by law authority to act alone for any purpose with the powers of two or more justices. . . .

Penalties, etc., imposed in respect of any offence committed within the Metropolitan Police District to be paid to the Receiver, and applied under 2 & 3 Vict. c. 71

S. 56. Every[1] penalty or forfeiture imposed by this or the special Act, or any Act incorporated therewith, or by any by-law in pursuance thereof, in respect of any offence which shall take place within the Metropolitan Police District, shall be recovered, enforced, accounted for, and, except where the application thereof is otherwise specially provided for, shall be paid to the Receiver of the Metropolitan Police District, and shall be applied in the same manner as penalties or forfeitures other than fines upon drunken persons, or upon constables for misconduct, or for assaults upon police constables, are directed to be recovered, enforced, accounted for, paid, and applied by an Act passed in the third year of the reign of her present Majesty, intituled An Act for Regulating the Police Courts in the Metropolis ;[2] and every order or conviction of any of the police magistrates in respect of any such forfeiture or penalty shall be subject to the like appeal and upon the same terms as is provided in respect of any order or conviction of any of the said police magistrates by the said last-mentioned Act ;[2] and every magistrate by whom any order or conviction shall have been made shall have the same power of binding over the witnesses who shall have been examined, and such witnesses shall be entitled to the same allowance of expenses as they would have had or been entitled to in case the order, conviction, and appeal had been made in pursuance of the provisions of the said last-mentioned Act.[2]

[1] Ss. 159 and 160 of the Railways Clauses Consolidation Act, 1845, are to the same effect as ss. 56 and 57 of this Act, and are incorporated with this Act by s. 52 thereof. Ss. 56 and 57 of the Act were therefore, it seems, unnecessary.

[2] The Metropolitan Police Courts Act, 1839,(*a*) which has been partially repealed by various later Acts. S. 46 of the Act of 1839 directs how the penalties and forfeitures are to be accounted for, and paid, to the Receiver of the Metropolitan Police District, and applied by him. The recovery and enforcement of the penalties and forfeitures are now regulated by the Summary Jurisdiction Acts, the sections of 2 & 3 Vict. c. 71 dealing therewith having been repealed by 47 & 48 Vict. c. 43, ss. 4 and 5. Appeals from orders and convictions also are now regulated by the Summary Jurisdiction Acts,(*b*) subject, however, to s. 50 of the Metropolitan Police Courts Act, 1839, which has not been repealed.

(*a*) 2 & 3 Vict. c. 71.
(*b*) See 47 & 48 Vict. c. 43, ss. 4 and 5.

S. 57. *Access to Special Act* 173

S. 57. Every[1] person who upon any examination upon oath[2] under the provisions of this or the special Act, or any Act incorporated therewith, shall wilfully and corruptly give false evidence, shall be liable to the penalties of wilful and corrupt perjury.[3]

Penalty for giving false evidence

[1] See s. 56, *supra*, and note (1) thereon.   [2] See s. 3, *supra*.
[3] See The Perjury Act, 1728 (2 Geo. II. c. 25) s. 2.

And with respect to access to the special Act, be it enacted as follows:

Clauses 58 and 59 are not incorporated either with the Public Health Act, 1875, or with the Diseases of Animals Act, 1894. In legal proceedings the special Act will be deemed to be a public Act, and will be judicially noticed, if it contain a clause to that effect, or if it was passed after 1850, and the contrary be not expressly provided by the Act (see 52 & 53 Vict. c. 63, s. 9).

S. 58. The undertakers shall at all times after the expiration of six months[1] after the passing of the special Act keep in their principal office of business a copy of the special Act, printed by the printers to her Majesty, or some of them, and shall also within the space of such six months[1] deposit in the office of the clerk of the peace of the county[1] in England... in which the undertaking[2] is situate, a copy of such special Act so printed as aforesaid; and the said clerk of the peace ... shall receive, and [he] and the undertakers respectively shall keep the said copies of the special Act, and shall allow all persons interested therein to inspect the same, and make extracts or copies therefrom, in the like manner, and upon the like terms, and under the like penalty for default, as is provided in the case of certain plans and sections by an Act passed in the first year of the reign of her Majesty, intituled An Act to Compel Clerks of the Peace for Counties and other Persons to take the Custody of such Documents as shall be directed to be deposited with them under the Standing Orders of either House of Parliament.[3]

Copies of special Act to be kept by undertakers at their office, and deposited with the clerk of the peace, and be open to inspection

[1] See s. 3.   [2] See s. 2.
[3] The Parliamentary Documents Deposit Act 1837 (7 Wm. IV. and 1 Vict. c. 83). By that Act the undertakers, and the clerk of the peace, are required, at all reasonable hours of the day, to allow all persons interested to inspect during a reasonable time, and make extracts from or copies of, the special Act, on payment by each person to the undertakers, or clerk of the peace, as the case may be, 'of one shilling for every such inspection, and the further sum of one shilling for every hour during which such inspection shall continue after the first hour, and after the rate of sixpence for every one hundred words copied therefrom' (s. 2). The penalty for default is a sum not exceeding £5 for every offence, recoverable summarily in the manner provided by the Act of 1837, s. 3.

Penalty on undertakers failing to keep or deposit such copies

S. 59. If the undertakers[1] fail to keep or deposit, as hereinbefore mentioned,[2] any of the said copies of the special Act, they shall forfeit twenty pounds for every such offence, and also five pounds for every day afterwards during which such copy shall be not so kept or deposited.[3]

[1] If the clerk of the peace fails to keep the copy deposited with him, he is liable under the Act of 1837 to a penalty not exceeding £5 for every offence (see s. 58, *supra*, and note (3) thereon).
[2] See s. 58, *supra*.
[3] As to the recovery of the sums forfeited, see s. 52, *supra*.

THE RAILWAYS CLAUSES CONSOLIDATION ACT, 1845.

(8 & 9 Vict. c. 20.)

[Clauses 140-161 (inclusive) of this Act are incorporated by s. 52 of the Markets and Fairs Clauses Act, 1847, with that Act, and any special Act which incorporates that section. In printing these clauses below, the word 'undertakers' has been inserted therein, instead of the word 'company,' pursuant to the directions in s. 52 of the Markets and Fairs Clauses Act, see *ante*, p. 171.]

With respect to the recovery of damages not specially provided for, and of penalties, and to the determination of any other matter referred to justices, be it enacted as follows:

S. 140. In all cases where any damages, costs, or expenses are by this or the special Act,[1] or any Act incorporated therewith, directed to be paid, and the method of ascertaining the amount or enforcing the payment thereof is not provided for,[2] such amount, in case of dispute, shall[3] be ascertained and determined by two justices;[4] and if the amount so ascertained be not paid by the undertakers or other party liable to pay the same within seven days after demand, the amount may be recovered by distress of the goods of the undertakers or other party liable as aforesaid; and the justices by whom the same shall have been ordered to be paid, or either of them, or any other justice, on application, shall issue their or his warrant accordingly.

Provision for damages not otherwise provided for

[1] Throughout these clauses, the expression 'the special Act' means not only the Act authorising the construction or regulation of the market or fair with which s. 52 of the Markets and Fairs Clauses Act, 1847, is incorporated, but also the Markets and Fairs Clauses Act, 1847; for s. 52 of the latter Act incorporates these clauses with both Acts.

[2] These clauses do not, it seems, apply to the recovery of damages sustained by reason of the exercise by undertakers of the powers of constructing their undertaking. See the Markets and Fairs Clauses Act, 1847, . 11, *ante*, p. 149.

[3] Damages, costs, and expenses to which this section applies can be recovered only in the manner provided by this section, and cannot be recovered by action.(*a*)

[4] As to the expressions 'justices' and 'justice' in these clauses, see ss. 3 and 55 of the Markets and Fairs Clauses Act, 1847, *supra*.

(*a*) Mayor of Blackburn *v.* Parkinson (1858) 1 E. & E. 71.

Distress against the treasurer

S. 141. If sufficient goods of the undertakers cannot be found whereon to levy any such damages, costs and expenses[1] payable by the undertakers, the same may, if the amount thereof do not exceed twenty pounds, be recovered by distress of the goods of the treasurer of the undertakers ; and the justices aforesaid or either of them, on application, shall issue their or his warrant accordingly ; but no such distress shall issue against the goods of such treasurer unless seven days' previous notice in writing, stating the amount so due, and demanding payment thereof, have been given to such treasurer, or left at his residence ; and if such treasurer pay any money under such distress as aforesaid he may retain the amount so paid by him, and all cost and expenses occasioned thereby, out of any money belonging to the undertakers coming into his custody or control, or he may sue the undertakers for the same.

[1] See s. 140, *supra*.

Method of proceeding before justices in questions of damages, etc.

S. 142. Where in this or the special Act any question of compensation, expenses, charges, or damages, or other matter, is referred to the determination of any one justice or more, it shall be lawful for any justice, upon the application of either party, to summon the other party to appear before one justice, or before two justices, as the case may require, at a time and place to be named in such summons ; and upon the appearance of such parties, or in the absence of any of them, upon proof of due service of the summons, it shall be lawful for such one justice, or such two justices, as the case may be, to hear and determine such question, and for that purpose to examine such parties or any of them, and their witnesses, on oath ; and the cost of every such inquiry shall be in the discretion of such justices, and they shall determine the amount thereof.

Publication of penalties

S. 143. The undertakers shall publish the short particulars of the several offences for which any penalty[1] is imposed by this or the special Act, or by any by-law of the undertakers affecting other persons than the shareholders, officers, or servants of the undertakers, and of the amount of every such penalty, and shall cause such particulars to be painted on a board, or printed upon paper and pasted thereon, and shall cause such board to be hung up or affixed on some conspicuous part of the principal place of business of the undertakers, and where any such penalties are of local application shall cause such boards to be affixed in some conspicuous place in the immediate neighbourhood to which such penalties are applicable or have reference ; and such particulars shall be renewed as often as the same or any part thereof is obliterated or destroyed ; and no such penalty shall be recoverable[2]

S. 143 Damages and Penalties

unless it shall have been published and kept published in the manner herein-before required.

[1] If a special Act relating to a market or fair incorporates all the clauses of the Markets and Fairs Clauses Act, 1847, the undertakers ought to publish particulars of the following offences:

1. The offences referred to in ss. 13, 15, 16, 19, 20, 22, 23, 27, 28, 29, 30, 37, 40 and 47, and probably also 26, 50, and 59, of the Markets and Fairs Clauses Act, 1847, and ss. 144 and 153 of the Railways Clauses Act.
2. Any offences for which a penalty is imposed by the special Act.
3. Any offences for which a penalty is imposed by any by-laws made by the undertakers and affecting persons other than their officers and servants.

[2] *Quære*, whether, if the undertakers have not published particulars of the offences referred to in ss. 50 and 59 of the Markets and Fairs Clauses Act, 1847, they could take advantage of that default, if sued for forfeitures under either of these sections. It should be noticed that s. 143, *supra*, speaks of 'penalties,' not 'forfeitures.'

S. 144. If any person pull down or injure any board put up or affixed as required by this or the special Act for the purpose of publishing any by-law[1] or penalty, or shall obliterate any of the letters or figures thereon, he shall forfeit for every such offence a sum not exceeding five pounds, and shall defray the expenses attending the restoration of such board.

Penalty for defacing boards used for such publication

[1] See the Markets and Fairs Clauses Act, 1847, s. 47, *ante*, p. 168.

S. 145. Every penalty or forfeiture imposed by this or the special Act, or by any by-law made in pursuance thereof, the recovery of which is not otherwise provided for, may[1] be recovered by summary proceeding before two justices[2]...

Penalties to be summarily recovered before two justices

[1] A penalty or forfeiture to which this section applies can be recovered only in the manner provided by this section, and cannot be recovered by action.(a)

[2] The remainder of this section (which related to the procedure to obtain the conviction of an offender, and an order against him to pay the penalty or forfeiture incurred, and costs), and the whole of ss. 146 and 147 (which related to the enforcement of such order by distress or by imprisonment in default of distress), were repealed by the Summary Jurisdiction Act, 1884.(b) That Act substituted for the procedure provided by the repealed enactments that provided by the Summary Jurisdiction Acts.

S. 148. Where[1] in this or the special Act, or any Act incorporated therewith, any sum of money, whether in the nature of penalty or otherwise, is directed to be levied by distress, such sum of money shall be levied by distress and sale of the goods and chattels of the party liable to pay the same; and the overplus arising from the sale of such goods and chattels, after satisfying

Distress, how to be levied

(a) L. & Brighton Rly. Co. v. Watson (1879) 4 C.P.D. 118.
(b) 47 & 48 Vict. c. 43.

such sum of money, and the expenses of the distress and sale, shall be returned, on demand,[2] to the party whose goods shall have been distrained.

[1] It is doubtful whether the provisions of this section, or of s. 149, *infra*, can be construed as applying to a distress for stallage, rent, or toll under s. 38 of the Markets and Fairs Clauses Act, 1847, see *ante*, p. 162. The words introductory to s. 52 of that Act, and to ss. 140-161 of this Act, seem to limit the scope of these two clauses to distresses to enforce orders or awards of justices.

[2] No action lies for the surplus until the demand has been made.(a)

Distress not unlawful for want of form

S. 149. No distress levied by virtue of this or the special Act, or any Act incorporated therewith, shall be deemed unlawful, nor shall any party making the same be deemed a trespasser, on account of any defect or want of form in the summons, conviction, warrant of distress, or other proceeding relating thereto, nor shall such party be deemed a trespasser *ab initio* on account of any irregularity afterwards committed by him, but all persons aggrieved by such defect or irregularity may recover full satisfaction for the special damage in an action upon the case.[1]

[1] See s. 148, *supra*, and note (1) thereon.

Application of penalties

S. 150. The justices by whom any such penalty or forfeiture shall be imposed may, where the application thereof is not otherwise provided for,[1] award not more than one half thereof to the informer, and shall award the remainder to the overseers of the poor of the parish in which the offence shall have been committed, to be applied in aid of the poor's rate of such parish [2]. . .

[1] S. 26 of the Markets and Fairs Clauses Act, 1847, makes express provision for the application of any forfeiture under that section. As to the application of penalties and forfeitures in respect of offences committed within the Metropolitan Police District, see s. 159, *infra*.

[2] The remainder of this section (which related to extra-parochial places) was repealed by the S.L.R. Act, 1875, having been rendered unnecessary by 31 & 32 Vict. c. 122, s. 7.

[**S. 151.** This section, which limited the time for the recovery of a penalty or forfeiture to within six months after the commission of the offence, was repealed by the Summary Jurisdiction Act, 1884, which substituted for the repealed enactment the provisions to the like effect of the Summary Jurisdiction Acts. See the Summary Jurisdiction Act, 1848.(b)]

Damage to be made good in addition to penalty

S. 152. If, through any act, neglect, or default on account whereof any person shall have incurred any penalty imposed by this or the special Act, any damage to the property of the undertakers shall have been committed by such person, he shall be liable to make good such damage as well as to pay such penalty; and the amount of such damages shall, in case of dispute, be determined by the justices by whom the party incurring such penalty

(a) Simpson *v.* Routh (1824) 2 B. & C. 682.
(b) 11 & 12 Vict. c. 43, s. 11.

S. 152 Damages and Penalties

shall have been convicted; and on non-payment of such damages on demand, the same shall be levied by distress, and such justices, or one of them, shall issue their or his warrant accordingly.

S. 153. It[1] shall be lawful for any justice to summon any person to appear before him as a witness in any matter in which such justice shall have jurisdiction under the provisions of this or the special Act at a time and place mentioned in such summons, and to administer to him an oath to testify the truth in such matter; and if any person so summoned shall, without reasonable excuse, refuse or neglect to appear at the time and place appointed for that purpose, having been paid or tendered a reasonable sum for his expenses, or if any person appearing shall refuse to be examined upon oath or to give evidence before such justice, every such person shall forfeit[2] a sum not exceeding five pounds for every such offence. *Penalty on witnesses making default*

[1] This section was repealed by the Summary Jurisdiction Act, 1884, ' so far as relates to any matter to which the Summary Jurisdiction Acts apply,' but for other matters remains in force. Thus it is still in force for the matters mentioned in s. 142 of this Act and s. 39 of the Markets and Fairs Clauses Act, 1847.
[2] Recoverable in the manner provided by s. 145, *supra*.

S. 154. It shall be lawful for any officer or agent of the undertakers, and all persons called by him to his assistance, to seize and detain any person who shall have committed any offence against the provisions of this or the special Act,[1] and whose name and residence shall be unknown to such officer or agent, and convey him, with all convenient despatch, before some justice, without any warrant or other authority than this or the special Act; and such justice shall proceed with all convenient despatch to the hearing and determining of the complaint against such offender. *Transient offenders*

[1] This section does not, it will be observed, authorise the seizure or detention of a person who has committed an offence against a by-law made under the Markets and Fairs Clauses Act, 1847.(*a*)

[S. 155. This section (which related to the form of convictions) was repealed by the Summary Jurisdiction Act, 1884.]

S. 156. No proceeding in pursuance of this or the special Act, or any Act incorporated therewith, shall be quashed or vacated for want of form, nor shall the same be removed by certiorari or otherwise into any of the superior courts.[1] *Proceedings not to be quashed for want of form, etc.*

[1] This section does not prevent the removal of a proceeding by certiorari where the justices have no jurisdiction.(*b*)

(*a*) See Barry *v.* Midland Rly. Co. (1867) I.R. 1 C.L. 130.
(*b*) R. *v.* Wood (1855) 5 E. & B. 49; Colonial Bank of Australia *v.* Willan (1874) L.R. 5 P.C. 417.

180   *Railways Clauses Act,* 1845   **S. 157**

Parties allowed to appeal to quarter sessions

S. 157. If any party shall feel aggrieved by any determination or adjudication of any justice with respect to any penalty or forfeiture under the provisions of this or the special Act, or any Act incorporated therewith, such party may appeal to the general quarter sessions ; [1] . . .

[1] The remainder of this section (which related to the procedure on appeal, was repealed by the Summary Jurisdiction Act, 1884, the effect of which Act is that (subject to s. 158, *infra*) all appeals to quarter sessions are now regulated by the Summary Jurisdiction Acts.

Courts to make such order as they think reasonable

S. 158. At the quarter sessions for which such notice [1] shall be given the court shall proceed to hear and determine the appeal in a summary way, or they may, if they think fit, adjourn it to the following sessions ; and upon the hearing of such appeal the court may, if they think fit, mitigate any penalty or forfeiture, or they may confirm or quash the adjudication, and order any money paid by the appellant or levied by distress upon his goods to be returned to him, and may also order such further satisfaction to be made to the party injured as they may judge reasonable ; and they may make such order concerning the costs, both of the adjudication and of the appeal, as they may think reasonable.

[1] ' Such notice ' originally referred to the notice of appeal provided for in the repealed portion of s. 157. It must now be taken to refer to the notice of appeal required by the Summary Jurisdiction Act, 1879, s. 31 (2).

[**Ss. 159 and 160.** These sections are in substance the same as ss. 56 and 57 of the Markets and Fairs Clauses Act, 1847, set out *ante,* p. 172. **S. 161** related only to Ireland, and was repealed by the S. L. R. Act, 1875.]

THE PUBLIC HEALTH ACT, 1875.
(38 & 39 Vict. c. 55.)

[Only those sections of this Act are here set out which relate more particularly to markets. Other sections, which bear indirectly on the subject, such as s. 161, which relates to contracts for lighting markets, are not set out, but many of these sections are referred to in the notes : it does not fall within the scope of this work to comment at any length upon these latter sections. The provisions of ss. 166 and 167 of this Act replaced the similar provisions of s. 50 of the Local Government Act, 1858 (21 & 22 Vict. c. 98), which this Act repealed. It has been considered unnecessary to set out the provisions of the repealed Act.]

S. 166. Where an urban authority [1] are a local board or improvement commissioners they shall have power,[2] with the consent of the owners and ratepayers of their district, expressed by resolution passed in manner provided by schedule III. to this Act, and where the urban authority are a town council they shall have power,[2] with the consent of two-thirds of their number, to do the following things, or any of them, within their district : [1]

Urban authority may provide markets

[1] To provide a market-place, and construct a market-house and other conveniences for the purpose of holding markets :
[2] To provide houses and places for weighing carts :
[3] To make convenient approaches to such market :
[4] To provide all such matters and things as may be necessary for the convenient use of such market :
[5] To purchase or take on lease land,[3] and public or private rights in markets and tolls [4] for any of the foregoing purposes :
[6] To take stallages, rents and tolls in respect of the use by any person of such market : [5]

But no market shall be established in pursuance of this section so as to interfere with [6] any rights, powers or privileges enjoyed within the district [8] by any person [9] without his consent.[10]

[1] Under the Public Health Act, 1875, there were three classes of urban authorities, viz. : (1) the local board, who were the authority in a local government district ; (2) the improvement commissioners, who were the authority in an Improvement Act district ; and (3) the borough or

town council, who were, and still are, the authority in a municipal borough. By the Local Government Act, 1894 (56 & 57 Vict. c. 73), ss. 21 and 23, local boards and improvement commissioners were superseded, as urban authorities, by the urban district councils constituted by that Act. The district subject to the jurisdiction of any urban district council (including a borough council) is now called an urban district. 'Their district,' and 'the district,' in the above section clearly refer to the urban district subject to the jurisdiction of the urban district council (or town council acting as district council) which establishes a market.

Rural district councils do not possess the powers which are given to urban district councils by ss. 166-168 of the Public Health Act, unless such powers be conferred upon them by an order of the Local Government Board under s. 276. It appears to have been the policy of the Board not to confer such powers on rural authorities.

² Urban district councils have no power to covenant or agree that they will not exercise the powers, or any of the powers, entrusted to them by this section, and such a covenant or agreement would be void.(a)

³ As to the powers of an urban district council to purchase lands or take lands on lease, see ss. 175 and 176 of this Act. S. 176 incorporates the Lands Clauses Acts, but prevents a council from enforcing the provisions of those Acts with respect to purchasing lands compulsorily until they have obtained a provisional order from the Local Government Board. A district council has no power to take lands on lease compulsorily.

⁴ 'Public rights' seems to mean rights vested in a public body : 'private rights,' rights vested in a private person. The clause enables an urban district council to purchase, or take on lease, market and toll rights enjoyed within the urban district. But they can, it seems, only effect such a purchase, or taking on lease, by agreement. Assuming that market rights which an urban district council desire to acquire are franchises, and therefore within the definition of 'lands' in s. 3 of the Public Health Act, and s. 3 of the Lands Clauses Consolidation Act, 1845,(b) yet it would appear that the provisions of these Acts relating to the compulsory purchase of lands do not extend to incorporeal hereditaments.(c) In the case of market-rights vested in a public body, the urban district council cannot acquire them by agreement unless the public body has power to sell them or let them on lease. S. 168, *infra*, contains provisions with regard to purchases by agreement from 'market companies.' A district council appears to have no power, under s. 166 or s. 168, to purchase or take on lease any rights in fairs.

One of the objects of clause [5] seems to be to enable a council to buy out persons who enjoy within the district saleable rights in markets and tolls, and who will not consent to the establishment of any market by the council except on the terms of their rights being purchased.

As to the transfer to a municipal corporation of the rights, powers, and property of trustees under a local Act for providing or maintaining a market in a borough, see 45 & 46 Vict. c. 50, s. 136, and *ante*, p. 29.

⁵ For the distinction between tolls and stallages, see *ante*, p. 55. The power here given to take tolls is expressed in very wide terms, and apparently authorises the taking of tolls from any person who uses the market in any manner, as by buying or selling articles or merely exposing

---

(a) Spurling v. Bantoft [1891] 2 Q.B. 384 ; cf. Ayr Harbour Trustees v. Oswald (1883) 8 App. Cas. 623.
(b) See G. W. R. Co. v. Swindon, etc., Rly. Co. (1884) 9 App. Cas. 787.
(c) See Pinchin v. London and Blackwall Rly. Co. (1855) 5 De G. M. & G. 851 ; Hill v. Midland Rly. Co. (1882) 21 Ch.D. 143 ; G. W. R. Co. v. Swindon, etc., Rly. Co., *supra*.

them for sale therein, or by using the weighing machines provided in the market-place. But this power is limited by s. 167, *infra*, which requires the approval of the Local Government Board for the tolls to be levied.

⁶ The interference here referred to seems to be limited to interference which would be actionable if its author were a person having no statutory powers.

⁷ 'Rights, powers, or privileges' here means rights, powers or privileges 'acquired adversely to the rest of the world and peculiar to' the person enjoying them ;(a) that is to say, rights, powers, or privileges 'in the nature of a franchise.'(b)

The repealed 21 & 22 Vict. c. 98, s. 50, contained the same provision to protect persons enjoying rights, powers, and privileges within the district. A municipal corporation owned a common law market, and this market had always been held in a market-place in which the occupier of an adjoining house had a prescriptive right to erect a stall. The corporation removed the market so as to interfere with his right. It was held that the removal was bad at common law (see *ante*, p. 38), and that by reason of the above provision the corporation could not justify the removal as an establishment of a new market under the Act.(c)

⁸ 'The district' means the urban district (see note (1), *supra*). With regard to the word 'enjoyed,' it is not clear whether a market franchise can be said to be enjoyed, as that word is here used, unless there be some actual exercise from time to time of the right. Assuming that the franchise be exercised by duly holding markets, it is not clear, again, what is the test whereby to decide whether or not the franchise is 'enjoyed within' a particular urban district. There seem to be three possible views, viz. (1) that the franchise is enjoyed only in the actual market-place in which the markets are held ; (2) that it is enjoyed in every part of the manor or other area within which the markets might lawfully be held ; (3) that it is enjoyed over the whole area within which the owner of the franchise can at common law prevent the levying of any rival market. If either the first or the second of these views be correct, cases can be suggested in which an urban district council has power to establish a new market without the consent of the owner of a neighbouring market, although the establishment of such new market, if it were established without statutory authority, would be an actionable disturbance of such neighbouring market—for instance, cases in which an old market is held outside, but within seven miles of, an urban district. In such cases, if the damage sustained by the owner of the neighbouring market be damage sustained by reason of the *lawful* exercise by the district council of their powers, his only remedy seems to be to seek compensation in the manner provided by s. 308 of the Act. On the other hand, if the third of the above views be correct, and the consent of each owner of a neighbouring market be necessary before the council can establish any market which would be deemed at common law to disturb the rights of such owner, then, assuming that a statutory market is entitled to the same measure of protection from a rival market as that to which a common law market is entitled (see *ante*, p. 87), it seems to follow that, as soon as one urban district council has established a market under this section, the consent of that council will be required by this section before a neighbouring urban district council can establish another market within seven miles.

⁹ 'Person' here includes any body of persons, whether corporate or incorporate ; see s. 4 of this Act.

¹⁰ If an urban district council establish a market without the consent of

---

(a) Fearon *v.* Mitchell (1872) L. R. 7 Q. B. 690, 696.
(b) Spurling *v.* Bantoft [1891] 2 Q. B. 384.
(c) Ellis *v.* Mayor of Bridgenorth (1863) 15 C. B. N. S. 52.

a person whose consent is required by this section, such person can maintain an action for an injunction or damages against the council. Such an action, however, is subject to the provisions of the Public Authorities Protection Act, 1893 (56 & 57 Vict. c. 61). As to the protection from personal liability given to members and officers of, and persons acting under the authority of, an urban district council, see s. 265 of the Public Health Act.

Incorporation of provisions of 10 & 11 Vict. c. 14 as to markets

S. 167. For the purpose of enabling any urban authority to establish or to regulate markets,[1] there shall be incorporated with this Act the provisions of the Markets and Fairs Clauses Act, 1847,[2] in so far as the same relate to markets ;[3] that is to say,

With respect to the holding of the market or fair, and the protection thereof ;[4] and

With respect to the weighing goods and carts ;[5] and

With respect to the stallages, rents and tolls :[6]

Provided that all tolls leviable by an urban authority in pursuance of this section [7] shall be approved by the Local Government Board.[8]

An urban authority may with respect to any market belonging to them[9] make by-laws for any of the purposes mentioned in section forty-two of the Markets and Fairs Clauses Act, 1847,[10] so far as those purposes relate to markets,[11] and printed copies of any by-laws so made shall be conspicuously exhibited in the market.[12]

[1] The section does not clearly direct whether or not a market purchased or taken on lease by an urban district council is to be held subject to the incorporated clauses of the Markets and Fairs Clauses Act, 1847, as limited by the proviso with regard to tolls. Law officers of the crown appear to have advised the Local Government Board that where a district council have acquired a market with rights of taking tolls therein, the council may continue to take the same tolls without the approval of the Board, but that such approval is required for any alteration of the tolls, if not justified by the rights acquired.(a) It seems that a district council which has purchased a common law market with tolls may, so long as they think fit to do so, levy the tolls previously leviable in such market, relying upon the remedies and incidents of the common law ; but may at any time, if they think fit, elect to regulate the market in accordance with s. 167, and to take the benefit of the incorporated provisions of the Markets and Fairs Clauses Act. If they elect to do that, it seems that their tolls require to be approved by the Local Government Board. Assuming that they can make such an election in the case of a common law market which they have taken on lease, then, after the election, the franchise would be exercised subject to restrictions, and with various modifications, which might not affect the reversioner when the lease expired.

A municipal corporation which, as such, owns a common law market is entitled to maintain such market as a common law market, and to rely upon its common law rights; and it is also entitled, as urban district council, to establish and regulate a market under the powers conferred by this Act. But it is not entitled to blow hot and cold with regard to any particular market, and to say that for one purpose it is a common law market, but for another a market established under these statutory powers.(b)

(a) See *First Report of the Royal Commission*, vol. ii. p. 4 (1888).
(b) See Ellis v. Corporation of Bridgenorth (1861) 2 J. & H. 67.

S. 167 Public Health Act, 1875 185

² 10 & 11 Vict. c. 14, set out *ante*, p. 141.
³ It is important to notice this limitation. A district council has no power under this or the preceding section to establish a fair.
In reading the incorporated clauses regard must be had to s. 316 of the Public Health Act, set out *infra*, p. 188. This Act does not expressly incorporate the definition clauses (ss. 2 and 3) of the Markets and Fairs Clauses Act, 1847, even for the limited purpose of construing the incorporated clauses. But it is submitted that, subject to s. 316 of this Act, the incorporated clauses must be construed in accordance with the above-mentioned definition clauses.
⁴ Sections 12-16, set out *ante*, p. 149. The reference to 'fair' is only for the purpose of identifying the sections referred to ; see note (3), *supra*.
⁵ Ss. 21-30, set out *ante*, p. 156. The provisions of the Markets and Fairs (Weighing of Cattle) Acts, 1887 and 1891 (see *post*, pp. 196, *et seq.*), apply to markets owned by an urban district council, if the council are authorised to take, and actually take, tolls in respect of cattle.
⁶ Sections 31-41, set out *ante*, p. 160.
⁷ This section (s. 167) reproduces sub-section (2) of s. 50 of the repealed Local Government Act, 1858, sub-section (1) thereof being reproduced by s. 166, *supra*. The words 'in pursuance of this section' occurred in sub-section (2) of the repealed enactment, and related to the whole section, including sub-section (1). The reproduction of the repealed enactment in two sections instead of one does not seem to have altered materially the effect of the words, except, perhaps, that it confirms the view that the approval of the Local Government Board is required only for tolls taken by a district council in markets established or regulated in accordance with the Markets and Fairs Clauses Act, and not for tolls taken in a common law market purchased under s. 166 and regulated as a common law market. S. 166 enables the district council to take tolls 'in respect of the use by any person of the market'; the earlier portion of s. 167, by incorporating ss. 31-41 of the Markets and Fairs Clauses Act, provides for the manner in which the tolls are to be levied ; the proviso limits the operation of these incorporated sections, so far as tolls are concerned, to tolls approved by the Local Government Board.
⁸ The effect of the proviso appears to be that an urban district council cannot levy a toll in any market regulated by them in accordance with the incorporated clauses of the Markets and Fairs Clauses Act, 1847, unless and until such toll has been approved by the Local Government Board (see note (1), *supra*). As the Act does not provide for the manner in which the approval is to be obtained, the district council must comply with the requirements of the Board for the purpose of obtaining their approval. No special mode of proving the approval of the Board is provided ; but see the Local Government Board Act, 1871 (34 & 35 Vict. c. 70), s. 5 ; and the Documentary Evidence Act, 1868 (31 & 32 Vict. c. 37), s. 2.
The proviso applies only to tolls, and not to stallages and rents. The latter are matters for contract between the council and any persons who desire stalls. The council seem to be under no obligation to provide stalls. If they ask for an unreasonable sum for stalls, perhaps the only remedy is to abstain from hiring them : see, however, *ante*, pp. 59 and 64.
The Local Government Board, when they have once approved a toll unconditionally, appear to have no power to compel a district council to reduce it. *Quare*, whether the Board could retain a control over tolls by approving them only on the condition that such approval should not extend to any toll sought to be levied after a specified date.
⁹ I.e. belonging to them as urban district council. These words seem to give to a district council the power to make by-laws with respect to any market belonging to them, whether it be a new market established

by them, or an old market acquired by them, in accordance with their powers.

¹⁰ See s. 42 of the Act, set out *ante*, p. 165. S. 50 (2) of the repealed Local Government Act, 1858, incorporated the provisions of ss. 42–49 of the Markets and Fairs Clauses Act, 1847, with respect to by-laws. S. 167 of the Public Health Act does not incorporate them. This distinction must be borne in mind in considering Ellis *v.* Corporation of Bridgenorth (1861) 2 J. & H. 67.

¹¹ Purposes relating to a fair or slaughter-house are excluded by these words; see note (3), *supra*.

¹² By-laws made under this section are subject to the provisions of ss. 182–186 of this Act, with regard to the making, altering, and repealing of by-laws, their validity, the penalties which may be imposed thereby, their confirmation by the Local Government Board, and their publication and proof. With regard to publication, the requirements both of this section and s. 185 ought to be complied with. The Act contains no express provisions rendering by-laws inoperative unless duly published, such as are to be found in ss. 48 and 49 of the Markets and Fairs Clauses Act, 1847, *supra*, p. 168. For the penalty imposed by this Act for destroying or defacing any board on which the by-laws are inscribed, see s. 306. For the recovery of penalties, see ss. 251 *et seq.*, and the Summary Jurisdiction Act, 1884.(*a*)

As to by-laws made under the repealed Local Government Act, 1858, s. 50 (2), see the saving clause in s. 326 of the Public Health Act; and as to by-laws made before the passing of the Local Government Act, 1894, see the saving clause in s. 87 of that Act. As to the proof of by-laws made by a borough council, see the Municipal Corporations Act, 1882, s. 24. As to the effect of a variance between the provisions of a by-law made under s. 167 of the Public Health Act and those of a local Act applying to the same district, see Savage *v.* Brook.(*b*)

Power for sale of undertaking of market company to urban authority

S. 168. Any¹ urban authority may purchase,² and the directors of any market company,³ in pursuance, in the case of a company registered under the Companies Act, 1862, of a special resolution of the members passed in manner provided by that Act,⁴ and in the case of any other company,⁵ of a resolution passed by a majority of three-fourths in number and value of the members present, either personally or by proxy, at a meeting specially convened with notice of the business to be transacted, may sell and transfer to any urban authority, on such terms as may be agreed on between the company and the urban authority, all the rights, powers and privileges and all or any of the markets, premises and things which at the time of such purchase are the property of the company, but subject to all liabilities attached⁶ to the same at the time of such purchase.

¹ Compare with this section ss. 51, 63, and 162 of this Act, under which an urban district council can purchase the properties of water and gas companies. Under those sections a purchase can be made only with the sanction of the Local Government Board, which is not the case under this section. But a district council cannot exercise their borrowing powers

---

(*a*) 47 & 48 Vict. c. 43.   (*b*) (1863) 15 C.B.N.S. 264.

for the purpose of making a purchase under this section, unless they have obtained the sanction of the Local Government Board.(a)

The words of this section, if read without reference to s. 166, may be thought to be wide enough to permit an urban district council to purchase from a market company, and hold, a market situate outside the urban district; and moreover to purchase a market without first obtaining the consent of the owners and ratepayers of the district, or two-thirds of the council in the case of a borough. But probably this section must be read as supplementary to s. 166, and as enabling the council to purchase only for the purpose of providing a market within their district, and only after obtaining the consent of the owners and ratepayers, or two-thirds of the council, as provided by s. 166.

² This section relates only to purchases, but an urban district council has power, under s. 166, *supra*, to take market rights on lease from a company which has power to lease them.

³ The Act gives no definition of 'market company,' and therefore, if a question arises whether or not a particular company is a market company within the meaning of this section, it must be decided upon the particular facts of the case.

⁴ 25 & 26 Vict. c. 89; see ss. 50–54, and schedule I., table A, rules 29-51, of that Act.

⁵ The words 'any other company' are very wide, and apparently include a company established or regulated by a local Act. This section seems to confer upon the directors of a company powers of sale, which, apart from the section, the company may not possess. In the case of a company which, apart from this section, can only sell its undertaking after complying with formalities or conditions not covered by this section, it is perhaps not clear that, upon the passing of the resolution required by this section, the directors of such company become entitled to sell the undertaking to an urban district council without such formalities or conditions being complied with. But it is submitted that such is the case. Questions, however, might sometimes arise between a company which desires to sell, or sells, its undertaking to an urban district council, and members of such company, or other persons, or between such persons and the council, which cannot be discussed here.

⁶ The object of these words seems to be to preserve, for persons having at the date of the transfer mortgages or charges upon the property transferred, all their rights against such property.

The question arises whether an urban district council, when they have purchased a market from a company under this section, may or must regulate it upon the terms upon which the company were bound to regulate it, or whether they may or must apply to the market the provisions of the Markets and Fairs Clauses Act, 1847, mentioned in s. 167, *supra*. May the district council continue to exercise rights and powers enjoyed by the company, though greater than such as would be enjoyed if the above provisions of the Markets and Fairs Clauses Act applied thereto, for instance, privileges giving a wider protection to the market or a better remedy for the recovery of tolls? If the powers of the company are narrower than those contained in the Markets and Fairs Clauses Act, may the district council apply the latter to the market after the transfer? Probably the district council may, so long as they think fit, regulate the market as the company had power to regulate it, relying entirely on the rights and powers which they have purchased, but may, whenever they think fit, elect to apply to the market the above provisions of the Markets and Fairs Clauses Act, provided that by so doing they do not impair any outstanding charges

---

(a) See ss. 233 *et seq.*,

created before the purchase upon the undertaking or the tolls. It seems that, upon applying these provisions, they must obtain for their tolls the approval of the Local Government Board; see note (1) to s. 167, *supra*. In some cases nice questions might arise out of the application of these provisions to the rights and powers purchased, similar to those which arose in Rutherford *v.* Straker.(*a*)

As to construction of incorporated Acts

S. 316. In [1] the construction of the provisions of any Act incorporated with this Act the term 'the special Act' includes this Act; . . . the term 'the limits of the special Act' means the limits of the district; and the urban or rural authority shall be deemed to be . . . 'the undertakers.' . . .

All penalties incurred under the provisions of any Act incorporated with this Act shall be recovered and applied in the same way as penalties incurred under this Act.[2]

[1] Immaterial portions of this section are omitted.
[2] See ss. 251 *et seq.*, and the Summary Jurisdiction Act, 1884.(*b*) As to who may be 'a party aggrieved,' within the meaning of s. 253 of the Public Health Act, so as to be entitled to sue for penalties incurred under s. 13 of the Markets and Fairs Clauses Act, see Ross *v.* Taylerson.(*c*)

(*a*) (1889) 42 Ch.D. 85 n. (*b*) 47 & 48 Vict. c. 43.
(*c*) [1898] 62 J.P. 181.

DISEASES OF ANIMALS ACT, 1894.

(57 & 58 VICT. C. 57.)

[The Contagious Diseases (Animals) Act, 1867,(*a*) empowered any local authority under that Act to provide proper places for the sale, lairage and slaughter of foreign animals, but did not, in any way, constitute such places markets. That Act was repealed, and its provisions re; laced by those of the Contagious Diseases (Animals) Act, 1869.(*b*) By the Act of 1869, the local authority was empowered to provide 'wharves, lairs, sheds, *markets*, houses, and places, for the landing, reception, sale, and slaughter of foreign animals:' the Markets and Fairs Clauses Act, 1847, was incorporated : and the by-laws and charges for using the wharves and other places were subjected to the approval of the Privy Council. The Contagious Diseases (Animals) Act, 1878,(*c*) repealed these provisions, and substituted (by s. 39) provisions generally similar to those contained in s. 32 of the Act of 1894, set out below, but differing in two respects, viz. (1) the section related to ' foreign animals,' instead of 'foreign or *other* animals,' and (2) the Privy Council was the controlling authority. Subsequently the Contagious Diseases (Animals) Act, 1886,(*d*) extended the provisions of s. 39 of the Act of 1878 to 'animals not being foreign,' and to 'carcases, fodder, litter, dung, and other things of and relating to such animals ' ; and under the Board of Agriculture Act, 1889,(*e*) the Board of Agriculture was substituted for the Privy Council as controlling authority. The Act of 1878 (except s. 34) was repealed by the Diseases of Animals Act, 1894, s. 78.]

S. 32. (1.) A local authority[1] may provide, erect, and fit up wharves, stations, lairs, sheds, and other places for the landing, reception, keeping, sale, slaughter, or disposal of foreign[2] or other animals,[3] carcases, fodder, litter, dung, and other things.[4]

[1] The local authorities under this Act are defined by ss. 3 and 38, and are :—
In the city of London, the common council :
In the county of London, for the purposes of the provisions of the Act relating to foreign animals, the common council ; for other purposes, the county council :
In the Improvement Act district of Hove, the Hove Improvement Act Commissioners :
In any borough (except a borough which contained, according to

---

(*a*) 30 & 31 Vict. c. 125, s. 47. (*b*) 32 & 33 Vict. c. 70, ss. 23–25.
(*c*) 41 & 42 Vict. c. 74. (*d*) 49 & 50 Vict. c. 32, s. 10.
(*e*) 52 & 53 Vict. c. 30.

the census of 1881, a population of less than 10,000), the borough council:
Elsewhere in an administrative county, the county council.
² I.e. 'brought to the United Kingdom from a country out of the United Kingdom.'(a)
³ 'Animals' here means cattle (i.e. bulls, cows, oxen, heifers, and calves) and sheep and goats, and all other ruminating animals, and swine.(b) The Board of Agriculture, however, have power, by order, to extend, for all or any of the purposes of the Act, the above definition of animals, so that the same shall for those purposes, or any of them, comprise any kind of four-footed beasts.(c)
⁴ The words 'other things' are probably to be construed as limited to things *ejusdem generis* with the things previously mentioned, which all bear some relation to animals.(d)

(2.) There shall be incorporated with this Act the Markets and Fairs Clauses Act, 1847,¹ except sections six to nine² and fifty-one to sixty³ thereof.

¹ 10 & 11 Vict. c. 14, set out *ante*, p. 141.
² The incorporation of those sections, which relate to the acquisition of lands, was rendered unnecessary by the provisions of s. 33 of this Act.
³ S. 52 relates to the recovery of damages and penalties. With regard to the recovery of penalties for offences against the incorporated clauses of the Markets and Fairs Clauses Act, 1847, or by-laws made under s. 47 thereof, see the note *ante*, p. 171.

(3.) A wharf or other place provided by a local authority under this section shall be a market within that Act ;¹ and this Act shall be the special Act ;² and the prescribed limits² shall be the limits of lands acquired³ or appropriated for purposes of this section ; and by-laws⁴ shall be approved by the Board of Agriculture,⁵ which approval shall be sufficient without any other approval or allowance, notice of application for approval being given, and proposed by-laws being published before application, as required by the Markets and Fairs Clauses Act, 1847.⁶

¹ It is not clear whether these words render the wharf or other place, when provided, a market for all purposes : for instance, for the purposes of the common law doctrine as to the protection of a market from rival markets, or as to sales in market overt.
² See the Markets and Fairs Clauses Act, s. 2, *ante*, p. 142.
³ The power to acquire lands for the purposes of this section is given by s. 33 of the Act. Under that section the local authority may by agreement purchase land or take it on lease or at a rent, or, after obtaining a provisional order for the purpose from the Local Government Board, may purchase land compulsorily. These powers with respect to acquiring land may be exercised by the local authority within or without their district ; see s. 33 (4).
⁴ The power to make by-laws is given by s. 42 of the Markets and Fairs Clauses Act, 1847, *ante*, p. 165.

(a) See s. 59 (1) of this Act.   (b) See s. 59 (1).
(c) See s. 22 (xxxvi.).
(d) Cf. the repealed 49 & 50 Vict. c. 32, s. 10.

S. 32   *Diseases of Animals Act*, 1894   191

³ I.e. shall not come into force unless and until approved by the Board of Agriculture.
⁴ See ss. 46 and 47 of that Act, *ante*, p. 167.

(4.) A local authority may charge for the use of a wharf or other place provided by them under this section such sums as may be imposed by by-laws,[1] and the same shall be deemed tolls [2] authorised by the Special Act.

[1] The by-laws, and therefore the tolls, cannot be enforced unless and until approved by the Board of Agriculture. (*a*) As to the powers of the Board of Agriculture with regard to reducing the tolls, see sub-section 7, *infra*.
[2] See ss. 31-41 of the Markets and Fairs Clauses Act, 1847.

(5.) All sums so received by the local authority shall be carried to a separate account, and shall be applied in payment of interest on money borrowed by them under the Contagious Diseases (Animals) Act, 1869,[1] the Contagious Diseases (Animals) Acts, 1878 to 1893,[2] or this Act, and in repayment of the principal thereof, and, subject thereto, towards discharge of their expenses under this Act.

[1] 32 & 33 Vict. c. 70.
[2] 41 & 42 Vict. c. 74 ; 47 & 48 Vict. cc. 13 & 47 ; 49 & 50 Vict. c. 32 ; 53 & 54 Vict. c. 14 ; 55 & 56 Vict. c. 47 ; 56 & 57 Vict. c. 43.

(6.) The local authority shall make such periodical returns to the Board of Agriculture of their expenditure and receipts in respect of the wharf or other place as the Board require.

(7.) The Board, if satisfied on enquiry that the tolls taken by the local authority for the wharf or other place may properly be reduced, regard being had to the expenditure and receipts of the local authority in respect thereof, and to any money secured on the tolls,[1] and to the other circumstances of the case, may require the local authority to submit to the Board, for their approval, a new schedule of tolls, and, on failure of the local authority to do so to the satisfaction of the Board, may, by order, prescribe such tolls as the Board think fit, in lieu of those before approved by the Board.

[1] As to borrowing for the purposes of the Act on the security of the tolls, see s. 42 (5). With regard to markets in the metropolis, see s. 28 (2)-(4) of the Contagious Diseases (Animals) Act, 1869, which was not repealed by the Act of 1878.

(8.) The provisions of this section shall apply to a wharf or other place provided by a local authority under the Contagious Diseases (Animals) Act, 1869,[1] or under the Contagious Diseases (Animals) Acts, 1878 to 1893.[2]

[1] See 32 & 33 Vict. c. 70, ss. 23-35.
[2] See 41 & 42 Vict. c. 74, s. 39 ; 49 & 50 Vict. c. 32, s. 10.

(*a*) See sub-section (3) *supra*.

APPENDIX.

THE FAIRS ACT, 1871.
(34 VICT. c. 12.)

An Act to further amend the Law relating to Fairs in England and Wales. [25th May 1871.]

WHEREAS certain of the fairs held in England and Wales are unnecessary, are the cause of grievous immorality, and are very injurious to the inhabitants of the towns in which such fairs are held, and it is therefore expedient to make provision to facilitate the abolition of such fairs:

1. This Act may be cited as 'The Fairs Act, 1871.' *Title*

2. In this Act the term 'owner' means any person or persons, or body of commissioners, or body corporate, entitled to hold any fair, whether in respect of the ownership of any lands or tenements, or under any charter, letters patent, or Act of Parliament, or otherwise howsoever. *Definition of 'owner*

3. In case it shall appear to the Secretary of State for the Home Department, upon representation duly made to him by the magistrates of any petty sessional district within which any fair is held, or by the owner of any fair in England or Wales, that it would be for the convenience and advantage of the public that any such fair shall be abolished, it shall be lawful for the said Secretary of State for the Home Department, with the previous consent in writing of the owner for the time being of such fair, or of the tolls or dues payable in respect thereof, to order that such fair shall be abolished accordingly: Provided always, that notice of such representation, and of the time when it shall please the Secretary of State for the Home Department to take the same into consideration, shall be published once in the 'London Gazette,' and in three successive weeks in some one and the same newspaper published in the county, city, or borough in which such fair is held, or if there be no newspaper published therein, then in the newspaper of some *Secretary of State may, on representation of magistrates, with consent of owner, order fair to be abolished* *Notice of representation to be published in newspapers*

O

county adjoining or near thereto, before such representation is so considered.

Order of Secretary of State to be published in newspaper

4. When and so soon as any such order as aforesaid shall have been made by the Secretary of State for the Home Department, notice of the making of the same shall be published in the 'London Gazette,' and in some one newspaper of the county, city, or borough in which such fair is usually held, or if there be no newspaper published therein, then in the newspaper of some county adjoining or near thereto, and thereupon such fair shall be abolished.

THE FAIRS ACT, 1873.

(36 & 37 VICT. c. 37.)

An Act to amend the Law relating to Fairs in England and Wales. [7th July 1873.]

Short title
1. This Act may be cited as 'The Fairs Act, 1873.'

Definition of terms
3. In this Act the term 'owner' means any person or persons, or body of commissioners or body corporate, entitled to hold any fair, whether in respect of the ownership of any lands or tenements or under any charter, letters patent, or otherwise howsoever.

Power to secretary of state to alter days of holding fairs
6. In case it shall appear to a secretary of state, upon representation duly made to him by the justices acting in and for the petty sessional division within which any fair is held, or by the owner of any fair in England or Wales, that it would be for the convenience and advantage of the public that any such fair shall be held in each year on some day or days other than that or those on which such fair is used to be held or on the day or days on which such fair is used to be held and any preceding or subsequent day or days, or on or during a less number of days than those on which such fair is used to be held, it shall be lawful for a secretary of state to order that such fair shall be held on such other day or days, or on the same day or days and any preceding or subsequent day or days, or on or during any less number of days as he shall think fit : Provided always, that notice of such representation and of the time when it shall please a secretary of state to take the same into consideration shall if such representation shall have been made by justices be given to the owner of such fair, and shall if such representation shall have been made by the owner of such fair be given to the clerk to the justices acting in and for

the petty sessional division within which such fair is held, and shall also be published once in the 'London Gazette,' and in three successive weeks in some one and the same newspaper, published in the county, city, or borough in which such fair is held, or if there be no newspaper published therein, then in the newspaper of some county adjoining or near thereto, before such representation is so considered.

7. When and so soon as any such order as aforesaid shall have been made by a secretary of state, notice of the making of the same shall be published in the 'London Gazette' and in some one newspaper of the county, city, or borough in which such fair is usually held, or if there be no newspaper published therein, then in the newspaper of some county adjoining or near thereto, and thereupon such fair shall only be held on the day or days mentioned in such order; and it shall be lawful for the owner of such fair to take all such toll or tolls, and to do all such act or acts, and to enjoy all and the same rights, powers, and privileges in respect thereof, and enforce the same by all and the like remedies, as if the same were held on the day or days upon which it was used to be held previous to the making of such order. {.marginnote: Order of secretary of state to be published in certain newspapers. All rights, etc., of owner to remain good}

THE WEIGHTS AND MEASURES ACT, 1878.

(41 & 42 VICT. c. 49.)

SIXTH SCHEDULE.

SECOND PART.

[*The following Enactments are re-enacted by s. 86 of the above-named Act, and are to have effect as if enacted in the body of the Act.*]

22 & 23 VICT. c. 56, ss. 6, 8, 12.

THE owners or managers of any public market in Great Britain where goods are exposed or kept for sale shall provide proper scales and balances and weights and measures or other machines, for the purpose of weighing or measuring all goods sold, offered, or exposed for sale in any such market, and shall deposit the same at the office of the clerk or toll collector of such market, or some other convenient place, and shall have the accuracy of all such scales and balances and weights and measures or other machines tested at least twice in every year by the inspector of weights and measures of and for the county, borough, or place where the market is situate; {.marginnote: Owners of markets to provide scales, etc.}

All expenses attending the purchase, adjusting, and testing thereof shall be paid out of the moneys collected for tolls in the market;

Such clerk or toll collector shall at all reasonable times, whenever called upon so to do, weigh or measure all goods which have been sold, offered, or exposed for sale in any such market, upon payment of such reasonable sum as may from time to time be decided upon by the said owners or managers, subject to the approval and revision of the justices in general or quarter sessions assembled if such market be in England. . . . .

For every contravention of this section the offender shall be liable, on summary conviction, to a fine not exceeding five pounds.

22 & 23 VICT. c. 56, ss. 7, 8, 12.

Power to clerks of markets to inspect goods sold, etc., and if weight found deficient to summon the offender

Every clerk or toll collector of any public market in Great Britain, at all reasonable times, may weigh or measure all goods sold, offered, or exposed for sale in any such market; and if upon such weighing or measuring any such goods are found deficient in weight or measure, or otherwise contrary to the provisions of this Act, such clerk or toll collector shall take the necessary proceedings for recovering any fine to which the person selling, offering, or exposing for sale, or causing to be sold, offered, or exposed for sale, such goods, is liable, and the court convicting the offender may award out of the fine to such clerk or toll collector such reasonable remuneration as to the court seems fit.

For every offence against or disobedience to this section the offender shall be liable on summary conviction to a fine not exceeding five pounds.

THE MARKETS AND FAIRS (WEIGHING OF CATTLE) ACT, 1887.

(50 & 51 VICT. c. 27.)

An Act to amend the Law with respect to Weighing Cattle in Markets and Fairs.   [8th August 1887.]

WHEREAS it is expedient to afford the like facilities for weighing cattle in markets and fairs as are afforded for weighing goods and carts under the Markets and Fairs Clauses Act, 1847, in markets and fairs to which that Act applies:

Short title

1. This Act may be cited as the Markets and Fairs (Weighing of Cattle) Act, 1887.

Application of Act

2. This Act, save as is herein-after provided, shall apply to all markets and fairs in which tolls are for the time being authorised

Markets and Fairs (Weighing of Cattle) Act, 1887

to be taken and actually are taken in respect of cattle by any company, corporation, or person; and every such company, corporation, or person is in this Act called 'the market authority.'

3. In this Act the word 'cattle' includes ram, ewe, wether, lamb, and swine. Interpretation

4. In or near to every market or fair to which this Act applies, the market authority shall provide and maintain sufficient and proper buildings or places for weighing cattle brought for sale within the market or fair, and shall keep therein or near thereto weighing machines and weights for the purpose of weighing cattle, and shall appoint proper persons to have charge of such machines and weights, and to afford the use of such machines and weights to the public for weighing cattle as may be from time to time required. Accommodation for weighing cattle to be provided

The market authority shall have the accuracy of such weighing machines and weights tested at least twice in every year by the local inspector of weights and measures of and for the county, borough, or place where the market is situate, and the cost of such testing shall be borne by such market authority.

If the market authority fail to comply with the provisions of this section, it shall not be lawful for them to demand, receive, or recover any toll whatever in respect of any cattle brought to the market or fair for sale so long as such failure continues, but this enactment shall not apply till after the first day of January one thousand eight hundred and eighty-eight.

Any person who demands or receives any toll in respect of cattle in any market or fair to which for the time being this Act applies, but in which the market authority have not complied with the provisions of this Act, shall be liable on summary conviction to a fine not exceeding five pounds.

5. Every person selling, offering for sale, or buying any cattle in a market or fair provided with accommodation for weighing cattle may require such cattle to be weighed, and the tolls payable in respect of the weighing shall be paid by the person requiring the cattle to be weighed to the person authorised by the market authority to receive the tolls. Cattle to be weighed at option of seller or buyer

6. Every person appointed by the market authority to weigh cattle sold in the market or fair, who— Penalty for refusal to weigh cattle or to give ticket, etc.

(*a*) refuses or neglects to weigh the same when required; or

(*b*) refuses or neglects to deliver to the seller or buyer a ticket specifying the true weight of the cattle weighed; or

(*c*) gives to any person a false ticket or account of any cattle weighed;

shall be liable on summary conviction to a fine not exceeding forty shillings and not less than half a crown.

Penalty for fraud	7. Every person who knowingly acts or assists in committing any fraud respecting the weighing of any cattle weighed in pursuance of this Act, shall for every such offence be liable on summary conviction to a fine not exceeding five pounds.
Tolls for weighing cattle	8. The market authority may from time to time (unless otherwise expressly provided by any Act) demand and receive in respect of the weighing of cattle tolls not exceeding the amounts specified in the schedule to this Act, or such other amounts as may be authorised by the Local Government Board to be taken by the market authority; and sections thirty-six to forty-one (both included) of the Markets and Fairs Clauses Act, 1847, shall apply to the tolls mentioned in this section, as if this Act were the special Act, and the market authority were the undertakers.
Power to exempt certain markets and fairs from provisions of Act	9.—(1.) The market authority of any market or fair may at any time apply to the Local Government Board to be exempted from the provisions of this Act on the ground that the sale of cattle at such market or fair is or is likely to be so small as to render it inexpedient to enforce the provision and maintenance of a place for weighing cattle and of a weighing machine under this Act; and thereupon the Local Government Board may by order declare that this Act shall not apply to such market or fair until after the expiration of a time not exceeding three years to be limited by such order. Any order made under this section may at any time be wholly or partially rescinded, altered, or extended by any subsequent order of the Local Government Board.

(2.) This Act shall not apply to any market or fair to which any order under this section applies so long as it is declared by such order that this Act shall not apply thereto.

THE SCHEDULE.

	Not exceeding
For every head of cattle other than sheep or swine .	Twopence.
For sheep or swine, every five or less number . .	One penny.

MARKETS AND FAIRS (WEIGHING OF CATTLE) ACT, 1891.

(54 & 55 VICT. C. 70.)

An Act to amend the Markets and Fairs (Weighing of Cattle) Act, 1887. [5th August 1891.]

WHEREAS it is expedient to amend the Markets and Fairs (Weighing of Cattle) Act, 1887 (herein-after referred to as the principal Act):

Markets and Fairs (Weighing of Cattle) Act, 1891

1. As from the passing of this Act the powers under section nine of the principal Act of the Local Government Board as to England and Wales . . . shall be transferred to and vest in the Board of Agriculture. . . .
   Transfer of powers under 50 & 51 Vict. c. 27, s. 9

2.—(1.) The market authority of every market and fair to which the principal Act for the time being applies shall, unless exempted by order of the Board of Agriculture from the requirements of this section, provide and maintain to the satisfaction of the Board sufficient and suitable accommodation for weighing cattle.
   Amendment of 50 & 51 Vict. c. 27, s. 4, as to accommodation for weighing cattle

(2.) Default in complying with the requirements of this section shall be deemed default in complying with the requirements of section four of the principal Act.

3.—(1.) The market authority of every market and fair held in any of the places mentioned in the schedule to this Act shall send to the Board of Agriculture returns, at such intervals, and in such form and with such particulars as the Board of Agriculture by order prescribe, showing, so far as the market authority can ascertain the same, the number of cattle entering and the number and weight of cattle weighed at the market or fair, and the price of the cattle sold thereat. Such market authority may, for the purpose of making a prescribed return, cause any cattle which have been sold at the market to be weighed without fee.
   Statistics as to weight and sale of cattle

(2.) The Board of Agriculture shall publish the returns so sent, or abstracts thereof, or extracts therefrom, in such manner as they think most expedient for the information of the public.

(3.) If a market authority wilfully makes default in complying with the requirements of this section, it shall for each offence be liable on summary conviction to a fine not exceeding twenty pounds, or in case of a continuing offence to a fine not exceeding ten pounds for every day during which the offence continues.

(4.) If any person makes any false or fraudulent statement in any return made in pursuance of this section he shall be guilty of a misdemeanour.

(5.) The Board of Agriculture may from time to time vary or add to the list of places in the schedule to this Act.

4.—(1.) An auctioneer shall not, unless exempted by order of the Board of Agriculture from the requirements of this section, sell cattle at any mart where cattle are habitually or periodically sold unless there are provided at that mart similar facilities for weighing cattle as are required by the principal Act and this Act in the case of cattle sold at a market or fair to which the principal Act applies.
   Application of Act to auction marts

(2.) Every auctioneer who in any place from which returns are required to be made under this Act sells cattle at any such mart as aforesaid shall, unless exempted as aforesaid, make the like returns to the Board of Agriculture with respect to cattle entering, weighed, and sold at that mart as are required by this Act to be made by a market authority, and shall be subject to the like penalty for making any false or fraudulent statement in any such return.

(3.) If any such auctioneer makes default in complying with the requirements of this section, the auctioneer, or, if he is in the employment of any person, the person by whom he is employed, shall for each offence be liable on summary conviction to a fine not exceeding twenty pounds, or in case of a continuing offence to a fine not exceeding ten pounds for every day during which the offence continues.

(4.) This section shall not come into operation until the first day of January one thousand eight hundred and ninety-two.

Construction and short title

6. This Act shall be construed as one with the principal Act, and may be cited as the Markets and Fairs (Weighing of Cattle) Act, 1891, and the principal Act and this Act may be cited together as the Markets and Fairs (Weighing of Cattle) Acts, 1887 and 1891.

SCHEDULE.

ENGLAND.

Ashford.
Birmingham.
Bristol.
Leicester.
Leeds.
Lincoln.
Liverpool (Stanley Market).
London (Metrop. Cattle Market).
Newcastle-on-Tyne.
Norwich.
Salford.
Shrewsbury.
Wakefield.
York.

THE PUBLIC HEALTH (CONFIRMATION OF BY-LAWS) ACT, 1884.

(47 VICT. C. 12.)

An Act to amend the Public Health Act, 1875, so far as relates to the Confirmation of By-laws.

[19th May 1884.]

BE it enacted by the Queen's most Excellent Majesty, by and with the advice and consent of the Lords Spiritual and Temporal,

Public Health (Confirmation of By-laws) Act, 1884

and Commons, in this present Parliament assembled, and by the authority of the same, as follows :

1. This Act may be cited as the Public Health (Confirmation of By-laws) Act, 1884, and shall be construed as one with the Public Health Act, 1875. <small>Short title and construction</small>

2. In this Act, if not inconsistent with the context, the following expressions have the meanings herein-after respectively assigned to them : (that is to say,) <small>Definitions</small>

'Incorporated enactments' means section one hundred and twenty-eight of the Towns Improvement Clauses Act, 1847, sections sixty-eight and sixty-nine of the Town Police Clauses Act, 1847, and section forty-two of the Markets and Fairs Clauses Act, 1847, which Acts are herein-after referred to as the incorporated Acts :

'Confirming authority' means, as regards by-laws, rules, and regulations confirmed prior to the nineteenth day of August one thousand eight hundred and seventy-one, or made under any of the incorporated enactments by reason of the incorporation thereof with any local Act and confirmed prior to the tenth day of August one thousand eight hundred and seventy-two, one of Her Majesty's principal secretaries of state ; and as regards other by-laws, rules, and regulations, the Local Government Board.

3. Every by-law made or to be made under any of the incorporated enactments by reason of the incorporation thereof with the Public Health Act, 1848, the Local Government Act, 1858, or the Public Health Act, 1875, or any local Act, or any provisional order, or any Act confirming such provisional order, and every rule and regulation made or to be made by an urban authority under section forty-eight of the Tramways Act, 1870, shall be deemed to have required or to require the confirmation of the confirming authority, and not to have required or to require any other confirmation, allowance, or approval. <small>Confirmation of by-laws</small>

4. This Act shall not invalidate the confirmation, allowance, or approval of any by-law, rule, or regulation confirmed, allowed, or approved prior to the passing of this Act, nor shall this Act apply to any by-law made or to be made under any of the incorporated enactments by reason of the incorporation thereof with any local Act, if such by-law has or will come into force without any confirmation, allowance, or approval, or if by the express provisions of the local Act and without reference to the provisions with respect to confirmation, allowance, or approval of by-laws in any of the incorporated Acts, such by-law is required to be confirmed, allowed, or approved otherwise than by the confirming authority. <small>Saving clause</small>

THE LOCAL TAXATION RETURNS ACT, 1860.

(23 & 24 VICT. C. 51.)

An Act to provide for an annual Return of Rates, Taxes, Tolls, and Dues levied for local Purposes in England.
[23rd July 1860.]

Clerks of bodies empowered to levy rates, etc., to make annual returns

1. The clerk to any corporation, justices, commissioners, district or other board, vestry, inspectors, trustees, or other body or persons authorised to levy or to order to be levied any of the rates, taxes, tolls, or dues mentioned in the schedule to this Act, or any other compulsory rates, taxes, tolls, or dues in England, (other than such as are levied for the public revenue of the United Kingdom,) shall make a return of the sums levied or received by or in respect of such rates, taxes, tolls, and dues, and of the expenditure thereof, to [*the Local Government Board*] in every year.

Contents of returns

2. Such returns shall show the amounts levied and expended respectively, with such other particulars and in such form as shall from time to time be ordered by [*the Local Government Board*].

Saving for cases where returns already required

5. Where any annual return is now by law required to be made to the secretary of state, or to any public department, under any Act of Parliament, this Act shall not render necessary any further or other return in respect of the same matters: Provided always, that the [*Local Government Board*] may, by [*their*] order published in the 'London Gazette,' direct that all or any of such returns now required as aforesaid shall in future be made under this Act, and shall be subject to the provisions and penalties thereof.

Abstracts of returns to be laid before Parliament

6. The [*Local Government Board*] shall every year cause the returns transmitted to [*them*] under this Act to be abstracted, and the abstract thereof to be laid before both houses of parliament.

Saving for companies and private rights of toll, etc.

8. This Act shall not extend to any tolls or dues taken by any railway, canal, or joint stock company as profits of their undertaking, or to any tolls or dues taken by prescription or otherwise as private property.

SCHEDULE.

Tolls and dues levied under the authority of parliament in respect of markets.

[NOTE.—Certain portions of the above Act, and the schedule thereto, which do not affect market authorities, or have been repealed by the S.L.R. Acts, 1875 and 1892, have been omitted. In ss. 1, 2, 5, and 6, the name of the Local Government Board has been inserted in the place of that of a secretary of state, the authority originally named in this Act, the powers and duties of a secretary of state under this Act having been transferred to the Local Government Board by the Local Government Board Act, 1871 (34 & 35 Vict. c. 70), s. 2, and schedule, part 1. See also the Local Taxation Returns Act, 1877, *infra*.

THE LOCAL TAXATION RETURNS ACT, 1877.

(40 & 41 VICT. C. 66.)

An Act to amend the Law with respect to the Annual Returns of Local Taxation in England, and for other purposes relating to such Taxation.

[14th August 1877.]

1. The annual return required by law to be made of any receipts or expenditure of a local authority, or of any rates, taxes, tolls, or dues, shall be made for the financial year ending on the twenty-fifth day of March, or on such other day as the Local Government Board may from time to time prescribe, upon the application of any particular authority in respect of their receipts and expenditure, or of any rates, taxes, tolls, or dues levied by them, or in respect of the receipts and expenditure, and of the rates, taxes, tolls, or dues, levied by any class of authorities. {Date for annual return of local taxation}

Every such return shall be sent to the Local Government Board and not to one of Her Majesty's principal secretaries of state, and shall be so sent within one month after the audit of the receipts and expenditure to which the return relates is completed, or if the audit is not completed within six months after the end of the financial year for which the return is to be made, then on the expiration of such six months, or if there is no audit, then within one month after the end of the said financial year.

For the purpose of any such return the date to which the accounts of any local authority are required by law to be made up, and the date at which such accounts are required by law to be audited, and the auditors are required to be elected or appointed, may be altered by the local authority, with the approval of the Local Government Board : Provided that nothing in this section shall prevent any accounts being made up and audited at shorter periods than twelve months, so that one of such shorter periods ends on the last day of the financial year for which the return of such accounts is to be made.

2. Every return to which this Act applies shall be made by the

Appendix

Obligation of clerk of local authority to send return
clerk of the local authority, or where no clerk is appointed or acting, by the treasurer or other officer keeping the accounts of the receipts and expenditure, rates, taxes, tolls, or dues, to which the return relates, and any such clerk, treasurer, or other officer who makes default in making any such return shall be liable to a penalty not exceeding twenty pounds for each offence, to be recovered by action on behalf of Her Majesty in the High Court of Justice.

Definition of 'local authority'
3. The expression 'local authority' in this Act means any justices, municipal or other corporation, board, guardians, sanitary authority, vestry, commissioners, inspectors, trustees, or other body of persons required by law to make to one of Her Majesty's principal secretaries of state, or to the Local Government Board, a return of their receipts and expenditure, or of any rates, taxes, tolls, or dues levied by them or under their direction.

4. The Local Government Board shall make such provision as may seem to them necessary for any change of the date of the accounts and audit of the accounts of any local authority which may be rendered necessary by the provisions of this Act, so as to cause as little inconvenience as possible to the local authority.

Short title
5. This Act may be cited as the Local Taxation Returns Act, 1877.

The Local Taxation Returns Act, 1860, and this Act may be cited as the Local Taxation Returns Acts, 1860 and 1877.

[NOTE.—The portions of this Act which have been repealed by the S.L.R. Acts, 1883 and 1894, are omitted.]

THE METROPOLITAN POLICE ACT, 1839.

(2 & 3 VICT. C. 47.)

Penalty on keeping fairs open within forbidden hours
38. The business and amusement of all fairs holden within the metropolitan police district shall cease at the hour of eleven in the evening, and shall not begin earlier than the hour of six in the morning; and if any house, room, booth, standing, tent, caravan, waggon, or other place shall, during the continuance of any such fair, be open within the hours of eleven in the evening and six in the morning, for any purpose of business or amusement, in the place where such fair shall be holden, it shall be lawful for any constable to take into custody the person having the care or management thereof, and also every person being therein who shall not quit the same forthwith upon being bidden by such constable so to do; and the person so then having the care or management of any such house, room, booth, standing, tent, caravan, waggon, or other place shall be liable to a penalty not more

The Metropolitan Police Act, 1839

than five pounds, and every person convicted of having been therein, and of not having quitted the same forthwith upon being bidden by a constable so to do, shall be liable to a penalty not more than forty shillings.

39. If it shall appear to the commissioners of police that any fair holden within the metropolitan police district has been holden without lawful authority, or that any fair lawfully holden within the said district has been holden for a longer period than is so warranted, it shall be competent to such commissioners to direct one of the superintendents belonging to the metropolitan police force to summon the owner or occupier of the ground upon which such fair is holden to appear before a magistrate at a time and place to be specified in the summons, not less than eight days after the service of the summons, to show his right and title to hold such fair, or to hold such fair beyond a given period (as the case may be); and if such owner or occupier shall not attend in pursuance of such summons, or shall not show to the magistrate who shall hear the case sufficient cause to believe that such fair has been lawfully holden for the whole period during which the same has been holden, the magistrate shall declare in writing such fair to be unlawful, either altogether or beyond a stated period (as the case may be); and the commissioners shall give notice of such declaration by causing copies thereof to be affixed on the parish church and on other public places in and near the ground where such fair has been holden; and if, after such notices have been affixed for the space of six days, any attempt shall be made to hold such fair if it shall be declared altogether unlawful, or to hold it beyond the prescribed period if it shall be declared unlawful beyond a certain period, the commissioners of police may direct any constable to remove every booth, standing, and tent, and every carriage of whatsoever kind conveyed to or being upon the ground for the purpose of holding or continuing such fair, and to take into custody every person erecting, pitching, or fixing, or assisting to erect, pitch, or fix, any such booth, standing, or tent, and every person driving, accompanying, or conveyed in every such carriage, and every person resorting to such ground with any show or instrument of gambling or amusement; and every person convicted before a magistrate of any of the offences last aforesaid shall be liable to a penalty not more than ten pounds. *Fairs within the metropolitan police district may be inquired into*

If declared unlawful, booths, &c., to be removed

40. Provided nevertheless that if the owner or occupier of the ground whereon any such fair has been holden shall, when summoned before the magistrate, enter into a recognisance in the penal sum of two hundred pounds (which recognisance such magistrate is hereby authorised to take) with condition to appear in the Court of Queen's Bench on the first day of the then next term and to *On entering into recognisance, question as to right of title to fair*

may be tried in the Queen's Bench

answer to any information which Her Majesty's Attorney or Solicitor General may exhibit against such owner or occupier touching his right and title to such fair, and to abide the judgment of the court thereon, and to pay such costs as may be awarded by the court, which costs the said court is hereby authorised to award, then, notwithstanding the magistrate may have declared such fair to be unlawful, the commissioners of police shall forbear from giving notice of such declaration, and from taking any further measures thereon, until judgment shall be given by the said court against the right and title to such fair ; and the magistrate taking such recognisance shall forthwith transmit the same to one of Her Majesty's principal secretaries of state, to the end that the same may be filed in the said court, and such further directions may be given thereon as to such secretary of state may seem fit.

[NOTE.—The words in the above sections which were repealed by 30 & 31 Vict. c. 134, s. 21, and the S.L.R. Act, 1874 (No. 2), have been omitted.]

THE METROPOLITAN FAIRS ACT, 1868.

(31 & 32 VICT. C. 106.)

Short title

1. This Act may be cited for all purposes as ' The Metropolitan Fairs Act, 1868.'

Power to summon owner and occupier of ground on which fair is held

2. Where any fair is holden or notice is given of any fair proposed to be holden on any ground within the metropolitan police district other than that on which a fair has been holden during each of the seven years immediately preceding, it shall be competent for the commissioner of police to direct one of the superintendents of the metropolitan police force to summon the owner or occupier of the ground upon which such fair is holden to appear before a magistrate forthwith, or at a time to be specified in the summons, to show his right and title to hold such fair ; and if such owner or occupier do not attend in pursuance of such summons, or does not show to the magistrate who hears the case sufficient cause to believe that such fair is lawfully holden, the magistrate shall declare in writing such fair to be unlawful, and the commissioner shall give notice of such declaration by causing copies thereof to be affixed on and near the ground where such fair is holden or proposed to be holden ; and after such notice has been affixed for the space of six hours the commissioner of police may direct any constable to remove every booth, standing, and tent, and every carriage of whatsoever kind, conveyed to or being upon the ground for the

purpose of holding or continuing such fair, and to take into custody every person erecting, pitching, or fixing, or assisting to erect, pitch, or fix, any such booth, standing, or tent ; and every person hiring, accompanying, or conveyed in every such carriage, and every person resorting to such ground with any show or instrument of gambling or amusement, and every person convicted before a magistrate of any of the offences aforesaid shall be liable to a penalty of not more than ten pounds.

3. A summons under this Act may be served on the owner or occupier of any ground personally or by leaving the same at his usual or last known place of abode, or, if the name of such owner or occupier or his place of abode is not known to the police, by putting up such summons in a conspicuous place on the ground where the fair is holden or proposed to be holden, and it shall not be necessary to name the owner or occupier in the summons, but he may be described as the owner or occupier of the ground. *Service of summons*

4. All powers conferred by this Act shall be deemed to be in addition to, and not in derogation of, any other powers conferred by any other Act of Parliament, and any such other powers may be exercised as if this Act had not passed. *Act cumulative*

5. This Act, so far as is consistent with the tenor thereof, shall be construed as one with the Acts relating to the metropolitan police. *Construction of Act*

MODEL BY-LAWS.

Issued by the Local Government Board for the use of Sanitary Authorities establishing or regulating a Market under the Public Health Act, 1875.
[Published 25th July 1877.]

[By a memorandum prefixed to these model by-laws, the Board suggests that by-laws should not be made 'for regulating the use of the weighing machines provided by the undertakers, and for preventing the use of false and defective weights, scales, and measures,' on the ground that clauses 21 to 30 of the Markets and Fairs Clauses Act, 1847 (10 Vict. c. 14) sufficiently provide for the regulation of the weighing machines and also (in conjunction with other statutes) for the prevention of the use of false or defective weights, scales, and measures, and do not require to be supplemented by by-laws. Similarly, the Board thinks that it is unnecessary that by-laws should be made 'for preventing the sale or exposure of unwholesome provisions in the market.' The Board points out that s. 167 of the Public Health Act, 1875, provides that all tolls leviable by the sanitary authority must be approved by the Board, but that such approval is not required in the case of stallages and rents.]

For regulating the use of the market-place and the buildings, stalls, pens, and standings therein, and for preventing nuisances or obstructions therein, or in the immediate approaches thereto.

1. A person resorting to the market-place for the sale of any cattle, goods, provisions, marketable commodities or articles shall not, for the purpose of sale or of exposure for sale, place or cause to be placed such cattle, goods, provisions, marketable commodities or articles in any part or parts of the market-place other than such as shall have been appropriated for the reception, deposit, or exposure for sale of the same, and shall be defined or described in a notice printed, painted, or marked in legible letters of such a colour as to be clearly distinguishable from the colour of the ground whereon such letters are printed, painted, or marked, and affixed or set up and continued in some suitable and conspicuous position at or near to such part or parts.

2. A person resorting to the market-place for the sale of any cattle, goods, provisions, marketable commodities or articles shall not, for the purpose of sale or of exposure for sale, bring the same or cause the same to be brought into such market-place before the hour of_____ in the forenoon of any day appointed for the holding of any market.

Model By-laws

3. A person resorting to the market-place for the sale of any goods, provisions, marketable commodities, or articles shall not allow such goods, provisions, marketable commodities or articles, or any part thereof, to remain in the market-place after the hour of ———— in the afternoon of any day appointed for the holding of any market.

4. Every tenant or occupier, or servant of a tenant or occupier of any building, stall, or standing in the market-place shall, before the hour of — ———— in the afternoon of every day during which such building, stall, or standing may have been used for the sale or exposure for sale of any goods, provisions, marketable commodities, or articles, extinguish or cause to be extinguished every fire or light in, upon, or in connection with such building, stall, or standing.

5. A tenant or occupier, or a servant of a tenant or occupier of any building, stall, or standing in the market-place used for the sale, or exposure or preparation for sale of any carcase or meat intended for the food of man, shall not cleave such carcase or meat elsewhere than upon a cleaving block, or chopping board, or otherwise than when properly attached to or suspended from the hooks provided for the purpose in, upon, or in connection with such building, stall, or standing.

6. A person who shall use any pen for the reception of any cattle brought into the market-place for the purpose of sale, or of exposure for sale, shall not place or allow to be placed in such pen a greater number of cattle than shall be compatible with the allowance in respect of the several animals placed in such pen of an extent of superficial space to be determined in accordance with the following regulations :

	ft.	in.	ft.	in
For every horse :— a space not less than		,,	by	,,
For every ox or cow :— a space not less than		,,	by	,,
For every mule or ass :— a space not less than		,,	by	,,
For every calf :— a space not less than		,,	by	,,
For every ram, ewe, wether, lamb, goat, kid or pig :— a space not less than		,,	by	,,

[*The following requirements have been suggested as generally suitable* :—*For every horse,* 8 *feet by* 2 *feet. For every ox or cow,* 8 *feet by* 2 *feet. For every mule or ass,* 5 *feet by* 15 *inches. For every calf,* 5 *feet by* 15 *inches. For every sheep, goat, or pig (of medium size),* 4 *feet (superficial).*]

7. A tenant or occupier of any building, stall, or standing in the market-place shall not cause or allow any goods, provisions, marketable commodities or articles to be deposited or exposed for sale in or upon such building, stall, or standing, so that such goods, provisions, marketable commodities or articles, or any part thereof, shall project beyond the line of such building or stall, or beyond the limits assigned to such standing, so as to obstruct the passage of any person or vehicle or of any cattle, goods, provisions, marketable commodities or articles in or through the market-place or any part thereof.

8. A tenant or occupier of any building, stall, or standing in the market-place, or a person resorting to such market-place for the sale of any goods, provisions, marketable commodities or articles, shall not for any longer time or in any other manner than shall be reasonably necessary for the conveyance of such goods, provisions, marketable commodities or articles, to or from such building, stall, or standing, or any part of such market-place, deposit, or cause, or allow to be deposited in any avenue or passage adjoining such building, stall or standing, or elsewhere in such market-place, or in any of the immediate approaches thereto, any hamper, crate, basket, box, barrel, or other receptacle for any goods brought into such market-place for the purpose of sale or of exposure for sale.

9. Every tenant or occupier of any building, stall, or standing in the market-place, shall cause such building, stall, or standing to be properly cleansed immediately before the reception, deposit, or exposure for sale therein or thereon and immediately after the removal therefrom of any goods, provisions, marketable commodities or articles.

10. Every tenant or occupier of any building, stall, or standing in the market-place shall, from time to time, as often as occasion may require, during any day on which such building, stall, or standing may be used for the reception, deposit or exposure for sale therein or thereon of any goods, provisions, marketable commodities or articles, cause all filth, garbage, and refuse which may be produced or may accumulate in the course of the trade or business carried on by such tenant or occupier to be placed in such receptacle (if any) as may be provided by the sanitary authority, or otherwise in a receptacle of suitable construction and of adequate dimensions to be provided by such tenant or occupier, in, upon, or in close connection with such building, stall, or standing.

He shall, from time to time, as often as may be necessary, cause the contents of such receptacle to be promptly removed, in such a manner and with such precautions as not to create a nuisance in the process of removal, to such place of deposit as shall, from

Model By-laws

time to time, be appointed by the sanitary authority, and shall be defined or described in a notice printed, painted, or marked in legible letters of such a colour as to be clearly distinguishable from the colour of the ground whereon such letters are printed, painted, or marked, and affixed or set up and continued in some suitable and conspicuous position at or near to such place of deposit.

11. A person resorting to the market-place and being in charge of any waggon, cart, truck, barrow, or other vehicle or of any beast of burden shall not cause or allow such vehicle or beast to stand in any avenue or passage in such market-place, or in any of the immediate approaches thereto, for any longer time than shall be reasonably necessary for the loading or unloading of any goods, provisions, marketable commodities or articles.

12. Every person resorting to the market-place for the sale of any goods, provisions, marketable commodities, or articles, or in charge of any waggon, cart, truck, barrow, or other vehicle, or of any beast of burden used for the conveyance of any goods, provisions, marketable commodities, or articles to or from such market-place shall, from time to time as often as occasion may require, and in such a manner as to prevent nuisance or obstruction, remove or cause to be removed from every avenue or passage in such market-place, or from the footway or roadway of any of the immediate approaches thereto, all vegetable or animal refuse, filth, litter, or rubbish which may have fallen or may have been thrown or deposited therein or thereon during the loading or unloading or the conveyance to or from such market-place of such goods, provisions, marketable commodities or articles.

13. Every tenant or occupier of any building, stall, or standing in the market-place shall cause every avenue or passage in connection with such building, stall, or standing, whether used by him alone or in conjunction with any other person, to be properly swept and cleansed once at least during each day appointed for the holding of any market.

14. A person resorting to the market-place for the sale of any cattle, goods, provisions, marketable commodities or articles, shall not cause or allow such cattle, goods, provisions, marketable commodities or articles to be brought or conveyed to or from such market-place, or any building, stall, or standing therein, or to stand, be placed, or exposed for sale in such a manner as to obstruct the passage of any person or vehicle, or of any other cattle, goods, provisions, marketable commodities or articles in or through such market-place or any part thereof or any of the immediate approaches thereto.

For fixing the days and the hours during each day on which the market shall be held.

15. A market_____ [*here specify the class or description of wares for which the market is intended*] shall be held on_____ [*here insert the day of the week*] in every _____ [*here insert week, fortnight, month, quarter, as the case may require*] throughout the year_____ [*or if the markets are not held periodically throughout the year, substitute the names of the months during which they are held.*]

On every day appointed for the holding of a market such market shall be held between the hours of_____ in the forenoon and _____ in the afternoon :

Provided that when any day herein-before appointed for the holding of a market shall be a day duly appointed for a solemn fast, or public thanksgiving, such market shall be held on the lawful day next following such first-mentioned day.

For regulating the carriers resorting to the market, and fixing the rates for carrying articles carried therefrom within the limits of the district.

16. A carrier resorting to the market-place shall not, at any time, while plying for hire and not actually hired, occupy a station in any part or parts of the market-place other than such as shall be appropriated as a stand or stands for carriers and shall be defined or described in a notice printed, painted, or marked in legible letters of such a colour as to be clearly distinguishable from the colour of the ground whereon such letters are printed, painted, or marked, and affixed, or set up, and continued in some suitable and conspicuous position at or near to the part or parts so appropriated.

17. A carrier resorting to the market-place shall not, while plying for hire, canvass for hire by calling out or otherwise to the annoyance of any person.

18. Every carrier resorting to the market-place shall at all times, while plying for hire, conduct himself with civility and propriety towards every person hiring or seeking to hire such carrier, and shall comply with every reasonable requirement of any person hiring such carrier.

19. Every carrier resorting to the market-place shall be entitled to demand and receive from every person hiring such carrier, a sum to be determined in accordance with the following table as the rate or charge for the carriage of any goods, provisions, marketable commodities or articles, from such market-place to any place or places within the limits of the district :

Table of rates for the carriage of goods, provisions, marketable commodities, or articles from the market-place.

Distance.	Weight.	Rate.
		s. d.
To any place within the distance of from the limits of the market-place	For a weight not exceeding lbs. For every additional lbs.	,, ,,
To any place beyond the distance of and within the distance of from the limits of the market-place	For a weight not exceeding lbs. For every additional lbs.	,, ,,
For every additional of distance beyond such last-mentioned distance	For a weight not exceeding lbs. For every additional lbs.	,, ,,

Penalties.

20. Every person who shall offend against any of the foregoing by-laws shall be liable for every such offence to a penalty of :

Provided, nevertheless, that the justices or court before whom any complaint may be made or any proceedings may be taken in respect of any such offence may, if they think fit, adjudge the payment as a penalty of any sum less than the full amount of the penalty imposed by this by-law.

INDEX.

	PAGE
ABOLITION of fair, order for	94, 193
ABUSE, loss of franchise by	90–92
loss of toll by	60
ACCOMMODATION, duty of lord to provide	34–36, 38
effect of not providing	35, 81, 83
ACCOUNTS of market revenue	111–113, 202–204
under M.F.C. Act	112, 170
Diseases of Animals Act	112, 113, 191
ACQUISITION of market-rights	17–27
by ordinance	17, 19
grant	18, 19
prescription or usage	23
statute	25, 141 et seq.
under Public Health Act	27, 181–188
Diseases of Animals Act	27, 189–191
ACTION for toll or stallage	66, 162
toll illegally levied	68
disturbance	74, 86, 89
AD QUOD DAMNUM, writ of	21
ALIENATION of market-rights	27–30
ALTERATION of days	xxxi., 50–52, 154, 194
AMUSEMENTS in fairs	1, 54, 109–111, 204
ANCIENT DEMESNE, tenants in, when exempt from toll	69, 73
ANIMALS, diseases of, regulations for	106
APPROACHES to market, under M.F.C. Act	148, 149
ARTICLE, meaning of	153, 156
ASSIZE of bread and ale	8, 92
AUCTION, may be a rival market	78
AUCTION-MART for cattle	199
AUCTION-ROOM, whether a shop	153
AUCTIONEER, causing crowd to collect	45
differential toll for	66
by-laws as to	165
BOARD OF AGRICULTURE	100, 102, 106, 113, 190, 191, 199
BOOTHS, licence for plays in	110
BOROUGH, provision of market by	181–189
transfer of market to	29, 182
sale or lease of market by	29
ancient market in	18, 184
market accounts of	111, 113, 191
exemptions from toll in	71–73
place for holding market in	34, 37, 183
See also DISTRICT COUNCIL	
BOROUGH ENGLISH, market on land that is	41

	PAGE
BRISTOL, Court of Pie Powder in	6
BY-LAWS	96–98
for whirligigs and swings	111
under M.F.C. Act	164–170
penalties for breach of	166, 171
penalty for defacing	177
confirmation of	166, 201
publication of	168
for markets under Public Health Act	184, 186
model	208
CALENDAR, reformed	xxxi., 51
CARRIERS, by-laws as to	165, 212
CARTS, weighing of, under M.F.C. Act	156–160
CATTLE, diseases of	106
weighing of	100, 196–200
under M.F.C. Act	156
meaning of term in M.F.C. Act	143
tolls for, under M.F.C. Act	161
markets under Diseases of Animals Act	189
statistics as to weight, etc., of	102, 199
CERTIORARI	179
CHANGE of day of market or fair	xxxi., 50–52, 154, 194
of place	37–39, 149
CHARTER	19–22
how proved	134
effect of statute on	26, 87, 93
CHURCHYARDS, markets and fairs in	42
CLERK OF THE MARKET	10
CLERK of market authority	99, 195, 196, 202
in metropolitan hay-markets	128, 129
COLLECTOR of tolls, defined	143
penalty for obstructing	163
payment of tolls to	161
duty of, to weigh and measure	99, 196
in horse-fairs	126
in metropolitan hay-markets	128, 129
COMMISSIONERS	19, 29, 202
COMMON LAW DISTANCE	76
COMPANY, sale of undertaking by	136
COMPENSATION for lands taken, damage, &c.	145, 149, 183
CONFIRMATION of by-laws	168, 200
CONSTRUCTION of market under M.F.C. Act	145
CONTAGIOUS DISEASES (ANIMALS) ACTS. See DISEASES OF ANIMALS ACT	
COPIES of Special Act	135, 173, 174
CORN, toll of	65
CORRECTION of market	8, 40
COSTERMONGERS in metropolis	6, 45
COUNTY COUNCIL, provision of cattle-market by	189–191
local authority as to weights	98
as to adulterated food	106
licensing authority for plays	110
COUNTY COURT, jurisdiction in action for tolls	67, 162
COURT OF THE CLERK OF THE MARKET	12
COURT OF PIE POWDER	6–8

Index

	PAGE
COURTS in markets and fairs	3
CRIMINAL JURISDICTION in markets and fairs	8
CROWN, markets and fairs belonging to	17, 93
prerogative to grant charters	2-6, 17-22
escheat and forfeiture to	28, 90
exempt from toll	69
not affected by M.F.C. Act	171
by sale in market overt	123
CUSTOM, evidence of	135
stallage regulated by	64
to erect stalls	64
to prevent sales in shops	79
CUSTOMARY TOLLS	56, 63, 65
DAMAGES for disturbance of market	74
when recoverable in addition to penalties	88, 178
by construction of market under M.F.C. Act	145, 149
recovery of, under M.F.C. Act	171, 175
distress for	176
tender of amends for	171
DANGEROUS structures in market-place	32
DAY, meaning of in grants	53
DAYS for holding markets and fairs	48
alteration of	50, 194
under M.F.C. Act	154, 165
DEFINITION of market and fair	1, 100
of toll, stallage, etc.	55
DEFINITIONS in M.F.C. Act	142-144
DEVOLUTION of market-rights	27, 41
DIFFERENTIAL TOLLS	66
DISEASES OF ANIMALS ACT, closing, etc., of markets under	106
erection of cattle-markets under	27, 189
DISPUTE as to tolls under M.F.C. Act	163
DISTRESS on goods in market	31
on cattle going to market	33
for toll or stallage	67, 68
under M.F.C. Act	162
for penalties, etc. under M.F.C. Act	175, 177
not unlawful for want of form	178
against treasurer of market authority	176
DISTRICT COUNCIL, provision of market by	27, 181-188
purchase of market by	181, 186
leasing of market by	30
lease of market to	181
by-laws of	97, 111, 164, 184
accounts of	112, 113
powers of, relating to abolition of fairs	94
change of days	52
DISTURBANCE of fair or market	74-80
by levying rival market	74, 88
grant no defence	80
by evading toll	82
by assaulting lord, etc.	85
by preventing goods coming to market	85
nature of action for	86
limitation of action for	86

	PAGE
DISTURBANCE of rights of stall-holder	86
of statutory market	87, 150
under statutory powers	80, 183
DUCHY OF LANCASTER	11, 73
DWELLING-PLACE, meaning of	152
ECCLESIASTICAL PERSONS exempt from toll	69
ESCHEAT of franchise	28
EVIDENCE, of market rights	134–137
in action for toll or stallage	67
disturbance	75, 76, 87
of grants	134
of ancient usage	23, 135
of acts of ownership	136
under M.F.C. Act:	
penalty for giving false	173
of completion of market	161
of by-laws	168–170
of alteration of Special Act	147, 148
under Public Health Act:	
of by-laws	164, 186
of approval of tolls	185
EXEMPTIONS from toll	69–73
EXTINCTION of franchise	93
FAIR, origin and nature of	1–6
distinguished from market	1, 100
abolition of	94, 193
when and how long to be held	48–54
alteration of days for	50–53, 94, 194
proclamation of	49, 126
FAIRS ACT 1871	94, 191
,, 1873	51, 194
FEAST DAYS, markets and fairs on	48–51
FOOD, sale of unwholesome	8, 104
FOREIGN CATTLE, market for	189
FORESTALLING	33, 129
FORFEITURE of fair or market	28, 90–93
for change of day	49
for taking outrageous toll	59
waiver of	93
effect of	93
of toll	92
FRANCHISE of market or fair	17
parliamentary	119
GOOD FRIDAY	50
GOODS, weighing of	99, 156–160, 184, 195–6
GRANT of market or fair	19–22
necessity of	3–5
validity of	20
form and contents of	20
how obtained	21
duration of	22
presumption of lost	22–24
repeal of	90, 130

GRANT, evidence of	134
of toll	56
to be exempt from toll	71
HAWKERS, in metropolis	6, 45
exempt from penalties under M.F.C. Act, s. 13	150
HAWKER'S LICENCE not required for selling in market	xxxi
HAY AND STRAW MARKETS in metropolis, sales	128
weighing	103
hours	53
HEREFORD FAIR	9, 79
HIGHWAY, markets and fairs in	42–47
stalls in	42, 63
weighing machine in	102
HIGHWAY ACTS	44
HIRING FAIRS or MOPS	5
HOLDING market or fair, where	31–47
when	48–54, 126
HOME SECRETARY, order of, abolishing fair	94, 193
changing days	51, 194
HORSES, sale of	126
IMMEMORIAL USER	22, 135
INCOME TAX	115
INCORPORATION OF M.F.C. Act	144
with Public Health Act	184, 188
Diseases of Animals Act	190
M. and F. (Weighing of Cattle) Act	198
of inhabitants to hold market	10
INHABITANTS, grant of market to	18
exemption from toll	71, 72
INJUNCTION against disturbance	74, 88, 184
INSPECTION of by-laws	167
of Special Act	173
INSPECTOR OF PROVISIONS	105, 154, 155
OF MARKET	105
OF WEIGHTS AND MEASURES	98, 195
JURISDICTION of lord of market	6–10, 96
JUSTICES, powers of under M.F.C. Act	143, 147, 161, 172
to settle disputes as to tolls	163
recovery of penalties and damages before	171, 175–180
licensing powers of	107–111
approval of charges for weighing	99
KEEPER of market or fair, penalty for obstructing	154
LAIRS, provision of	189
LAND-TAX	114
LAND, market may be held on whose	39
LANDS, meaning of in M.F.C. Act	142, 144
compensation for taking or injuring	145
entry upon when taken	148
additional	148
LANDS CLAUSES ACTS	145
LASTAGE	56

	PAGE
LEASE of market rights and tolls	27–30
lands, markets and tolls to District Council	181
LETTERS patent, grants made by	19–22
evidence of	134
LICENCES for sale of intoxicating drinks	107
theatrical performances	109
LICENSED HAWKERS	xxxi., 150
LICENSED PREMISES near markets exempt from closing	108
LIMITATION of actions for disturbance	86
of proceedings for penalties	179
LOCAL GOVERNMENT BOARD, powers of, over weighing-tolls	101
market-tolls	184, 185, 188
by-laws	167–70, 186, 201
returns of accounts to	113, 202–204
model by-laws of	208
LONDON, CITY OF, shops in, market overt	122
exemption from toll	71, 73
market authority under Diseases of Animals Act	189
clerk of the market in	11
market charter of Edw. III.	77
See also METROPOLIS	
LORD OF THE MARKET	18, 19
his jurisdiction	6–10
LORDS OF MANORS, grants to	18
LOSS OF TOLL. *See* DISTURBANCE and FORFEITURE	
LOST GRANT, presumption of	23, 37, 48, 58, 59, 135
MARKET, defined	1, 100
early history of	2–6
MARKET AUTHORITIES	18, 19, 181, 189
MARKET COMPANY, sale by	186
MARKET COURTS	3, 6, 8–13
MARKET DAYS	48–52, 154, 165
change of	xxxi., 50, 154, 194
MARKET HOURS	53, 126, 165
MARKET OVERT, sale in	120–125, 190
sale of horses in	126
MARKET-PLACE	31–47
failure to provide	35
extent of	36
removal of	37–39
nuisances in	32
rights of public in	31
upon what land	39–42
on highways and in churchyards	42
under M.F.C. Act	148, 161
by-laws regulating use of	165, 208
MARKETS AND FAIRS CLAUSES ACT	141–174
why passed	25
nature of markets under	26, 88, 121
extent of	141
how cited	144
construction of	142
how incorporated with special Act	144
incorporation with Public Health Act	184
incorporation with Diseases of Animals Act	190

Index

	PAGE
MARKETS AND FAIRS CLAUSES ACT, incorporation with Weighing of Cattle Act	198
MART	1, 199
MEAT, sale of unwholesome	8, 104, 154
METES AND BOUNDS	34
METROPOLIS, street markets in	6, 45
hay and straw markets in	53, 128
hours of fairs in	54, 204
suppression of unlawful fairs in	134, 205
application of penalties under M.F.C. Act in	172
METROPOLITAN FAIRS ACT, 1868	134, 206
MANAGEMENT ACT, 1855	46
POLICE ACT, 1839	44, 54, 204
STREETS ACT, 1867	45
MONOPOLY of market-owners	2, 74
MORTGAGE of market-rights and tolls	27-30
MUNICIPAL CORPORATION. *See* BOROUGH.	
NEGLECT TO TAKE TOLL	92
NEGLIGENCE of market-owner	32, 146
NON USER of franchise	90
NUISANCE, rival market when a	44-46
in market-place	32
by steam organ in fair	111
slaughter-house may be	155
by-laws against	165
ORDINANCE for a market	17, 19
OUTRAGEOUS TOLL	59
OWNERS of markets and fairs, who are	18, 52, 95
duty to provide a market-place	33
liable for negligence	32
PEDLARS	xxxi., 150
PENALTIES under M.F.C. Act, publication of	171, 176
application of	172, 178
recovery of	171, 175-180
for slaughtering cattle	155
for selling outside market	150
whether in substitution for damages	89
for obstructing market-keeper	154
toll-collector	163
selling unwholesome meat, etc.	154
fraud, etc. in weighing	158-160
taking excessive toll	162
breach of by-laws	166
omitting to render accounts	170
giving false evidence	173
neglecting to deposit copies of Act	174
refusing inspection of Act	173
Public Health Act	188
Diseases of Animals Act	106, 171
Weights and Measures Act, 1878	99, 196
M. and F. (Weighing of Cattle) Acts	101, 197, 199
Local Taxation Returns Acts	204
Hay and Straw Acts	103, 129

	PAGE
PENALTIES under Horse Stealing Acts	. 126
Sale of Food and Drugs Act	. 105
PENNAGE	. 55
PESAGE	. 56
PICCAGE	. 55
PIE POWDER, Courts of	3, 6–8
PILLORY	9, 92, 96
PLACE for holding market or fair. *See* MARKET-PLACE	
PLEADINGS in action for tolls or stallage	. 67
disturbance	. 86
POISAGE	. 56
PRESCRIBED limits or area	142, 150, 183, 190
PRESCRIPTION, acquisition of market by	22–24
exemption from toll by	. 72
PRESCRIPTIVE rights in markets	. 38
toll	. 59
PRESUMPTION of lost grant	22–24
of disturbance	. 74
PROCLAMATION of fair	49, 126
PROTECTION from disturbance	2, 74–89, 181
of statutory markets	87, 150, 183
PROVISIONS, sale of unwholesome	8, 104, 154
PUBLIC HEALTH ACT, acquisition of market-rights under	27, 181–188
PUBLIC rights in market	31–33, 38, 39
PUBLICITY of market	4, 121
QUARTER SESSIONS, allowance of by-laws by	. 166
appeals to	. 180
approval of weighing charges by	. 99
QUIT OF TOLL	69–73
QUO WARRANTO, information	. 132
Placita de	. 131
proceedings as evidence	. 137
writ of	. 131
RAILWAYS CLAUSES CONSOLIDATION ACT	171, 175–180
RANKNESS OF TOLLS	. 60
RATEABILITY of markets and fairs and tolls	. 117
REASONABLENESS of toll and stallage	58–61, 64
RECEIVER of profits and tolls	. 30
REGRATING	33, 129
REGULATING the market	. 96
REMOVAL of market or fair	37–39, 149
RENT of market, recovery of	. 28
stall. *See* STALLAGE	
RESTITUTION of stolen goods	. 123
horses	. 127
RETURNS of tolls and profits. *See* ACCOUNTS	
weight and sales of cattle	. 199
RIVAL market, disturbance by levying	74–89
what amounts to	. 78
RURAL DISTRICT COUNCIL. *See also* DISTRICT COUNCIL	. 182
SALE in market overt	. 120
of horses	123, 126
of hay, straw, etc. in metropolis	. 128

                                                              PAGE
SALE by sample 62, 83, 152
    in shop 79, 150
    toll payable on 55, 62
    of market-rights 27–30
        by company 186
SAMPLE, sale by 62, 83, 152
SCAVAGE 56
SCIRE FACIAS, for abuse or non-user 90–93
    grant improperly obtained 21
    procedure on 130
SECRETARY OF STATE. *See* HOME SECRETARY
SHEWAGE 56
SHOP, sales in, when a disturbance 79, 83, 88
    what is a, under M.F.C. Act, s. 13 152
    in city of London, market overt 122
SHOP HOURS ACTS 54
SHOW, licence for 110
SLAUGHTER-HOUSES 155, 189
SOIL of market place, ownership of 40–42
SPECIAL ACT, defined 142, 190
    incorporation of M.F.C. Act with . . . 144
    custody and inspection of 173–174
    errors and omissions in 147
    construction of 142
STALLAGE, defined 55
    when due 63
    in kind 65
    variable and differential 66
    recovery by action 66
        distress 68
    exemptions from 69–73
    under M.F.C. Act 160–164
STALLS, rights of public as to 31, 32
    what are 40
    rateability of 118
    in highways 42–45
    customary right to 39
    occupation of, may qualify for vote . . . 119
STATISTICS as to weight and sale of cattle . . . 199
STATUTE, market-rights acquired by 25–27
    common law market modified by . . 26, 87, 93
STATUTE FAIRS, or STATUTE SESSIONS 5, 44
STOURBRIDGE FAIR 40
STRAW. *See* HAY AND STRAW
STREETS. *See* HIGHWAY
SUMAGE 56
SUNDAYS, markets and fairs on 50
SURRENDER of franchise 93
SWINGS, by-laws for 111

TENDER of amends 171
THEATRICAL performances in fairs 109
TOLL, nature of 55
    not incident to market or fair 4, 56
    grant of 56–58
    prescriptive 57, 59

224 Index

	PAGE
TOLL, must be reasonable	56–58
payable on what articles	61–63
on sale by sample	62
payable by whom	62
exemption from	69–73
recovery of, by action	66
,, by distress	67
remedies for unlawful	68
not lost by non-user	92
power of Commissioners of Woods to relinquish	93
lease of	27, 28
receiver of	30
accounts of statutory	113, 202–204
taxes on	114–116
not rateable	117
TOLLS under Public Health Act	181, 184
Diseases of Animals Act	191
M. and F. (Weighing of Cattle) Acts	196–198
TOLLS FOR WEIGHING	99, 101, 104, 161, 183, 198
TOLLS, STALLAGES AND RENTS, under M.F.C. Act	160–164
recovery of	162
disputes concerning	163
list of	164
for weighing and measuring	161
TOLL-COLLECTOR. *See* COLLECTOR OF TOLLS	
TOLL-FREE market	58
TOLL-THROUGH	56
TOLL-TRAVERSE	56
TOLL-TURN	56
TOWN POLICE CLAUSES ACT	44
TRANSIENT OFFENDERS, arrest of	179
TRONAGE	56
TRUSTEES OF MARKETS	18, 19, 29, 202–204
TUMBREL	9, 92, 96
UNDERTAKERS, defined	142
URBAN DISTRICT COUNCIL. *See* DISTRICT COUNCIL	
USAGE, acquisition of market-rights by	22–24
evidence of	135
VARIABLE TOLLS and stallages	66
VIEW OF FRANKPLEDGE	8
WAKES	4
WEIGHTS AND MEASURES	10, 98–104, 156–160, 195–200
WEIGHING AND MEASURING, tolls for	161, 198
offences concerning	158–160, 197
WHARFS, provision of	189
WHEAT, toll of, in kind	65
WHIRLIGIGS, by-laws for	111
WINCHESTER, St. Giles' Fair	9
WITNESSES, penalty for making default	179
WITNESSING of sales	3
YORK FAIR	9

Spottiswoode & Co. Printers, New-street Square, London.

www.ingramcontent.com/pod-product-compliance
Lightning Source LLC
Chambersburg PA
CBHW021403230426
43666CB00006B/624